The Giants and
the Dodgers

The Giants and the Dodgers

Four Cities, Two Teams, One Rivalry

ANDREW GOLDBLATT

McFarland & Company, Inc., Publishers

Jefferson, North Carolina, and London

Consulting Editor: John Bergez

Library of Congress Cataloguing-in-Publication Data

Goldblatt, Andrew.
    The Giants and the Dodgers : four cities, two teams, one rivalry /
Andrew Goldblatt.
       p.   cm.
    Includes bibliographical references and index.

    ISBN 0-7864-1640-8 (softcover binding : 50# alkaline paper)

    1. San Francisco Giants (Baseball team)—History. 2. Los
Angeles Dodgers (Baseball team)—History. 3. New York Giants
(Baseball team)—History. 4. Brooklyn Dodgers (Baseball
team)—History. I. Title.
GV875.S34G64   2003
796.357'09794—dc21   2003008029

British Library cataloguing data are available

On the front cover: John McGraw (left) and Wilbert Robinson (courtesy
National Baseball Hall of Fame Library, Cooperstown, N.Y.)

Manufactured in the United States of America

McFarland & Company, Inc., Publishers
  Box 611, Jefferson, North Carolina 28640
   www.mcfarlandpub.com

Acknowledgments

This book was John Bergez's idea. As an editor and fan, he longed to see a contemporary treatment of the Giant-Dodger rivalry in print. After a couple of false starts, he met me. I had the requisite baseball and literary backgrounds, and like the teams themselves, I started life in New York and moved to California. Thus was born what for me has been the collaboration from heaven. John handled the business side while I researched and wrote. Whenever I ran into a problem with the text, he proposed a deft solution. Although I am listed as sole author, this book would not have existed — or been nearly as good — without him.

My thanks to Leonard Koppett and David Biesel for encouragement early in the process, to Henry Staat and Jules Tygiel for encouragement late in the process, and to Jeanne Woodward for the supreme kindness of compiling the index. I am much indebted to Leon Nehmad for accompanying me to the National Baseball Library in Cooperstown and providing invaluable research assistance, and to Janice Schachter and Janet Keller for being my eyes, ears, and hosts in New York and Los Angeles, respectively. Above all, I wish to express my abiding gratitude to my wife and first reader, Christa, the reason I feel like such a lucky man.

Contents

Introduction:
The New York Game

What does a tomato mean?

On April 20, 1937, Dick Bartell of the National League champion New York Giants stepped into the batter's box at Brooklyn's Ebbets Field to begin the new baseball season. The epitome of combative little infielders, he'd earned the nickname "Rowdy Richard" for tagging baserunners across the teeth and inviting them to start something if they didn't like it.

On the mound stood Van Lingle Mungo. Outsized and ill-tempered, he was the fastest pitcher Bartell ever saw—faster even than Bob Feller, Bartell claimed—and threw curveballs that started at a right-handed batter's ribs. A year earlier he'd lumbered across the diamond to cover first on a Bartell drag bunt and slammed into the pint-sized shortstop. "I hurtled through the air like a basketball shot at the buzzer," Bartell recalled. Bartell had charged Mungo, only to have Mungo take him down so hard he couldn't play for two weeks. To make matters worse, in the ensuing melee Bartell's best punch blackened the eye of his own manager, Bill Terry.

Bartell expected 1937's inaugural pitch to be one of those brushback curves, but instead Mungo threw a fastball that blazed past the plate at the letters. "Stee-rike one," called Beans Reardon, the same umpire who had separated Bartell and Mungo the year before. Bartell looked back at Reardon to argue, only to feel a thump against his chest.

Someone in the stands had nailed him with a rotten tomato.

The largest crowd to date for an opening day at Ebbets Field hooted

Van Lingle Mungo. He drank as hard as he threw, which made his bad temper worse and cost him $15,000 in fines — more, he claimed, than any player of his day. (Transcendental Graphics)

in joyous derision as Bartell tamely requested time out, retreated to the clubhouse, and changed into another uniform. Snickered veteran sportswriter Roscoe McGowen in the next day's *New York Times,* "Mungo and a rabid Brooklyn fan threw consecutive strikes."

On the surface, Bartell's tomato was proof that the old days weren't any more polite than ours. But there was more to it than that. The tomato juice spattered across Dick Bartell's shirt symbolized the bad blood that had characterized the rivalry between the Giants and Dodgers for nearly half a century — and continues to characterize it to this day. No two baseball teams have competed so intensely for so long as the Giants and Dodgers. From its roots in New York's teeming boroughs to its present incarnation in California's world-class cities, the rivalry was, and remains, baseball's best, providing fans with some of the biggest thrills, fiercest personalities, and hottest emotions in professional sports.

Leonard Koppett, dean of baseball writers and a close observer of the Giants and Dodgers on both coasts, proclaimed the rivalry "the richest in American sports." Historian Doris Kearns Goodwin wrote, "Even in years when the two teams were not contending for the pennant, every meeting was regarded as a separate war, to be fought with implacable hostility." Echoed former Dodger shortstop Maury Wills: "Grudges got carried not only from game to game but from year to year. It was like a war all the time." Summed up ex-Giant shortstop and manager Alvin Dark: "I was involved with big league baseball for 28 years and I've never seen anything like the rivalry between the two teams."

But there's even more to the tomato that hit Dick Bartell. Through the Giant-Dodger rivalry we can see how citizens of four great American cities (if you count Brooklyn as an independent city, which it was until 1898) used the medium of athletic competition to forge a common identity and define themselves against a potent political, economic, and cultural *other.* Without their beloved Dodgers — and formidable Giant squads pitted against them — Brooklynites would not have retained their distinct identity into the 20th century. And the more the San Francisco Bay Area grew to resemble Southern California, the more vociferously Giant fans expressed their contempt for the Los Angeles Dodgers.

Group rivalry has existed ever since two tribes depended on the same waterhole. Just how naturally humans fall into the us-versus-them dynamic was demonstrated in a 1954 study known as the Robbers Cave Experiment. Psychologists brought 22 fifth-grade boys of similar economic, ethnic, religious, and family background to an isolated camp in Oklahoma's Robbers Cave State Park. The boys were divided into two groups of 11. Neither group knew the other existed. The psychologists gave the boys a few days to bond among themselves, accomplished in large part through baseball workouts. But soon the boys grew restless; they didn't want practices, they wanted games against opponents.

At stage two of the experiment, each group was informed of the other's existence. The boys immediately "became insistent in their desire to challenge the other group of boys to play competitive games, especially baseball." The psychologists planned a tournament, including ballgames, lasting several days, and offered prizes like switchblades (different times, those) to the overall winners. In the beginning, "even though the boys hurled invectives starting with the first contest of the tournament," they still displayed good sportsmanship, giving three cheers for the losers. But by the end of the second day they'd cast off all pretense of mutual respect, and on day four one group ransacked the other's cabin, then returned to its own cabin and loaded socks with stones to prepare for the counterattack. The psychologists stepped in when fistfights broke out.

Without intervention, it's likely the boys eventually would have graduated to mortal combat — purely on the basis of an artificial group identity! It sounds silly, yet we routinely encourage young men (and, increasingly, women) to fight for arbitrary social constructs like nations or "ways of life," and we shower adulation on them when they do. Often this is appropriate. But the same impulse fuels racism, terrorism, and genocide. The task of every civilized society is to direct the explosive energy of group rivalry toward wholesome ends and away from destructive ones.

Evidence suggests the ancient Egyptians used basic sports like running, swimming, and wrestling for the safe expression of competitive impulses and for training young men in war. By the time the Greek city-states reached their height, athletics were pursued for their own sake, organized into Olympic games and mythologized through such figures as Hercules and Atalanta (a woman who could outrun any man). The Romans preferred blood sport, which may explain why the Catholic Church, whose proselytes often served as fodder for imperial spectacles, did little to encourage the development of competitive games over the next thousand years. Nor did Protestants find much redemptive about sports.

Then came the Industrial Revolution, the most sweeping change in the way people lived since the invention of agriculture 10,000 years before. Millions of families moved from farms to cities, exchanging the arduous but essentially healthy routines of rural life for the arduous but enervating conditions of factories and tenements. The number of office workers also multiplied as business and government bureaucratized. By the 1850s, respectable citizens in America's rapidly industrializing northeast worried that long hours, little exercise, bad air, and overcrowding were making the average laborer physically and mentally unfit for anything but insurrection. Following their counterparts in England, they rehabilitated the reputation of competitive sports, extolling the concept of "muscular Christianity," in which team games were seen as promoting fitness, fairness, unselfishness, and other virtues transferable to daily life.

Baseball had already been invented by then, in Manhattan by a group of office workers calling themselves the Knickerbockers. Their New York Game, the latest of many American variations on English cricket, was more calisthenic than competition, an excuse for Alexander Cartwright and his middle-class buddies to engage in frolicsome ballchasing across Madison Square. The set of 20 rules the club adopted in 1845 laid the foundation for the game played today. But one of the formulators of those rules, D. L. Adams, later admitted that "there was no rivalry, as no other club was formed until 1850, and during these five years base ball had a desperate struggle for existence."

Enter Brooklyn.

Although Giovanni da Verrazano saw Manhattan first (in 1524), Henry Hudson was responsible for its European settlement, extolling its sheltered harbor and fertile soil to the Dutch West India Company. In 1626 Peter Minuit bought the island from Lenape tribespeople who had no concept of private property. By 1653 Nieuw Amsterdam, as it was called, had 800 residents. The English took over in 1664 as part of a global struggle with the Netherlands, renaming the small town New York. Surrounded by wilderness and occasionally hostile natives, Dutch and English settlers cooperated, and gradually their town expanded northward from the base of the island. By the time George Washington took the presidential oath of office there in 1789, New York had grown into the fledgling nation's largest city, with 33,000 inhabitants. Ten years later that number had nearly doubled.

With the 1825 opening of the Erie Canal, Manhattan became the port of choice for shippers delivering goods to inland markets. Through tariffs, the harbor brought in a substantial share of the federal government's revenue, establishing New York City as the country's locus of political, economic, and cultural clout. Talented and ambitious individuals from the rest of the nation gravitated to it. So did immigrants from Europe. In the 1840s Irish and German newcomers willing to work for low wages sparked a fresh burst of industrialization, turning the city into America's top manufacturing center. New York grew rich, powerful, and glamorous, but also arrogant, corrupt, and squalid.

Brooklyn, just across the East River from New York, started as several Dutch farming villages, the foremost of which, Breuckelen ("marsh-land"), eventually subsumed the rest and gave the area its name. When the British took over, they designated the region Kings County. The 1790 census put the county's population at about 4,500, nearly a third of which was African American (including slaves; the Peculiar Institution persisted in New York State into the 1820s). The advent of steamboat ferries in the early 1800s opened the area to settlement by Manhattan's expanding man-agerial and professional classes, and soon Brooklyn was growing at an even faster pace than New York City.

With a port of its own, farms by Sheepshead Bay, and commercial dis-tricts crowded with shopkeepers and tradesmen, Brooklyn became a bustling, if unspectacular, neighbor to Gotham, charting a middle course in contrast to Manhattan's extremes. It quickly developed two reputations, one it was proud of, one it was not. Brooklynites liked living in "The City of Churches," a reference both to their Christian devoutness and to the spired skyline. But they resented being thought of as a moon to Manhat-tan's planet. Yes, they owed much of their prosperity to working in or sup-plying goods to New York, but they were decent, regular folks, as opposed to those scammers on the other side of the river, and their city was dis-tinguished in its own right, if only for the lack of misery and decay that, in their minds, typified Manhattan.

The first known competitive baseball game in the metropolitan area was between genteel teams from New York and Brooklyn. On October 22, 1845, a blustery cold day, eight members of the New York Ball Club squared off against eight Brooklynites in the Elysian Fields of Hoboken, New Jer-sey. They didn't abide by all the Knickerbockers' rules, which is why base-ball historians consider the *real* first game an all-Manhattan affair between the Knicks and the New York Club on June 19, 1846. But they did follow the three-out-per-inning regulation that made the New York Game more interesting than the one-out Massachusetts Game, and per Alexander Cartwright's dictum, they agreed that the first team to score 21 or more aces (runs) over an equal number of innings won. The Brooklynites, recent converts from cricket, were trounced 24–4, but novelty and sportsman-ship took the edge off losing. At the postgame banquet, "the good feeling and hilarity that prevailed, showed that the Brooklyn players, though defeated, were not disheartened," reported the *New York Morning News*. Three days later the New York Ball Club won a rematch played on Brook-lyn's Myrtle Avenue, 37–19.

The intercity rivalry took off in the 1850s, when the New York Game went from curiosity to craze. Manhattan enthusiasts started the Gothams around 1850, followed in the middle of the decade by the Eagle, Empire, and Baltic clubs, and later by the powerful Mutuals. But that was nothing compared to Brooklyn, where writer Henry Chadwick, a Scottish immigrant and former cricketer, promoted the game in a variety of publications. (Chadwick also became baseball's first statistics freak, inventing the box score and the rudiments of the scoring system — pitcher as 1, catcher as 2, etc.) The Excelsiors started in 1854, followed by the first working-class team, the Eckfords, and then the Atlantics, who gained immortality in 1870 by stopping the 92-game unbeaten streak of the first openly professional team, the Cincinnati Red Stockings. "Verily Brooklyn is fast earning the title of the 'City of Baseball Clubs,' as well as the 'City of Churches,'" noted *Porter's Spirit of the Times* in 1857. By 1858, Brooklyn had 71 organized teams to Manhattan's 25.

In the summer of 1858 the Brooklyn clubs challenged New York to a best-of-three series between all-star teams, to be played at a neutral location, the Fashion Race Course on Long Island. The impending clash created so much anticipation that the sponsors were emboldened to charge a 50-cent admission fee, the first known instance of spectators paying to watch baseball. At the July 20 opener "the stands were well filled, while the entire homestretch was filled with a triple row of carriages, besides hundreds which were upon the field and outside the course," vouched the *Spirit of the Times*. New York won a squeaker, 22–18. But Brooklyn came back on August 17 with a 29–8 blowout. In the rubber game, played on September 10, Brooklyn took a 2–0 lead in the top of the first but gave up seven in the bottom of the inning and never recovered, losing 29–18.

That was New York's last hurrah, though. As Brooklyn teams triumphed in one contest after another in early 1859, the *Spirit of the Times* huffily asked, "Is New York to rank second to the village over the other side of the river?" The answer was yes. "If we are ahead of the big city in nothing else, we can beat her in baseball," bragged the *Brooklyn Eagle,* which also accepted as fact that "nowhere has the National game of Baseball taken firmer hold than in Brooklyn and nowhere are there better players."

By the time the Giants and the Dodgers came along, in other words, the baseball rivalry between New York and Brooklyn had been flourishing for more than 30 years.

One thing that makes the Giant-Dodger rivalry the best in baseball is how often both teams have been good, how rarely they've both been bad, and how tenaciously the underdog has battled in between. At the rivalry's peak, from 1946 to 1971, the Giants and Dodgers finished either one-two or within five games of first place an amazing nine times. Earlier, the Giants regularly contended while the Dodgers took on the spoiler role. Later, the

Dodgers dominated and the Giants became determined underdogs. And get this: over the course of the entire rivalry—from 1890 to 2002, 113 seasons in all—the Giants and Dodgers finished under .500 in the same year just *six* times.

The only rivalry that comes close to the Giants and Dodgers is that of the Boston Red Sox and New York Yankees. But it started later (1903) and didn't really get going until the Red Sox sold Babe Ruth to the Yankees in 1919. It's also a lopsided affair, not so much a rivalry as an adult version of the schoolyard bully beating up the skinny kid. In the 83 seasons since the Ruth deal, the Yankees have finished ahead of the Red Sox 65 times (78 percent). The Giant-Dodger rivalry is much more balanced: over its 113 seasons the Giants have finished ahead of the Dodgers 59 times, the Dodgers ahead of the Giants 54 times. And you can't beat this for parity: from 1890 to 2002, the Giants hold a mere 1,099-1,073 edge over the Dodgers in games played against each other.

Another factor that makes the Giant-Dodger rivalry the best in baseball is its huge cast of mythic heroes, battlegrounds, and moments: John Montgomery Ward, Roger Connor, and Amos Rusie; Ned Hanlon, Bill Dahlen, and Wee Willie Keeler; John McGraw and Wilbert Robinson; the Polo Grounds and Ebbets Field; Mathewson, Terry, Hubbell, and Ott; Leo the Lip; Red Barber and Russ Hodges; Jackie; Willie; Snider and Hodges and Campy and Pee Wee and Skoonj; Thomson, Branca, and the Shot Heard 'Round the World; Walter O'Malley and Horace Stoneham; McCovey and Cepeda versus Koufax and Drysdale; Marichal and Roseboro; Garvey, Lopes, Cey, and Russell; Tommy Lasorda; Joe Morgan and the Little Shot Heard 'Round the World; Piazza and Karros; Bonds and Kent.

And then there are the fans. Through the decades (and, remarkably, in two sets of cities 3,000 miles apart) Giant and Dodger partisans have rooted so passionately against each other that, just as during the Civil War, conflicting loyalties have divided neighborhoods and even family members—with less dire consequences, of course, although more than one Giant-Dodger game has threatened to turn into a riot, and once an argument between fans ended in murder. By imbuing their team with every civic and personal virtue and attributing every dastardly vice to the other, Giant and Dodger fans have attained a quasi-religious clarity that renders the world simple and vivid. And who doesn't long for that? Or the solidarity that comes with it—so encompassing that on April 20, 1937, not a soul fingered Dick Bartell's assailant to authorities?

Except for boy meets girl, there's no human story more timeless than good versus evil. And there's no good versus evil story in baseball more timeless—or exciting—than the Giants and the Dodgers.

PART I

1883–1901: "Even Members of the Gentler Sex Have the Fever"

	Giants	Dodgers
Where They Played	Polo Grounds I, 1883–88 Polo Grounds II, 1889–90 Polo Grounds III, 1891–1901	Washington Park I, 1884–90 Eastern Park, 1891–97 Washington Park II, 1898–1901
Owners	John B. Day, 1883–92 Edward Talcott, 1893–94 Andrew Freedman, 1895–1901	Charles Byrne, 1884–97 Charles Ebbets, 1898–1901
Managers	John Clapp, 1883 James Price, 1884 John Montgomery Ward, 1884 Jim Mutrie, 1885–91 Pat Powers, 1892 John Montgomery Ward, 1893–94 George Davis, 1895 Jack Doyle, 1895 Harvey Watkins, 1895 Arthur Irwin, 1896 Bill Joyce, 1896–98 Cap Anson, 1898 John B. Day, 1899 Fred Hoey, 1899 Buck Ewing, 1900 George Davis, 1900–01	George Taylor, 1884 Charles Hackett, 1885 Charles Byrne, 1885–87 Bill McGunnigle, 1888–90 John Montgomery Ward, 1891–92 Dave Foutz, 1893–96 Billy Barnie, 1897–98 Mike Griffin, 1898 Charles Ebbets, 1898 Ned Hanlon, 1899–1901

	Giants	Dodgers
Best Players	Buck Ewing, Roger Connor, John Montgomery Ward, Mickey Welch, Tim Keefe, Amos Rusie, George Davis	Adonis Terry, Bob Caruthers, Dave Foutz, Wee Willie Keeler
Wore Both Uniforms but Shouldn't Have	John Montgomery Ward	Tom "Oyster" Burns
League Championships, **World Championships**	**1888, 1889** (in **1894** the Giants finished second but won the Temple Cup)	1889, **1890**, 1899, **1900**
Won-Lost vs. Each Other (1890–1901)	88–86 (.506)	86–88 (.494)
Won-Lost vs. Rest of League	National League, 1883–1901 1,238–1,053 (.540)	American Association, 1884–89 410–354 (.537) National League, 1890–1901 797–667 (.544)

By the end of the 1860s the New York Game had become baseball, the national pastime. Soldiers who had learned to throw, catch, and hit during Civil War encampments took the game home to every hamlet and hollow. New York publications with nationwide readerships further spread enthusiasm. Fans (then called cranks) showed a willingness to pay for superior play, and teams began to professionalize.

New York and Brooklyn fans remained the most fervent, especially about games against each other. "No other game throughout the year arouses the same amount of excitement that the Atlantic-Mutual games do," reported *Wilkes' Spirit*. "There is a certain amount of party feeling imparted to the game which appears to make the spectators feel as if they themselves were involved in the strife, and not merely lookers-on." The August 1865 match between Brooklyn's Atlantics and New York's Mutuals drew an estimated 18,000 cranks. For perspective, consider that three decades later the Giants and Dodgers averaged only 4,000 fans per home game.

The New York area also continued to produce the best players. The Cincinnati Red Stockings, baseball's first openly all-professional team, created a sensation in 1869 when they barnstormed from coast to coast without losing a game, but they fielded only one Cincinnati native, first baseman Charlie Gould. Brothers Harry and George Wright, the manager and top player respectively, grew up in Harlem. Third baseman Fred Waterman was a New Yorker too. Pitcher Asa Brainerd honed his craft with New York's Knickerbockers and Brooklyn's Stars and Excelsiors. Chief substitute Dick Hurley learned to play ball at Columbia University. Even team president Aaron Champion was an ex-New Yorker.

The Red Stockings' success led to a showdown between the professionalizers and baseball's amateur founders, who still controlled the game's ruling body, the National Association. In March 1871 the professionals broke away and formed the first major league, the National Association of Professional Base Ball Players (National Association for short, which made for some confusion with the amateur National Association). Teams in the new league included New York's Mutuals and Brooklyn's Atlantics and Eckfords. But the first professional circuit was in trouble from the start. The Eckfords dropped out after 1872, and the Atlantics folded after going 2–42 in the league's last season, 1875.

William Hulbert, owner of the Chicago franchise that would later become the Cubs, organized the National League in early 1876. He invited the strongest teams from the National Association to join him. He also invited the Mutuals, even though they embodied the evils that had ruined the Association. They skipped out on road trips. They drank and caroused, encouraging similar behavior in the stands and scaring away middle-class patrons. They engaged in *hippodroming*, or sleazy promotional stunts. Worst of all, they conspired with gamblers to throw games. But how could you have a major league without a team in America's biggest city?

When the Mutuals decided against taking their last road trip of the year, an enraged Hulbert put principle ahead of pragmatism and expelled them from the league. From 1879 to 1882 the upstate towns of Buffalo and Troy had National League teams, but not Manhattan and Brooklyn. Even before the grudge-carrying Hulbert died in 1882, the league was seeking reliable owners for a New York franchise. When the American Association arose that same year, it became clear that the first major league to establish viable roots in the New York area would gain a competitive advantage.

Young Manhattanite John B. Day flourished in the tobacco business, but in his heart he yearned to play baseball. He took up pitching for a team in New Jersey. Legend has it that the Nationals, a club from the District of Columbia, needed a pitcher for a game against a local Brooklyn nine. The Brooklyn team recommended Day, and the Nationals accepted him sight unseen. Good thing, too: he arrived wearing a frilled shirt, tight-fitting mauve pants, sky blue silk socks, and crimson-laced tennis shoes. After Brooklyn scored 12 runs off him in the first inning, the scornful Washingtonians banished him to the stands.

While moping over his performance, Day was accosted by small-time Massachusetts hustler James Mutrie, also eager for diamond glory. Mutrie convinced the gaudily garbed tycoon that he, Mutrie, had the experience to build a team better than those on the field. In 1880 the duo formed an independent outfit called the Metropolitans. A Wall Street bootblack asked Day why the Mets, as they were known, played in Brooklyn when a polo field at Sixth Avenue and 110th Street went virtually unused. Day took the suggestion and leased the original Polo Grounds, drawing big crowds.

Encouraged, Day and Mutrie scheduled 60 exhibitions against National League clubs in 1881. They won just 18, but that was enough for the newborn American Association to invite the Mets to join. Day and Mutrie cagily refused, and sure enough, the stronger, more prestigious National League offered them membership a year later. Attempting to corner the New York market, Day and Mutrie went back to the American Association, put the Mets there, and insisted on a brand-new franchise in the National League. Rather than concede New York to the other league, the N.L. bosses agreed.

New York's National League team, originally known as the Gothams, played its first game on May 1, 1883, and beat the Boston Red Stockings at the Polo Grounds in front of Ulysses S. Grant and 15,000 less-distinguished citizens. Although the American Association Mets were doing better in the standings, Day and Mutrie (the manager of the Mets) saw that the N.L. offered a more promising future, and began transferring the Mets' stars to the Gothams. They went for big players in the mold of Roger Connor, the 6'3", 220-pounder whose career record for home runs (138) stood until Babe Ruth broke it. Mutrie himself switched to the Gothams in 1885, and in the jubilation of an 11-inning win in front of eight thousand fans in Philadelphia proclaimed his players "My big fellows! My *giants*!" The name stuck, as did Mutrie's equally spontaneous rallying cry, "We are the people!"

Wary of the favoritism Day and Mutrie were showing their National League club, the American Association hedged its position with a franchise in Brooklyn. Before the 1883 season, real estate magnate and baseball enthusiast Charles Byrne pooled resources with a pair of casino operators, Joseph Doyle (his brother-in-law) and Ferdinand Abell, to start a team in the minor Interstate League. Byrne set up a grandstand on Fifth Avenue between Third and Fifth Streets and named it Washington Park in honor of the Founding Father who lost the Battle of Long Island there in 1776. (Today that land is Byrne Park.) He let Doyle manage, and hired 23-year-old Manhattan native Charles Ebbets to sell scorecards and tickets.

Byrne's team drew 6,000 cranks to its first home game, a May 12, 1883, victory over Trenton. It finished first and did well financially. The American Association, unperturbed by the ownership group's gambling interests, offered Byrne and his partners a franchise for 1884, and they accepted. Team nicknames came and went in those days, but before long Byrne's outfit was

James Mutrie. In modern terms he was the Giants' general manager, and team captain Buck Ewing was the field manager. (National Baseball Hall of Fame Library, Cooperstown, N.Y.)

commonly referred to as the Trolley Dodgers, in honor of the pedestrians scrambling to avoid the streetcars hurtling down the city's crowded thoroughfares. In some accounts, the term was a slur used by New Yorkers, who saw in the "primitive" mass transit system (Manhattan had elevated trains by the late 1870s) proof of the City of Churches' inferiority. As often happens, the targets of the epithet turned it into an endearment. Soon the name was so commonly used it was contracted to plain old Dodgers.

The Giants and Dodgers met for the first time as major league teams on April 18, 1884, in an exhibition at Washington Park. New York's Mickey Welch trounced Brooklyn's star pitcher, William "Adonis" Terry, 8–0. The Dodgers fared poorly in their inaugural American Association campaign, finishing 33½ games behind Mutrie's champion Mets. In 1885 they passed the Mets (who had lost Mutrie and pitcher Tim Keefe to the Giants) but were still 26 games from the top. With Byrne managing, the Dodgers leaped to third in 1886. Byrne's magic wore off in 1887, though, and the team fell back to sixth.

After 1887, Byrne snapped up ex-Met Darby O'Brien, added outfielder Tom (later known as "Oyster") Burns from the American Association's Baltimore club, and traded for catcher Doc Bushong and outfielder-pitchers Bob Caruthers and Dave Foutz from the American Association's St. Louis Browns (eventually to become the Cardinals). He appointed moustachioed Bill McGunnigle to manage, and in 1888 the Dodgers enjoyed their best season yet, finishing second, just six and a half games behind St. Louis.

Rechristened the Bridegrooms after several players married within weeks of each other, the 1889 Dodgers set a major league record by drawing over 350,000 customers. They battled defending champ St. Louis to the wire. The key games came a month before the end of the season. On September 7 the Bridegrooms trailed the Browns 4–2 through eight innings at a packed Washington Park. The Browns, stalling since they took the lead in the sixth, claimed it was too dark to continue playing, and lit candles by their bench to dramatize the point. The umpire ruled that the game would go on. The Browns tested him by leaving the field. The ump declared a forfeit. Bottle-hurling Brooklyn cranks so intimidated the departing St. Louis club that it refused to return to Washington Park the next day, forfeiting that contest also. The Bridegrooms won the pennant by two games.

The World Series in those days was known as the Dauvray Cup Championship, after a big silver trophy designed by actress Helen Dauvray, wife of Giant shortstop John Montgomery Ward. The first team to win six games won the series, and the first team to win three World Series in a row gained permanent possession of the Cup. Which National League team would Brooklyn, as American Association champion, meet for the coveted prize? None other than the New York Giants.

1. 1889: "I Do Mind Being Robbed"

The 1889 World Series was the first time the Giants and Dodgers played for something more than pride, and spirits ran high on both sides. In addition to the usual antagonisms, an element of class had crept in: the National League Giants appealed to the refined element, charging 50 cents admission, resting on Sundays, and prohibiting consumption of alcohol, while the American Association Dodgers played to a rougher crowd, charging just 25 cents, taking the field on the Lord's day (to the consternation of many in the City of Churches), and letting patrons drown in beer if they wished.

The Brooklyn Bridge had opened six years earlier, guaranteeing that partisans of both teams would mix in large numbers at each game. With a tad of anxiety, the *New York Times* declared: "The rivalry between New York and Brooklyn as regards baseball is unparalleled in the history of the national game. It is not confined to the players or the attachés of the clubs, but the patrons take part in it. Old men, middle-aged men, beardless youths, small boys, and even members of the gentler sex have the fever, and when the champions of the two teams meet heated arguments as to the merits of the nines are sure to follow."

Nearly 8,500 cranks assembled for the opener, played at the new Polo Grounds. The old Polo Grounds had been claimed for construction of a grand entrance to the north end of Central Park (Douglass Circle), so John Day moved his team uptown, to a pastoral lot that would eventually become the corner of Eighth Avenue and 155th Street in Harlem. At the west end of the lot, nearly abutting the Hudson River, loomed a steep, craggy hill called Coogan's Bluff, after James J. Coogan, who later became Manhattan's borough president. The land beneath was expansive enough to fit two ballfields. Day built a wooden grandstand around the south end.

The Giants figured to win handily. Jim Mutrie's big fellows were the reigning champs, having won the World Series the year before. They faced stiffer competition in the National League than the Bridegrooms did in the American Association. And they had *six* Hall of Famers. Catcher Buck Ewing hit .327 (league norm: .264), and his strong arm was a key weapon in an era when teams routinely stole over 200 bases. First baseman Roger Connor led the N.L. in RBIs and slugging average, and also finished among the top five in triples, homers, walks, and on-base percentage. Shortstop John Montgomery Ward struck out only seven times in 479 at-bats and stole 62 bases. Bombastic outfielder "Orator Jim" O'Rourke hit .321 and finished third in the league in doubles. And then there were the pitchers, Tim Keefe and Mickey Welch. Though wins are widely presumed to have come wholesale back then, only Keefe, Welch, and three others from that first generation of major league hurlers reached the 300-victory plateau.

Who did the Bridegrooms offer in opposition? Left fielder and leadoff man Darby O'Brien ranked third in the American Association in runs scored. Right fielder Oyster Burns hit a productive .304, driving in an even hundred runs. And first baseman Dave Foutz finished second in RBIs. But most of the position players hit underwhelmingly. Without good fielding and strong performances from pitchers Adonis Terry and Bob Caruthers (who were also such good hitters they batted sixth or seventh), the Bridegrooms would never have won the pennant.

On the streets of New York and Brooklyn, a $100 bet on the Giants would get you only $75 more if they won. But Church City savant Henry Chadwick took a more sanguine view of the Bridegrooms' prospects: "To win will give the Giants but little honor, comparatively speaking, in addition to what they have already earned, while to lose means the most costly defeat the club has ever sustained; while with Brooklyn, if they win, it will be the greatest event in the history of the game in that city since the defeat of the Red Stockings by the Atlantics in 1870, while if they lose it will only give them another year of preparation to win in 1890, and be nothing to their discredit."

John Day and Charles Byrne each got to name an umpire. Day inexplicably selected the American Association's John Gaffney. Not only was Gaffney considered inferior to former N.L. arbiter John Kelly, widely expected to get Day's nod, but he was on bad terms with John Montgomery Ward, who had once given him a black eye. "He swore vengeance against Ward and the New York team at the time, and that old feeling may come back," fretted the *Times*. Worse yet, Charles Byrne was indirectly tempting Gaffney, a failed manager, with another shot at running a team; scuttlebutt had Bridegroom manager Bill McGunnigle being replaced after the World Series by Baltimore's Billy Barnie, who in turn would be replaced by Gaffney.

It didn't take long for Day to suffer the consequences of his choice. The Bridegrooms, batting in the bottom of the first (despite playing on the road — many baseball customs hadn't yet crystallized) scored five runs off a tired Tim Keefe. But the Giants chipped away at Adonis Terry, and in the seventh took a commanding 10–6 lead, helped by what may have been the first seventh-inning stretch. "Somebody cried, 'Stretch for luck!' And instantly the vast throng on the grandstand rose gradually and then settled down, just as long grass bends to the breath of the zephyr," recorded the *Sporting News*.

Brooklyn put a pair across in their half of the seventh to close within two. With darkness approaching, the Giants batted quickly in the eighth to speed up the game. The Bridegrooms just as strategically stalled. The ploy worked. With two out and a man on second, Darby O'Brien hit what should have been an inning-ending grounder to Giant second sacker Danny Richardson, but in the dimming light Richardson muffed it and a run scored. Then Brooklyn's Hub Collins hit one over Orator Jim O'Rourke's head to tie the game, and Oyster Burns hit one past George Gore in center to give Brooklyn the lead; it's likely neither O'Rourke nor Gore saw the balls off the bat.

Dave Foutz slapped a double past third base to score Burns, giving Brooklyn a 12–10 edge, then intentionally let John Montgomery Ward tag him out. That retired the side, which meant each team had batted an equal number of innings. The Bridegrooms appealed to the umpires to call the game on account of darkness. Byrne's umpire readily agreed. It was up to Day's man, John Gaffney. He surprised everyone by assenting. The Bridegrooms carried the first win of the Series—and their captain, Darby O'Brien — out of the Polo Grounds.

New Yorkers were enraged. They streamed over the Brooklyn Bridge for the second game, held at Washington Park, and swelled the crowd to over 16,000, six thousand more than had ever seen a World Series game before. Spectators formed a wall around the outfield. "Thousands of human faces could be seen in all directions, and save a few tilts, in which dyed in the wool 'cranks' took part, the best of good nature prevailed," noted the *Times*. Behind a strong effort from pitcher Ed "Cannonball" Crane, the Giants picked up a 6–2 win against the Bridegrooms' 40-game winner, Bob Caruthers.

Back at the Polo Grounds for the third game, Giant captain Buck Ewing said that "it's a hundred dollars to a toothpick that we win today." He sparked the Giants' first-inning rally, slamming a double to knock in outfielder "Silent Mike" Tiernan and coming home on a John Montgomery Ward single. But pitcher Mickey Welch, widely credited with inventing the change-up, had no heater to set up his off-speed stuff. The Bridegrooms tied the game with a pair in the second, then took the lead in the third. At the end of five Brooklyn was in front, 8–5.

The Giants put together a couple of runs in the sixth to make the score 8–7. They brought in Hank O'Day to relieve the exhausted Welch, who did not appear again in the Series. O'Day held Brooklyn scoreless in the sixth, seventh, and eighth. But he couldn't prevent the Bridegrooms from stalling in hopes of having another game called for darkness. The crowd of over 5,000, consisting mostly of Giant cranks, knew exactly what the Bridegrooms were up to and hissed the Brooklyn squad remorselessly.

Roger Connor led off the Giant ninth with a single against Bob Caruthers, brought in to close the game. With one out, Orator Jim O'Rourke and third baseman Art Whitney worked Caruthers for walks to load the bases. Giant cranks went into a frenzy. Their big fellows were going to pull this one out!

Except umpire John Gaffney chose that moment to call the game on account of darkness.

Objective observers pointed out that Mickey Welch had given up eight runs in five innings, and had he been replaced earlier, the Giants would have won. But New York manager Jim Mutrie blamed the Bridegrooms: "The days of such tactics are gone by, and it comes with poor grace from the Brooklyn men to resort to them. Such methods are disgusting and do not tend to elevate the national pastime. The Brooklyns played like schoolboys." Everyone else, starting with John Montgomery Ward and Orator Jim O'Rourke, loudly blamed Gaffney, whom the fans so harassed he needed an escort from the Polo Grounds.

Thanks to sub-40-degree weather and a howling wind — this was late October, after all — only 3,045 cranks showed up at Washington Park for game four. A good thing for the city of Brooklyn, too, because if more New Yorkers had witnessed what followed, a riot might have ensued. Trailing 7–2 in the top of the sixth against Adonis Terry, the Giants rallied for five to tie. They'd have scored six, but Gaffney denied them a run by declaring George Gore out for being hit by the ball during a rundown, no more an out then than it is now. Gaffney also had to decide whether a pickoff throw that hit O'Rourke in the third base coach's box constituted interference. Giant captain Buck Ewing threatened to pull his team off the field if the call went for Brooklyn, and Gaffney relented, allowing John Montgomery Ward to cross the plate with the tying run.

All that did, however, was give the Bridegrooms a pretense for stalling. They argued for 22 minutes— until it got dark. Then Terry struck out Connor to end the Giant sixth and the Bridegrooms came to bat. Shortstop Germany Smith hit a grounder that Giant second baseman Richardson booted for an error. With two out, Hub Collins walked. Oyster Burns hit a fly ball to left that O'Rourke never saw. The Giants were still looking for it when Burns crossed the plate with a home run. At that

William "Adonis" Terry. The lady-killing pitcher started five of the nine 1889 World Series games for the Bridegrooms. (National Baseball Hall of Fame Library, Cooperstown, N.Y.)

point — you guessed it — John Gaffney called the game on account of darkness.

New Yorkers went apoplectic. Glossing over the fact that he was responsible for Gaffney's presence, John Day fulminated, "Three times have we lost in this series through trickery and we shall do so no more. Unless the Brooklyn club plays on its merits the same as the New Yorks are doing, the series will end at once. This kind of ballplaying and umpiring is enough to kill the game. I do not mind losing games on their merit, but I do mind being robbed of them."

He and Bridegroom owner Charles Byrne met in Brooklyn the next day with their captains and the two umpires. After Day let off enough steam to power a locomotive, the parties reached an agreement. All subsequent games in New York would begin an hour earlier, at two o'clock, and all games in Brooklyn would begin at two-thirty. Only the team captains could talk to the umpires, and no one would dispute calls—the most common ruse for delaying games.

The game that followed suggested Day's tantrum had been unnecessary, as the Giants clobbered the Bridegrooms, 11–3. But game six would not have been the best of the series had the New York owner failed to assert himself. The Bridegrooms touched Hank O'Day for their only run in the second; they would have scored more had Adonis Terry and third baseman George Pinkney not been thrown out on the basepaths. But through 26 outs it looked as if that wouldn't matter, because Terry was shutting out the mighty Manhattanites.

John Montgomery Ward was New York's last chance. Down to his last strike — and with most Giant cranks leaving Washington Park — he slapped a single. Brooklyn catcher Joe Visner had nowhere near Buck Ewing's arm, and Ward took immediate advantage, stealing second. Then he took off for third and was safe again. Up came big Roger Connor. Bill McGunnigle, determined to show that his Bridegrooms played "manly" ball, declined to relieve Terry or intentionally walk Connor.

Again Adonis Terry came within a strike of ending the game. But Connor belted a liner that ate up Bridegroom shortstop Jumbo Davis to bring home Ward and tie the score. Reported the *Times*, "From the outset the New York cranks were compelled to hold their peace and listen to the exultant remarks and shouts of the Brooklynites. Their corked-up enthusiasm knew no bounds ... hats, canes, and umbrellas were thrown in the air."

The game went into extra innings. Both sides were retired one-two-three in the 10th. O'Day put away the Bridegrooms on three fly balls in the top of the 11th. But Terry got off to an ominous start in the bottom of the frame, yielding a single to little-used Mike Slattery. One out later, Ewing grounded Slattery to second. That brought up John Montgomery Ward.

After his do-or-die single in the ninth, Ward had the psychological, and quite likely the physical, edge over the tiring Terry. He also had the remaining Giant cranks roaring for him. But the best he could produce was a roller to Bridegroom shortstop Jumbo Davis. Ward was very fast, however, and Davis had to hurry. He didn't hurry enough: Ward beat out the throw. Slattery, going to third on the play, kept running. By the time Bridegroom first baseman Dave Foutz reacted, Slattery crossed the plate with the winning run. "The game in which the representatives of New York and Brooklyn took part ... surpasses, perhaps, anything ever seen on a baseball field," the *New York Times* marveled about a game that, if not for John Day's tirade and the changes that followed, probably would have been called with Brooklyn ahead after eight.

That cliffhanger tied the series at three wins apiece, but it broke the Bridegrooms. They fell behind early and lost the next game 11–7 at the Polo Grounds, then lost a 16–7 blowout at Washington Park. Facing elimination, they again pitted Adonis Terry against Hank O'Day. Before anyone was out, they put two runs across. But once O'Day warmed up on that frigid afternoon, he shut down the Bridegrooms, giving up just two hits the rest of the way. The Giants got one run in the bottom of the first on a Ward triple, then tied it up in the sixth when Ward singled, stole second, advanced to third on a groundout, and came home on a sacrifice fly.

The deciding run scored anticlimactically. In the bottom of the seventh, Slattery reached on a force and stole second. With two outs, Bridegroom catcher Doc Bushong made a mistake worse than Mickey Owen's half a century later: he missed strike three to Buck Ewing, and by the time he recovered the ball, Slattery had scored all the way from second with the series clincher.

Brooklyn had a chance to even the game in the ninth when O'Day flubbed a Jumbo Smith comebacker for an error, but Bushong lined into a double play. It still wasn't over: Darby O'Brien coaxed out a walk. But Ewing threw him out trying to steal second, and on that dismal note, the 1889 World Series ended. "We are the people!" shouted triumphant Giant fans, banging a gong to alert the rest of Manhattan to its glorious victory over rival Brooklyn.

John Gaffney never got that managerial job in Baltimore (or any other). Charles Byrne rehired Bill McGunnigle, who was so popular with his players that they presented him a gold watch and diamond-studded locket after the Series.

2. The 1890s: "The Hottest Baseball Locality on Earth"

The 1889 World Series could have been the first of many between the Giants and Dodgers. But the Players League, organized by John Montgomery Ward, dashed the possibility.

The new league aimed to increase the players' autonomy and income, both severely circumscribed by the reserve clause, which prohibited a player from signing with any but his current team. Led by John T. Brush of the N.L.'s Indianapolis club, the owners also planned to rank players by skill level and pay the same salary to everyone at the same level. Ward, a labor activist and aspiring lawyer, responded by securing financial backing in eight cities, including New York and Brooklyn, and starting the Players League. Overnight it lured away most National League regulars and several key players from the American Association.

Ward's revolt imperiled the National League; it now had to compete against two other leagues with almost all its best players gone. Through complicated backroom dealing, it seduced Charles Byrne and his popular, profitable, intact Brooklyn Bridegrooms from the American Association. But in gaining a top draw and damaging one of its competitors, the National League permanently altered baseball's best rivalry. Never again would the Giants and Dodgers battle for a world championship. They would, however, compete for the pennant every year, meeting as many as 22 times during the regular season, which allowed the rivalry to sink even deeper roots among players and fans.

Most of the National League Giants defected to the Players League

John Montgomery Ward. No fool for a client he: when the Giants sought a court injunction to stop him from bolting to the Players League, he argued his own case and won. (National Baseball Hall of Fame Library, Cooperstown, N.Y.)

Giants (Ward became shortstop and manager of the Players League's Brooklyn entry). John Day, whose new recruits possessed nowhere near the turnstile charm of the "real" Giants, averaged fewer than a thousand customers per game and lost money in buckets. To remain solvent, he sold shares of his team to colleagues like John T. Brush. He lost the franchise in 1892 when Edward Talcott, working with Brush, gained a controlling block of stock.

Only two good things came out of the Players League for the Giants. The upstart circuit built a magnificent grandstand on the north side of the Polo Grounds, which they occupied for the next 20 years. And in the search for pitchers to replace Keefe, O'Day, and Crane, the Giants found Amos Rusie, first in the line of wild fastballers that includes Bob Feller, Nolan Ryan, and Randy Johnson. Rusie won more than 30 games four straight seasons, led the league in strikeouts five times, and was one of the main reasons pitchers were pushed to 60 feet, six inches from home plate in 1893.

After the Giants won the Temple Cup (a playoff between the N.L.'s first- and second-place teams) in 1894, Talcott sold his interest to Andrew Freedman, a real estate speculator and prominent cog in Manhattan's Tammany Hall Democratic machine. In earlier times, Tammany gave needed leverage to the Irish and other disadvantaged immigrants, but by the 1890s it had devolved into the most corrupt political organization in America. A hot-headed egomaniac, Freedman changed managers at a whim and humiliated the players. By century's end he'd run the franchise into the ground.

For Brooklyn, the move to the National League paid immediate dividends, as the Bridegrooms won the 1890 pennant. But the triumphs of 1889 and 1890 inflated Charles Byrne's opinion of his baseball acumen. In 1891 he built Eastern Park in distant Ridgewood, too far from his fan base and too close to windy Jamaica Bay. He also fired Bill McGunnigle and replaced him with John Montgomery Ward. In Byrne's defense, who wouldn't want Ward on his team? Ward managed tolerably well, but not as well as he played shortstop, and he went back to the Giants after 1892. Byrne's next managerial appointments, Dave Foutz and Billy Barnie, did no better; from 1893 to 1898 the Dodgers never finished higher than fifth.

But Byrne did bestow one lasting gift on Brooklyn: Charles Hercules Ebbets. An architectural draftsman, Ebbets rose from jack-of-all-trades to Byrne's right-hand man, buying shares in the club. Upon Byrne's death in January 1898, the other Dodger stockholders named Ebbets their managing partner. He abandoned Eastern Park and built a new grandstand a few blocks from the old Washington Park, calling the new digs Washington Park also. When manager Billy Barnie lost 20 of the first 35 games in 1898, Ebbets first replaced him with Mike Griffin, then took over the team himself, compiling an abysmal 38–68 record. In need of a real manager, he formed a partnership with Harry von der Horst, owner of the legendary but under-attended Baltimore Orioles, and secured the services of Ned Hanlon.

Though notorious for vicious, underhanded tactics, Hanlon's Orioles were baseball's first think tank, inventing the Baltimore Chop (in which the batter hits the ball straight down, so it bounces too high for the fielder to throw him out), perfecting the bunt and hit-and-run, and giving the pitcher backup duties on throws from the outfield. Their record over the last five years under Hanlon: a jaw-dropping 452–214 (.679). Hanlon brought with him Hall of Famers Hughie Jennings, Joe Kelley, and Brooklyn native Wee Willie Keeler, whose formula for success, "I hit 'em where they ain't," was an early example of the semiliterate sagacity his townspeople became famous for. The Dodgers won pennants in 1899 and 1900, and their name changed again, this time to Hanlon's Superbas, after a vaudeville act as successful as they were.

The first National League regular season contest between the Giants and Dodgers took place on May 3, 1890, in Brooklyn. Bob Caruthers sailed to a 7–3 victory over Mickey Welch in front of 3,774 at Washington Park. The rivals got into their first brawl a few weeks later, on June 12, 1890, when Darby O'Brien, coaching at third, deceived the Giants into thinking he was a baserunner and drew an errant pickoff throw. Two days later Tom Lovett hurled the rivalry's first shutout, a 16–0 Brooklyn romp. How intense was that first year? Although Brooklyn won the pennant with an 86–43 record (.667), it went just 10–8 (.556) against the sub-.500 Giants.

Lovett made rivalry history again in 1891 when he threw its first no-hitter, a 4–0 triumph at Eastern Park that was also Brooklyn's first no-hitter in the National League. Six weeks later Amos Rusie got the Giants even, fastballing his way to a 6–0 no-hitter at the Polo Grounds. On September 26, 1891, Rusie won both ends of the first doubleheader in rivalry history, although the second game was called after six innings on account of darkness. By 1896 the rivalry inspired the *Sporting Life* to deem the New York-Brooklyn area the "hottest baseball locality on earth."

Though the rivalry prospered, the City of Churches did not, undone by the huge success of the Brooklyn Bridge. Used by a quarter of a million people each day, the Bridge made commuting to Manhattan so easy that Brooklyn's population surged from 570,000 in 1880 to nearly 900,000 in 1894. The city government piled up a huge deficit providing streets and utilities for the new inhabitants. Property taxes soared, angering the city's established businesses and residents. Worse yet, an irremediable water shortage loomed.

New York spent more than twice as much per capita on its citizens but was in far better financial shape thanks to its stupendous tax base; the businesses in a single skyscraper paid as much tax in a year as several hundred Brooklyn homeowners. Manhattan also possessed a seemingly bottomless water supply. To many of Brooklyn's civic leaders, the only way out of its problems was to consolidate with New York.

What about Tammany Hall, though? Predominantly Republican Brooklynites shuddered at the thought of subservience to Manhattan's crooked Democratic machine. But supporters of consolidation argued that the upstanding people of Brooklyn, together with Manhattan's reformers and honest businessmen, could overcome Tammany's hold on the municipal levers. They asked the state legislature to authorize a nonbinding referendum on creation of a Greater New York City that would include not just Manhattan and Brooklyn, but the Bronx, Queens, and Staten Island. The referendum was held in November 1894.

Manhattanites, envisioning renewed development in Brooklyn that would allow them to escape their crowded, shabby tenements, voted by more than 60 percent for consolidation. So did residents of Queens. The Bronx and Staten Island also came out in favor. But in Brooklyn, proponents of consolidation had to overcome mountains of civic pride. Why can't we just connect ourselves to New York's water supply and leave it at that? asked the *Brooklyn Eagle*. In the end, Brooklynites passed the referendum by a mere 277 votes out of more than 129,000 cast.

It was nonbinding, however, and Brooklyn's municipal patriots immediately launched a campaign against the merger, invoking both highminded, Jeffersonian ideals of local control and low-minded anxieties about immigrants pouring over from Manhattan's slums. In 1895 they talked the legislature out of going forward.

It proved a temporary respite, however. State Republican Party chairman Thomas Platt craved the mayoralty of New York and figured he'd have an easier time getting it with Brooklyn's Republican votes added to the tally. The state's Republican governor, Levi P. Morton, had been vice president under Benjamin Harrison and wanted to run for president in 1896. Platt made Morton a deal: he would help Morton win the presidential nomination at the upcoming Republican Convention if Morton signed legislation chartering a greater New York City. Over a storm of protest from both sides of the East River, Morton signed a bill that turned Brooklyn into a borough of New York effective January 1, 1898. Fat lot of good it did either man: Morton lost the presidential nomination to William McKinley, and Platt never became mayor.

In the cold and rain of New Year's Eve, 1897, New Yorkers gathered at City Hall and celebrated wildly when San Francisco mayor James Phelan pressed a button that sent an electric pulse 3,000 miles to unfurl the new flag of Greater New York. At a more somber convocation in front of Brooklyn's City Hall — henceforth Borough Hall — the editor of the *Brooklyn Eagle,* anti-consolidation crusader St. Clair McElway, reminded the crowd that "though borough it may be, Brooklyn it is, Brooklyn it remains, and Brooklynites are we!"

More than a century later, Brooklyn still mourns its loss of autonomy. "We are linked to the rest of New York City by means of a questionable act of municipal empire building," rued Kenneth Adams, chair of the Brooklyn Chamber of Commerce, in 1999. Newspaper columnist and Brooklynite Pete Hamill lamented, "An inner voice always seems to whisper: there was another place here once and it was better than this." To a city robbed of independence, the Dodgers became a symbol — many would say *the* symbol — of its distinct identity. And for the next six decades, games against the Giants took on overtones of civil war.

But Brooklyn fans almost didn't get to keep their Dodgers. The American Association collapsed at the end of 1891, and to forestall further competition, the National League absorbed four A.A. franchises. The expansion turned the N.L. into a big league (which is where we get that term) of 12 teams. Too many for those days, and as the 1890s wore on, talk of contraction arose. With the consolidation of Brooklyn into New York, wouldn't it be unfair for one city to have two entries in the National League when other cities had none?

Charles Ebbets came to the rescue by doing some consolidating of his own with the Baltimore Orioles. But even if he hadn't arrived in the nick of time, the following argument, advanced by John B. Foster (later a Giant official) in the *Sporting Life,* might have saved the Dodgers for Brooklyn: "As long as the present generation exists there always will be the feeling of rivalry between the sections of Brooklyn proper and New York proper that there has been in the past. It will be plenty strong enough to create a vast amount of baseball sentiment."

When the National League contracted in 1900, it retained Brooklyn, shedding teams in Cleveland, Louisville, Washington, and Baltimore instead. As owners of the Orioles, Ebbets, von der Horst, and Hanlon profited handsomely.

In looting the once-proud franchise, however, they failed to make away with one very valuable nugget: its manager, the bellicose but brilliant John Joseph McGraw.

PART II

1902–1931: Little Napoleon and Uncle Robbie

	Giants	Dodgers
Where They Played	Polo Grounds III, 1902–11 Hilltop Park, 1911 Polo Grounds IV, 1911–31	Washington Park II, 1902–12 Ebbets Field, 1913–31
Owners	Andrew Freedman, 1902 John T. Brush, 1902–12 Harry Hempstead, 1912–19 Charles Stoneham, 1919–31	Charles H. Ebbets, 1902–25 Edward McKeever, 1925 Steve McKeever and Joseph Gilleaudeau, 1925–31
Managers	Horace Fogel, 1902 George "Heinie" Smith, 1902 John McGraw, 1902–31	Ned Hanlon, 1902–05 Patsy Donovan, 1906–08 Harry Lumley, 1909 Bill Dahlen, 1910–13 Wilbert Robinson, 1914–31
Best Players	Christy Mathewson, Iron Joe McGinnity, Roger Bresnahan, Larry Doyle, Ross Youngs, Frankie Frisch, Bill Terry, Travis Jackson	Bill Dahlen, Jimmy Sheckard, Nap Rucker, Zack Wheat, Jake Daubert, Burleigh Grimes, Dazzy Vance, Babe Herman
Wore Both Uniforms but Shouldn't Have	Fred Merkle	Leon Cadore
League Championships, **World Championships**	1904, **1905,** 1911, 1912, 1913, 1917, **1921, 1922,** 1923, 1924	1916, 1920
Won-Lost vs. Each Other	369–276 (.572)	276–369 (.428)
Won-Lost vs. Rest of League	2,295–1,574 (.593)	1,838–2,025 (.476)

Say you were born in a podunk village to immigrant parents who, though educated, barely scraped by. You're the oldest of seven kids, not counting the half-sister by your dad's first marriage. Ever wish the house was a little less crowded? Here's something to haunt you the rest of your life: when you're 11 an epidemic kills your mom, your half-sister, and three siblings. Your father, mad with grief, expects you to help him earn a living and raise the younger children. When he catches you playing baseball instead, he beats you so badly you run away. Barely a teenager, you eke out a living as a newsboy and as a snack vendor on passenger trains.

You start to make your way in the world, but at 22 you come down with malaria. A year later you catch typhoid fever and nearly die. You celebrate your recovery by marrying a vivacious 20-year-old beauty, but after just two years together she dies a slow, agonizing death. At the age of 28 your right knee is dislocated, and the next year your other knee is so badly damaged it sometimes gives out on you. And then, just after your 30th birthday, a projectile hits you smack in the face, afflicting you with excruciating sinus infections the rest of your life.

How nice a guy would you be?

Such were the tribulations of John Joseph McGraw, the most successful manager in baseball history. A lot of good things happened to him also, like playing infield for the legendary Baltimore Orioles of the 1890s. But those who despised McGraw as a churlish bully—a legion that included every Brooklyn fan—usually overlooked this catalog of emotional and physical traumas when wondering how anyone so successful could behave as if the whole world was against him.

Plenty of managers have been pugnacious paranoiacs, but none have won like McGraw, who led the Giants to 10 pennants and three world championships—and might have had another of each had Fred Merkle not committed the infamous boner of 1908, turning a game-winning single in the heat of a pennant race into an inning-ending force-out. McGraw's 33 years as a manager (including two and a half with Baltimore) and 2,673 career victories rank second only to Connie Mack, whose winning percentage of .486 McGraw bested by a whopping .100 points.

How did he do it? He had a keen eye for talent and, except for a few years under owner Harry Hempstead, could buy, sell, trade, and release players as he saw fit. He ran his team with an iron hand: "Any *mental* error, any failure to think, and McGraw would be all over you. And I do believe he had the most vicious tongue of any man who ever lived," recalled Fred Snodgrass, a Giant outfielder for five seasons. And he rode umpires—or anyone else in the way of victory—with a relentlessness that has no modern equivalent.

McGraw's vices—fighting, gambling, and drinking (the last undiminished by Prohibition)—frequently got him in trouble. But he was also a one-man benevolent society, doling out cash to indigent ex-players and finding Polo Grounds jobs for struggling alumni like Mickey Welch, Amos Rusie, and even former owner John B. Day. And after the game, provided he hadn't been tippling, he was a quiet, charming individual, an honored member of Gotham's smart set.

McGraw chose his friends well. The best he ever had was Oriole teammate Wilbert Robinson. They were, perhaps, the oddest couple in baseball history. McGraw was small, Robinson large; McGraw from a poor, broken family, Robinson from a middle-class, loving one. Their biggest contrast was in temperament. Arlie Latham, whom McGraw hired as baseball's first full-time coach, said, "Robbie sleeps in a salve factory and McGraw eats gunpowder every morning for breakfast and washes it down with warm blood." Nonetheless, McGraw and Robinson formed a tight bond. They went into business together, starting the Diamond Café, a combination men's club, bowling alley, and saloon, near Baltimore's theater district. It was wildly successful.

Wilbert Robinson, 10 years older than McGraw, was a butcher's son from Bolton (later annexed to Hudson), Massachusetts. When he was 20 his father died and left him the butcher shop, but he forsook the secure life of a village meatcutter for the vicissitudes of professional baseball. At 5'9" and well over 200 pounds he was built to play catcher. Over time he made himself a decent hitter, on June 10, 1892, slapping seven hits in a nine-inning game, a record tied but never exceeded.

When Harry von der Horst and Ned Hanlon merged the Orioles with the Dodgers in 1899, they sent most of Baltimore's stars to Brooklyn. But McGraw and Robinson refused to go. They made more money from the Diamond Café than they did from baseball. They'd bought nice new row houses next door to each other. And McGraw probably realized that with everyone else gone to Brooklyn, he was the logical choice to become Baltimore's new skipper, even though he was just 26. With the older, calmer Robinson as his deputy, McGraw took to managing as if he'd been born to it. He also had his best season as a player, batting .391 and compiling an on-base percentage (.547) no National Leaguer topped until Barry Bonds in 2002.

Prodded by Giant owner Andrew Freedman, who (because he couldn't take advantage of it himself) deplored the multiple-team, or *syndicate*, ownership that made Brooklyn the runaway champion of 1899, the National League decided to cut four of its 12 franchises in early 1900, including Baltimore. Once more McGraw and Robinson became property of Ned Hanlon's Brooklyn team. But again Hanlon couldn't budge them from Baltimore, so he sold them to the Cardinals. At first McGraw and Robinson did not go to St. Louis. But the Cardinals lured them out of early retirement with huge contracts (at $9,500, McGraw's was probably the highest of any player's) that included, amazingly, a rescission of the reserve clause.

The contraction of the National League created an opportunity for the Western League, run by ambitious, authoritarian Byron Bancroft "Ban" Johnson. Johnson renamed his circuit the American League, set up shop in Cleveland, Washington, and Baltimore, three of the eastern cities abandoned by the N.L., and went major in 1901, promising cleaner baseball and a more orderly atmosphere. McGraw and Robinson fled St. Louis as soon as they could, returned to Baltimore, and became part owners of the American League's new Orioles. McGraw also managed the team.

One of the players McGraw tried to sign for his new club was Charley Grant, star of an African American outfit in Chicago. His attempts to pass Grant off as a Cherokee went awry when Charles Comiskey, owner of the White Sox, recognized Grant and tattled to Ban Johnson. McGraw was a strong character, and he wasn't afraid of Ban Johnson. But he wasn't a crusader, either. He dropped Grant, leaving the integration of major league baseball to a later time and more resolute individuals.

That was just the first of McGraw's problems with the American League. He and Ban Johnson, all smiles at the league's inception, were soon snarling at each other. Johnson promised clean baseball, and here was McGraw grabbing the belts of runners at third so they couldn't score on sacrifice flies. Although the Orioles played well, they had the third-worst attendance in a league that lacked — and desperately wanted — a franchise in New York, where Freedman's hapless Giants survived purely by dint of monopoly. Johnson's intention to move the Orioles to New York ranked among the worst-kept secrets in baseball.

McGraw's 1902 started well enough: he married Blanche Sindall, destined to become nearly as popular a figure at the ballpark as he. But early in the season Ban Johnson twice suspended him for umpire baiting. Though he longed to own and manage a New York team, he grew convinced that Johnson would never let him represent the American League in the country's biggest market, so he did what lots of players did with the return of two-league baseball: switched teams under questionable circumstances. He sold his half of the Diamond Café to Wilbert Robinson in exchange for Robinson's shares in the Orioles, then sold the Oriole stock to a group fronting for none other than Andrew Freedman and partners. Freedman, at last enjoying the benefits of syndicate baseball, signed McGraw to a lucrative four-year contract with the Giants and, at McGraw's instruction, transferred several Orioles to New York, including Hall of Famers Roger Bresnahan and Iron Man Joe McGinnity.

McGraw insisted on, and got, total control of his new team. Why did the tyrannical Freedman yield the reins? In November 1901 the political promise of Brooklyn's consolidation with New York bore fruit as reformer Seth Low was elected mayor, ousting (for a time) the Tammany Hall lowlifes. Freedman decided to sell the Giants and visit Europe until the good government fad blew over. The franchise would be a lot more valuable with McGraw running it than Horace Fogel or Heinie Smith, a point proved when McGraw's first game with the Giants, on July 19, 1902, drew almost 10,000 fans. The Giants got their first win under McGraw a few days later in Brooklyn, attracting a crowd of 7,000. They played .397 ball under the fiery 29-year-old, unimpressive until you compare it to Heinie Smith's barrel-bottom .156. That September Freedman sold his interest in the Giants for an estimated $200,000 to John T. Brush, a genuine baseball man and a fan of McGraw's.

With Wilbert Robinson back in Baltimore tending the Diamond Café, McGraw needed a new best friend. He found one in Christy Mathewson, eight years his junior. Like Robinson, Mathewson complemented McGraw. But Mathewson and Robinson were very different. The heroic ethos modern ballplayers are expected to live up to was established, in large part, by the talented, humble Mathewson. Tall, proportioned, blond, and blue-eyed, he refused to play on Sundays (not the sacrifice it sounds, since back then most cities banned athletic events on the sabbath), spoke like the college boy he was, and though more capable of mischief than popularly imagined, went about his business with an earnestness Robinson would have found peculiar. Under McGraw he developed into the National League's greatest pitcher and the game's most popular figure. The two men became so close that they and their wives rented an apartment together.

In 1903 McGraw's Giants finished an amazing 34½ games better than the year before, and in 1904 and 1905 they won pennants to establish themselves as the National League's premier attraction. Where once they looked to Brooklyn for rivalry, they now looked to the Chicago Cubs of Tinker, Evers, and Chance and the Pittsburgh Pirates of Honus Wagner. At the same time the Dodgers, still called the Superbas, were fading. Charles Ebbets and Ned Hanlon lost players to the American League, lost attendance, and lost any love they might have had for each other. Ebbets outflanked Hanlon by buying out Harry von der Horst to become the majority owner, but the deal left him too poor to pay decent players. The result: the most lopsided era in the rivalry's history. New York finished

Christy Mathewson. He combined an unhittable "fadeaway" (screwball) with intelligence and control to win 20 or more games in 13 seasons. (National Baseball Hall of Fame Library, Cooperstown, N.Y.)

ahead of Brooklyn every year from 1903 to 1914 by an average of 33 games, dominating head-to-head competition 175–85 (.673).

Such imbalance could have killed the rivalry. But Brooklynites, still smarting from their consolidation into greater New York, heartily reviled McGraw and the Giants, darlings of Broadway and Wall Street. How they chafed when Bill Dahlen, their star shortstop, was traded to New York on December 12, 1903, and cracked, "Brooklyn is all right, but if you're not with the Giants, you might as well be in Albany." Recalled Tommy Holmes (not the player, but the *Brooklyn Eagle* sportswriter) "The Brooklyn faithful felt that all was not lost if their nondescript heroes could now and then lower the boom on the swaggering men of McGraw. And so Giant games at Washington Park became sell-outs, and frequently thousands were turned away."

For decades Brooklyn had absorbed multitudes of Irish, Italian, and Jewish immigrants who found just enough gold on Manhattan's streets to move their families to nicer homes across the East River. Just as they shed their European ways upon arrival in New York, most shed their Giant-rooting tendencies once they got to Brooklyn. But not all. Brooklyn always had a cadre of Giant fans, former Manhattanites unable to switch loyalties plus a few natives eager to identify with a winner. As a consequence, there were days when attendees at Giant-Superba games in Brooklyn merited combat pay. A list of every lowlight would take too much space, so two examples will have to suffice.

On June 23, 1910, a Superba fan at Washington Park heckled Giant third sacker Art Devlin without cease. Apparently children nearby heard his "Devlin, you dog!" as "Yellow Dog!" and began chanting it non-stop. Before long the whole section joined in. Devlin asked the crowd to desist, which only egged it on the more. After the Superbas were retired in the sixth, Devlin snapped. He flew into the stands and hit a man named Bernard Roesler so hard that he knocked him unconscious. As rowdies surged to get a piece of Devlin, teammates Larry Doyle and Josh Devore came to his defense. In seconds all the Giants were throwing punches, including McGraw. Bill Klem, commonly reckoned the greatest umpire of all time, plunged into the fracas and ordered McGraw to withdraw his players while Superba employee George Lundquist bravely repelled fans trying to get on the field.

Devlin, almost hit by a bottle as he retreated, was taken to jail. Brooklyn-born Wee Willie Keeler, ending his career as a Giant benchwarmer, went to bail him out, but someone from the coroner's office beat him to it. At the indictment two days later Roesler, sporting a pair of shiners, insisted he had no part in heckling Devlin and announced his intention to file suit for $5,000. But then as now, ballplayers got off easy. Devlin was paroled and Roesler's suit was never filed. The National League suspended Devlin for five days and fined Doyle and Devore $50 each.

Then there was opening day at Washington Park in 1912, when an estimated 25,000 fans jostled for room in a ballpark designed to accommodate 18,000. Two hours before game time the grandstand, in the words of the *Brooklyn Eagle's* Thomas Rice, "was packed to a point where the smallest kind of a riot would literally have endangered thousands of lives." Fans milled in the outfield, clogged the baselines, and sat on the players' benches. The Superbas' small security force tried to clear space to play, but all that did was agitate the crowd. Bat-wielding Superbas and Giants charged the fans, but the bluff gained only a few feet of playing room. Finally New York mayor William Gaynor called in the police.

Unlike the players, the cops used their clubs. To see what was happening, grandstand occupants stood on their seats. Fans in the rear wadded up paper and threw it at the standees. Fights broke out. Officials realized their best hope for restoring order was to play the game. "The only ones who saw the game at all were those in the top rows of the stand, the squad of policemen lined up in front of the crowd, and the boys who were standing on chairs and benches along the base lines," complained the *New York Times*, which, like the rest of the press, got its information from two men who climbed the backstop. The umpires ruled any ball that went into the crowd a ground-rule double. The Giants had 12 such hits and were routing the Dodgers 18–3 when Bill Klem, worried that someone might be killed, called the game after six innings.

Wilbert Robinson played some minor league ball after the American League franchise he and McGraw founded moved to New York and became the Yankees, then retired and went back to his bar. But without a major league team in Baltimore, business at the Diamond Café slowed. In 1909 McGraw invited him to spring training to work with Giant pitchers and catchers. The jovial Robinson was such a hit that McGraw brought him back in 1910 and 1911.

That third year he worked with failing phenom Rube Marquard, mockingly known as the "$11,000 Lemon" for the price McGraw paid to bring him to the majors. Under Robinson's tutelage Marquard progressed from thrower to pitcher, winning 24 games and leading the league in strikeouts. But that wasn't enough to keep the Giants ahead of the Cubs, and as pennant pressure increased, the ballclub tightened. McGraw, hearing one of his players recall how much fun Robinson had been in spring training, invited his old buddy back for the stretch drive. "The psychological effect was wonderful. In a little while the young fellows relaxed and became natural again," he acknowledged. The Giants won their first pennant since 1905.

McGraw hired Robinson full-time in 1912, and the rotund ex-catcher made a pitcher of rookie Jeff Tesreau to give the Giants an invincible three-man rotation. The 23-year-old Tesreau went 17–7. Marquard won 26, including 19 straight, a record that started and ended against Brooklyn (under modern scoring rules he would have earned a victory for an April relief stint against the Superbas and won 20 in a row). Christy Mathewson won 23. The Giants claimed their second straight pennant.

Once again McGraw and Robinson were making things happen together. But gone were the days when McGraw could share credit for success. Yielding the spotlight to Mathewson or Marquard was one thing; they were players. But every plaudit for Robinson's coaching was one less for the Little Napoleon, as admirers had taken to calling him. Opinions differ as to whether the rift between McGraw and Robinson opened after the 1912 season and grew over the next year, or whether it all sprang from one terrible argument after the Giants won again in 1913 but lost the World Series because, according to McGraw, Robinson misread a sign. Whichever, a quarter-century of close friendship ended abruptly, and the fired Robinson spoke only business to McGraw for the next 17 years.

Concurrently, Charles Ebbets was firing his manager, Bill Dahlen — the same Dahlen who'd said such cutting things about Brooklyn when traded to New York a decade earlier. Ebbets was alone in his loyalty to Dahlen, whose 251–355 (.414) record over four seasons did nothing to rehabilitate him among Brooklynites. Several prospective successors were mentioned, including first baseman Jake Daubert and ex-Giant Roger Bresnahan. But Ebbets surprised everyone by appointing 50-year-old Wilbert Robinson.

It was a brilliant move. Robinson had won over the New York press years before, assuring that even in futility the Superbas would receive favorable ink, which would increase attendance at the expensive new ballpark Ebbets had just built. Equally important was Robinson's skill with pitchers. For years the Superba staff consisted of stalwart Nap Rucker — deemed by John McGraw one of the four best pitchers in National League history — and anyone who stood half a chance of throwing the ball over the plate. Robinson made mound masters of journeymen like Jeff Pfeffer and Sherrod Smith. He purchased a sagging Marquard from the Giants and revived his career. And eventually he nurtured a pair of Hall of Famers, Burleigh Grimes and Dazzy Vance. In the decade before Robinson's arrival, the Superbas played less than .400 ball. In 18 seasons under him they still had some sad-sack finishes, but posted an overall .506 record.

John McGraw and Wilbert Robinson. After they fell out they occasionally posed together, but remained at arm's length. (National Baseball Hall of Fame Library, Cooperstown, N.Y.)

"I will follow McGraw's general system just as closely as is possible," Robinson vowed at his introductory press conference. He could not have told a bigger lie. Wilbert Robinson was the anti–McGraw, and everyone knew it, Brooklyn fans better than most. In him they recognized a kindred spirit, a salt-of-the-earth type used and abused by strutting, imperious New York, and they embraced him unconditionally, calling him Uncle Robbie and renaming the Superbas the Robins in his honor. For a time the team adopted robin's egg blue as a uniform color. Later in his tenure, when his lax discipline contributed to slapstick play, it was with as much affection as despair that Brooklynites referred to their team as the Daffiness Boys.

With McGraw in New York and Robinson in Brooklyn, the Giant-Dodger rivalry gained a whole new dimension. And it retained that dimension until the Little Napoleon and Uncle Robbie were dying old men.

3. 1911–1913: "Repositories of Twin Heartbeats"

Baseball parks had been made of wooden grandstands since the game's beginnings. They were cheap to build and easy to alter. But they were vulnerable to rot, collapse, and fire, and by the beginning of the 20th century they were also overcrowded; from 1901 to 1910 major league attendance increased more than 70 percent. In 1909 Ben Shibe of the Philadelphia Athletics applied to ballparks the newly invented techniques of ferro-concrete construction, in which steel rods reinforced concrete pillars. Like Camden Yards in modern times, Shibe Park inspired a frenzy of stadium building.

The Giants had no choice but to rebuild: in the first hours of April 14, 1911—Good Friday—fire consumed the Polo Grounds. It had been baseball's largest grandstand, double-decked and capable of seating almost 30,000, and had been home to the Giants for two decades. Now only the left field bleachers remained. For ailing owner John T. Brush, there was no question the team would put up a steel and concrete stadium at the same site, provided the Coogans gave him a long-term lease that made the investment worthwhile. James J. Coogan's widow Harriet readily obliged, and Brush's architects went to work designing the fourth — and final —facility known as the Polo Grounds.

Where to play in the meantime, though? That question was answered by Frank Farrell, owner of the New York Yankees. Ever since the Yankees transferred from Baltimore in 1903, the Giants had tried to undercut them; for Brush they represented competition, while for John McGraw they were an unhappy reminder of Ban Johnson. But when the cheek-turning Farrell offered the Giants shelter at Hilltop Park, less than a mile north of the Polo Grounds at Fort Washington Avenue and 168th Street, Brush gratefully accepted, turning down a similar offer from Charles Ebbets. The Brooklyn owner's offer was undoubtedly motivated more by public relations than pity, because he knew that many Giant and Superba home dates would conflict.

Brush commenced reconstruction of the Polo Grounds without soliciting bids. He paid contractors their cost plus a set profit to work around the clock. By late June, 800 laborers had erected a rudimentary infrastructure and 6,000 new seats to go with the 10,000 untouched by the fire. Just 75 days after the conflagration, the Polo Grounds reopened on a blistering hot day — "many persons were fearful that the big fire was still burning," quipped the *Times* — and a disappointing turnout of only 6,000 watched Christy Mathewson shut out Boston. The stadium was formally dedicated on April 19, 1912, in a ceremony spoiled by cold weather and the sinking of the *Titanic* a few days before. The Giants took the field against the Superbas and won 6–2 behind Mathewson. Fred Merkle hit the park's first home run, a shot to deep center against Superba ace Nap Rucker. McGraw was ejected for disputing an out call on an attempted steal.

The Polo Grounds wasn't finished until early 1923. In its enduring configuration it seated nearly 56,000 fans. To fit into upper Manhattan's rectangular street grid it was given a grossly elongated design; as the *Sporting News* said, "Envision a huge bathtub with a baseball diamond crammed inside." Its copious foul territory and deep, narrow outfield favored pitchers. But the left field line ended just 280 feet from home plate (an overhanging upper deck made the home run distance even shorter) and the right field line was a ludicrous 260, so it was also a pull hitter's paradise. Team offices and both clubhouses were in a tower behind center field, and after games players and fans walked out of the stadium shoulder to shoulder. The field as a whole sloped downward, so that in some places the base of the outfield wall was eight feet lower than the infield, a problem partially rectified by raising the outfield four and a half feet in 1949.

One of John T. Brush's last acts as Giant owner was to invite the Yankees to play at the new park. In repaying a kindness and providing the Yankees with a truly big league home, Brush also secured a steady rental income to defray the debts amassed in building the new stadium. But like so many small gestures, this one had enormous consequences. In 1920 the Yankees turned the Polo Grounds into the birthplace of the lively ball era as Babe Ruth, in his first year with the team, blasted 54 homers. He'd set a record the year before in Boston with 29, but this was equivalent to Barry

The steel-and-concrete Polo Grounds. In more ways than one, the longest home the Giants ever had. (Transcendental Graphics)

Bonds, after his 73-homer season in 2001, hitting *130* in 2002. The reason for the jump? That short right field fence at the Polo Grounds. Ruth hit only five additional homers on the road, but a staggering 20 more at home.

Ruth's exploits ushered in an age of binge scoring so popular with fans it saved the sport from the Black Sox scandal that broke the same year. In 1920 the Giants drew a National League record 929,609 customers, but Ruth's Yankees, performing at the same venue, brought in 1,289,422. And they did it by turning deadballers like John McGraw and Wilbert Robinson into relics. A jealous Charles Stoneham, the Giants' new owner, sent the Yankees an eviction notice. Though he soon withdrew it, the Yankees took the hint and arranged for construction of their own stadium just across the East River in the Bronx. They left the Polo Grounds after 1922.

McGraw despised the newfangled baseball: "I think the game far more interesting when the art of making scores lies in scientific work on the bases." But with Ruth dominating the sports pages, he knew the Giants needed a slugger. In 1926 he found Mel Ott, a high-kicking, dead-pulling lefty who feasted off the Polo Grounds' short right field fence to set a National League record with 511 homers. In time, the desire for power hitting became such an organizational obsession that it all but obliterated the Little Napoleon's legacy.

"Baseball is still in its infancy," Charles Ebbets told his fellow baseball executives in December 1909, eliciting snickers. But this was no Hot Stove humbuggery. Ebbets believed it, and following Ben Shibe's example, laid plans for an eponymous steel and concrete stadium big enough to hold record throngs.

He wouldn't build it in the Superbas' old neighborhood. Back in 1898 Washington Park was centrally located, but with the advent of municipal consolidation and interborough subway lines, Brooklyn was spreading out, and districts closer to Manhattan were decaying. Red Hook, just west of the park, was becoming an industrial wasteland, as the smoke from its many stacks and the stench from the Gowanus Canal attested, and residential Park Slope, on the east, was getting down at the heels. If Ebbets announced his intentions, though, the owners of prospective ballpark sites would raise their prices, so he created a dummy corporation and hired a gentleman otherwise innocent of Superba connections to purchase land for him just east of Prospect Park in a squatter-dotted garbage dump called Pigtown.

Pigtown lay at the conjunction of Flatbush, Bedford, and Crown Heights, affluent neighborhoods that Ebbets rightly figured would eventually expand into the underdeveloped area. He shelled out $100,000 for dozens of contiguous lots there, far less than he would have paid had the owners been aware of his plans. On January 2, 1912, he finally went public, and two months later, surrounded by borough politicians, broke ground with a silver shovel. "Dig up a couple of new players, Charlie," someone cracked.

"I want to build a structure that will fill all demands upon it for the next 30 years," Ebbets wrote a month later, in part to assuage disappointment that the new stadium wasn't constructed as quickly as the Polo Grounds. The extra time helped Ebbets realize his vision of ballpark as cultural center, as vital to a city (or borough) as a symphony hall or theater district. He designed a grand entrance, a domed, 27-foot-high marble rotunda with bat-and-ball chandeliers and tiled floors in a red-stitch motif.

But even with the additional building time, Ebbets Field had flaws. Some were fleeting: at the first game, an April 5, 1913, exhibition against the Yankees, thousands of ticket holders couldn't get in because someone forgot the key to the bleacher gates, and when Shannon's 23rd Regiment Band, a regular performer at Superba games, readied to play "The Star-Spangled Banner," it was discovered that someone had forgotten the

American flag. But other problems were more serious. Not a blade of grass sprouted from the outfield. The Superbas complained that the hitting background made it hard for them to judge the speed and break of pitches, and in the field, the passage of pop-ups from shadow to light and back made catching the ball an adventure. There was also one enduring boo-boo: the stadium was built without a press box. All these problems were overcome, but not before they reinforced Brooklyn's waxing reputation for vaude-villian bumbling.

Ebbets Field came no closer to symmetry than the Polo Grounds. The original dimensions were 419 feet down the left field line, 450 to center, 500 to deepest right center, and a mere 301 down the right field line. But every few years the team brought the fences a little closer, especially after the second deck was extended into center field in the early '30s. By 1948 left field was 343 feet from home, center field 384 feet, the right-center field depths 403, and the right field corner just 297. Although there was plenty of foul territory behind home plate, there was little down the sidelines, giving the park an intimate feel. Overall it favored right-handed gap hitters and left-handed sluggers.

Ebbets Field. The 38-foot right field wall and scoreboard contained 289 different angles, confounding fielders. (Courtesy Los Angeles Dodgers, Inc.)

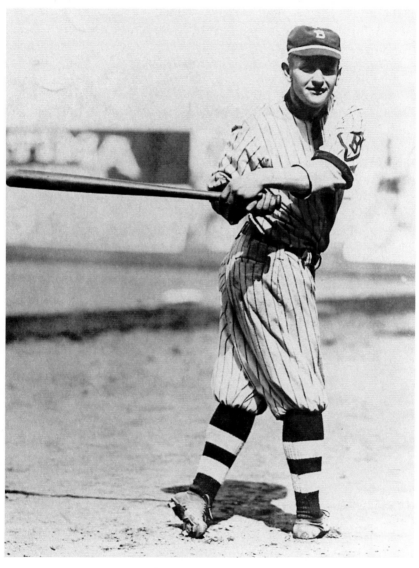

Casey Stengel. A born comedian, in his first game at Ebbets Field after Brooklyn traded him to Pittsburgh he doffed his cap — and a sparrow flew out of it. (National Baseball Hall of Fame Library, Cooperstown, N.Y.)

The first Giant-Dodger game at Ebbets Field took place on April 26, 1913. Brooklyn's center fielder, 22-year-old Charles Dillon "Casey" Stengel — so fresh to the local scene that the *Times* misidentified him as "Jake" — broke a 3–3 tie in the seventh with a two-run, inside-the-park homer to the flagpole in dead center, enthralling the capacity crowd of 25,000 and giving the Superbas their first win in their new home. "It was an epoch-making swat, a swat that should be recited in heroic verse to do it justice, a swat that knew no brother in that or any other game that has been played on Ebbets Field," kidded Thomas Rice in the *Eagle*.

No baseball stadium has ever been more of a green cathedral than the one at the heart of the Borough of Churches. For 45 years Ebbets Field united a complex, combustible mix of races, ethnicities, religions, and neighborhoods. With the exception of Coney Island, no civic landmark brought more Brooklynites together, and even Coney Island couldn't compete with it for affirming the borough's unique identity.

At the same time, however, the boundless affection Brooklynites felt for Ebbets Field revealed how much like New Yorkers they were: intensely proud of where they lived and absolutely fanatical about their team. Years later, New York sportswriter Jerry Izenberg said of Ebbets Field and the Polo Grounds, "They were more than ballparks. They were repositories of twin heartbeats to which this city marched."

But Brooklyn's repository cost Charles Ebbets $750,000, which he didn't have. He raised capital by selling half the team to his contractors, the brothers Ed and Steve McKeever. For 12 years the arrangement worked fine, but ultimately it led to strife, drift, paupery, and a new regime that looked upon Ebbets Field with a cold, cold eye.

4. 1916: "He Pissed on My Pennant"

In 1915 the Giants finished last for the only time under John McGraw. In the spring of 1916, the Little Napoleon insisted his team would battle the Boston Braves for the pennant. That became a joke when the Giants lost their first eight games. But then they went on the road and won 17 straight.

Only to come home and lose 10 of 15.

Up and down the Giants went. A July 4 doubleheader home loss to Brooklyn dropped them to sixth place, three games under .500. "The big jam of fans who came over from Brooklyn were a happy lot, but the New York citizens who still have any confidence left in the Giants were as cheerless as a toothache," reported the *Times*.

John McGraw had seen enough. From late July to the end of August he tore apart and rebuilt his team like a home mechanic determined to find that rattle in his engine. His first move was the hardest: trading Christy Mathewson. McGraw loved Matty, who still has more wins than any other National League pitcher. By his 36th birthday Mathewson had worn out, though, and he had a chance to manage in Cincinnati, so McGraw let him go. By throwing in two other future Hall of Famers, Edd Roush and Bill McKechnie (the latter in the Hall for his managerial talents), McGraw persuaded the Reds to part with Buck Herzog, third baseman on those pennant-winning Giant clubs of 1911, 1912, and 1913. Then McGraw picked up pitcher Slim Sallee for cash, agreed with Wilbert Robinson to exchange Fred Merkle for backup catcher Lew McCarty, and acquired another infielder, Heinie Zimmerman, for the previous year's batting champion, Larry Doyle.

Much motion, little movement. On September 7, 1916, after splitting another home doubleheader against the Robins, the Giants stood three games under .500, just as they had on July 4. They trailed the first-place Phillies by 13½ games with just 33 to go. So much for that pennant prediction.

Adding to McGraw's frustration was the rise of rival Brooklyn. After placing fifth in Uncle Robbie's first year, the Robins improved to third in 1915, finishing ahead of the Giants for the first time in 13 years. And after the September 7 twin bill at the Polo Grounds they were just one percentage point out of first place.

To McGraw winning was serious business, but to Wilbert Robinson a loose, joking ballclub pulled out the close ones. "Like Falstaff, he was not only witty himself but the cause of wit in others," the *Times'* John Kieran said of Uncle Robbie. During spring training in 1916 a group of Robin players, recalling Gabby Street's 1908 catch of a ball dropped from the Washington Monument, debated whether a ball could be caught from an airplane. Uncle Robbie claimed that even though he was 52 years old and close to 300 pounds, he could do it. So the players hired stunt aviatrix Ruth Law to drop a ball. As she was about to take off she realized she'd left her baseball at her hotel, so she improvised, borrowing a grapefruit from a member of her ground crew. At the appointed spot she dropped the grapefruit.

Casey Stengel described what happened next. "Robbie got under the grapefruit, thinking it was a baseball, which hit him right on this pitcher's glove he put on, and you know, the insides of it flew all over, seeds on his face and uniform, and flipped him back right over on his back." Uncle Robbie bawled, "Jesus! I'm killed! I'm blind! It's broke open my chest! I'm covered with blood! Jesus! Somebody help me!" until he realized he hadn't been hurt. Other managers would have burned with humiliation seeing their players laugh at them, but before long Robinson was laughing too.

Still, happy ballclubs go nowhere without talent. In 1916 the Robins had just enough. Uncle Robbie loved to give struggling veterans a second chance — Stengel and pitcher Sherrod Smith, at 25, were the team's youngest regular performers — and in 1916 they all came through. Three vets dated back to pre-Robbie times: first baseman Jake Daubert, second baseman George Cutshaw, and the ultimate Dodger, left fielder Zack Wheat. The dignified, popular Wheat still holds the franchise records for games played, at-bats, hits, doubles, triples, and total bases. A left-handed line drive hitter and smooth defender, he was the clubhouse leader for 18 years and was elected to the Hall of Fame in 1959.

The rest were Robinson imports, including three popular ex-Giants:

Rube Marquard, whose dead arm revived under old mentor Robbie; Chief Meyers, the best catcher in the league when New York won its three straight pennants from 1911 to 1913, but a fading 35-year-old in 1916; and Fred Merkle, subbing at first base while sciatica kept Jake Daubert out of the lineup.

With the Giants seemingly out of the race, their fans switched allegiance to the rival Robins. To Brooklynites it was odious front-running, but New Yorkers saw nothing heretical in wishing a pennant on Robinson, Marquard, Meyers, and Merkle. "New Yorkers consider Brooklyn as a part of the real works, so why not enjoy a part of the World Series in Colonel Ebbets' magnificent ball park? It's

Rube Marquard. He arranged his own 1915 sale from the Giants to the Robins, talking McGraw into naming a price ($7,500), then calling Robinson to ask, "How would you like to have a good left-handed pitcher?" (National Baseball Hall of Fame Library, Cooperstown, N.Y.)

better than trips to some other cities, isn't it?" rationalized the *New York Sun's* Joe Vila. On September 9 the Robins beat the Boston Braves while Pol Perritt of the Giants started and won both ends of a doubleheader against the Phillies. Fully aware that Perritt's sweep put the Robins in first place, the Polo Grounds crowd of 33,000 cheered wildly and carried the young hurler to the clubhouse.

The Giants kept on winning. And winning. And winning. On September 25 they took a doubleheader from the Cardinals for consecutive victories 20 and 21, breaking the all-time win streak set by the Providence Grays in 1884. Three days later they pulled off another doubleheader sweep, twin shutouts of the Braves, impelling the brawniest among the 35,000 fans to carry the whole team off the field. The win streak finally ended at 26 on September 30. It has yet to be surpassed.

The Robins were too busy fending off the Phillies to admire their rivals' achievement. They were also distracted by a damaging controversy.

No one had ever charged more than three dollars for a World Series ticket before, but Ebbets announced that if the Robins got in, he would charge five. Even the cheapest seats would cost a dollar. Disaffected Brooklynites stopped going to the ballpark. "Ebbets, the players and the newspapers have been amazed at the slim attendance lately for single games, but there seems to be no way to stir up the folks who should be giving the club generous support," wrote Thomas Rice.

But then came the last series of the year, at home against the Giants, who despite their record win streak were out of contention. They could play spoiler, though: the Robins had just a half-game lead over the Phillies. Knowing John McGraw would do everything in his power to thwart Wilbert Robinson, Robin fans forgot Charles Ebbets's perfidy. A healthy Monday crowd of 15,000 turned out for the opening game.

In the top of the first, junkballing Jack Coombs gave up two infield singles and a walk to load the bases with two outs. He went 3–0 on Giant center fielder Benny Kauff, then coolly lobbed strike after strike until Kauff tired of fouling them off and struck out. The Giants, meanwhile, played tentative ball. With one out in the bottom of the fourth, shortstop Art Fletcher juggled a Jake Daubert grounder for what should have been an error but was ruled a hit. Daubert took off for second as Ferdie Schupp (ERA for the season: 0.90 in 140 innings) struck out the next batter, but Giant second baseman Herzog mishandled the throw and Daubert was safe again. Zack Wheat then hummed a liner to left to score the game's first run.

Though his offerings "didn't appear as if they would any more than break through tissue paper," as the *Times* put it, Coombs limited the Giants to six singles as the Robins won, 2–0. In Philadelphia, the Phillies split a doubleheader against Boston to fall a full game back. Brooklyn's magic number was three.

The next day, October 3, nearly 11,000 fans passed through the Ebbets Field rotunda. New York plated three in the first with the help of three Brooklyn errors. The Robins scored a run in the second, but the Giants got it back in the top of the third. In the bottom of the third, four of the first five Brooklyn batters got hits off New York's Rube Benton. McGraw brought in ace Pol Perritt. Mike Mowrey greeted Perritt with a single to tie the game, and then the Robins took a 5–4 lead on Ivy Olson's RBI groundout.

While Robin fans went wild, McGraw stewed. His men tied the game in the top of the fifth, but fell behind again in the bottom of the inning on a two-out, bases-empty hit batsman, a wild pitch, and a single by the balsa-batted Olson. It was an exciting, seesaw contest, hardly the best ever played but not a comedy of errors either. There were four more innings to go, and a pennant depended on the outcome. So what was John McGraw's next move?

He left.

The Little Napoleon had done a lot of impulsive things during his quarter century in the major leagues, but this might have been the most bizarre, and was certainly the least explicable. When he did offer his justification — before skipping out on the team for the season — he only made things worse, alleging the Giants were throwing the game: "I never laid down in a game to any man, no matter how good a friend, and my players can verify the statement that I insisted on them fighting for every one of these Brooklyn games. But today they played their own game. They missed my signs, displayed miserable judgment in every department of play, and almost turned the game into a farce."

The players adamantly denied the charges, but New York sportswriters largely sided with McGraw, citing rumors that the Giants had conspired to throw the race in favor of old mates Robinson, Marquard, Meyers, and Merkle. Before the series, Thomas Rice of Brooklyn's *Eagle* predicted such a controversy: "We believe the Superbas are going to play better ball than the Giants. We know if they do the moralists will say the Giants didn't try." John McGraw was no moralist, but Rice got everything else right. He reminded fans that Brooklyn had won 13 of its 19 previous games against the Giants, including a split just as the Giants were starting their win streak, and that the Giants were due for a letdown. "Can any sane man say that the winning of two straight by the Superbas from the Giants in the present series, when the Superbas are going better than they have at any time this year, while the Giants have every reason in the world to be experiencing a relaxation, was illogical?" He might have added that the Giants had been careening from brilliant to wretched all season long.

The Robins went on to win 9–6, while the Phillies, playing far worse than the Giants, blew a twin bill to the Braves to eliminate themselves. Wilbert Robinson was elated. "It has been a long, hard fight, but I think the players showed their mettle when they stuck to their task and refused to give up." While he stood on a clubhouse bench, the team did a triumphal snake dance around him.

"I am sorry for Wilbert Robinson's sake that we did not make a better showing," McGraw said. But Uncle Robbie wasn't buying. "Manager McGraw's suspicions in this matter are ridiculous," he responded. Privately he believed the walkout had less to do with the Giants' poor play than McGraw's jealousy of his success. "He pissed on my pennant," he fumed.

5. 1924: "Better Than a Free Trip to Mars"

To build a baseball dynasty you need a nucleus of good young play-ers. John McGraw understood that, which was why he won pennants in clusters. Wilbert Robinson probably understood it too, but couldn't help himself: he loved old pros down on their luck and marginal prospects looking for a last shot, the sort of players unlikely to sustain superior per-formance. After the Robins won the pennant in 1916, they finished sev-enth, fifth, and fifth. They won again in 1920 (with the Giants in second place, seven back — the first one-two finish by the rivals) but slogged around .500 in 1921, 1922, and 1923.

The Robins returned to contention in 1924, even though their regu-lars averaged nearly 31 years of age. Zack Wheat, 36, still patrolled left field. Utilityman Jimmy Johnston also remained from the 1916 champs (as did 38-year-old shortstop Ivy Olson for a few games). Right fielder Tommy Griffith was 34. Center fielder Eddie Brown was 32 and getting a chance with Brooklyn after twice failing to impress McGraw in New York. Fas-tidious first baseman Jacques Fournier, 34, found refuge with the Robins after Hall of Famer Jim Bottomley supplanted him in St. Louis. Only sec-ond baseman Andy High and catcher Zack Taylor were under 29.

The pitchers were old-timers too, but the workhorses, Burleigh Grimes and Dazzy Vance, were Hall of Famers. The irascible Grimes was one of 17 hurlers permitted under a grandfather clause to continue throw-ing spitballs after the pitch was banned in 1920. To look more menacing he refused to shave on pitching days, earning the nickname "Old Stubblebeard." Fastballer Vance had been "as wild as a vodka soaked Bolsheviki in front of a red flag," as the *Sporting News* put it, and flunked opportunities with the Pirates and Yankees before receiving a last chance from Robinson, under whose encouragement he led the league in strikeouts seven straight seasons. Grimes was 30, Vance 33. The other four Robins with more than 100 innings pitched were also over 30.

By contrast, John McGraw had five Hall of Famers in his 1924 lineup, and the oldest was first baseman George "Highpockets" Kelly at 28. Outfielder Ross Youngs, 27, McGraw's favorite player after Christy Mathewson's departure, had hit over .300 every year since 1918. Second baseman Frankie Frisch, a Bronx native, was only 25. Outfielder Hack Wilson was in his first full season at 24. Shortstop Travis Jackson was just 20. Two more Hall of Famers deemed unready for everyday play rode the bench: Bill Terry, 25, and Fred Lindstrom, 18.

No surprise, then, that in 1924 the Giants vied for their fourth consecutive pennant, a feat no National League team had ever accomplished. And no surprise that their leader, John McGraw, attained new heights of popularity in New York. He'd become a civic institution, one of the few constants in a metropolis changing at breakneck speed. Even Brooklynites tempered their reaction to him and his club. The Robins opened their home season against New York on April 24 and lost 7–4 in front of 24,000 fans who actually applauded Frisch for two spectacular defensive plays. "If the old interborough rivalry still exists it was not to be found in the cheering. The time was when the Giants could do nothing right in Brooklyn but lose, but those days apparently are gone," the *Times* noted.

Of course, Brooklyn fans had no way of knowing how decisive those early Giant-Robin matches would be. On July 4 the Giants were in first place, eight and a half ahead of the surprising third-place Robins. The difference between them was entirely attributable to their games against each other, of which the Giants had won 13, the Robins just four.

After the holiday the teams went west, where the Giants slaughtered the second-place Cubs to open a nine and a half game lead. A nation accustomed to seeing New York on top conceded the season. Even the Giant players turned complacent. After they blew four straight to the charging Pirates in late August, McGraw decided some motivation through fear was in order, and sent home backup catcher Eddie Ainsmith and scrub pitcher (and former Robin) Leon Cadore for violating curfew. If he thought that would focus his team for an Ebbets Field series at month's end, he was wrong. In front of crowds that, according to Joe Vila, "would rather see the Giants lambasted than take a free trip to Mars," the Robins whipped the McGrawmen three straight. Suddenly, it was a race again. The Giants went into September just two games up on Pittsburgh and four ahead of Brooklyn.

The series with the Giants gave Uncle Robbie's men five straight victories, but they were just warming up. They played doubleheaders each of the first four days of September — and won all eight games. That amazing feat vaulted them past Pittsburgh into second place, just three percentage points behind the Giants. On September 5 rookie Rube Ehrhardt shut out the Braves. The next day, pitching the first game of yet another doubleheader, grizzled Bill Doak whitewashed Boston. That gave the Robins 15 straight victories, still the franchise record. Coupled with a Giant loss to Philadelphia in the opening game of a Polo Grounds twin bill, it put Brooklyn in first place.

For a couple of hours the Robins reveled in the lead. But they lost their second game to Boston, snapping the win streak, while the Giants won their nightcap against Philadelphia to regain first place. Then the Pirates swept a doubleheader in St. Louis to pass the Robins. In the course of one afternoon, Brooklyn had gone from second to first to third. Even so, the Robins stood just half a game behind the Giants, with a match against their rivals at Ebbets Field the next day.

An overflow crowd literally broke down the door to see the game. Starting time was three o'clock. The stands were sold out by one. Management decided to put fans on the field, but when the field got too full the gates were closed with thousands more Robin rooters still outside. Some blatantly crashed the turnstiles. Others scaled the park's sheer brick walls (a 13-year-old boy suffered a concussion when he fell). Hundreds more massed behind a locked service door between the grandstand and bleachers, smashed it off its hinges, and streamed onto the field. Though unable to control the mob, the police managed to squeeze Bill Klem (who always seemed to be around when the rivalry went haywire) into the park.

In the top of the third the Giants, leading 1–0, had Ross Youngs on second, Bill Terry on first, and Hack Wilson up with one out. Wilson hit a shrieking liner into left center field. The crowd parted to give Zack Wheat a chance to catch the ball, but the runners couldn't see the action. Youngs waited on second, so that if Wheat made the grab he couldn't be accused of leaving the base early. But Terry, anticipating a hit, took off from first. He all but smacked into Youngs. Once he realized Wheat had caught the ball he hightailed back to first while Youngs sprinted for third, then home. Klem called Youngs safe, and another run went on the board. But Robin starter Burleigh Grimes demanded the ball, ran to first, and tagged Terry — who was called out for passing Youngs. That retired the side and erased

Youngs's run. Klem and crew got an earful from the Giants, but it's questionable how much they heard over the gleeful crowd.

The Giants scored another run in the fourth, but then the Robins went to work against Giant starter Jack Bentley. Five-foot six-inch second baseman Andy High singled. Shortstop Johnny Mitchell doubled him to third. Zack Wheat doubled them both home, then scored on a single by Eddie Brown to put the Robins up 3–2. Hundreds of straw hats and newspapers filled the air.

But the Giants tied the game in the seventh, and in the eighth they really unloaded on Grimes, blasting five hits that, combined with a walk and an error, produced five runs to make the score 8–3. It looked like the game's decisive turn. But the Robins got a run back in the eighth, then mounted a bottom of the ninth comeback. Jacques Fournier singled. Eddie Brown lifted a deep fly that sent Giant center fielder Hack Wilson into the crowd — which ripped off his cap and glove, tore his uniform, and never let him near the ball. The umpires called it a ground-rule double. Wilson and John McGraw called it a mugging, to no avail.

McGraw pulled the left-handed Bentley in favor of righty Hugh McQuillan to face the Robins' right-handed third baseman, Milt Stock. The platoon advantage didn't help, as the underrated Stock singled home Fournier to bring the Robins within three. McQuillan bore down after that, retiring Tommy Griffith (a lefty) and Zack Taylor. That forced Wilbert Robinson to make a crucial decision. He was down to his last out with the tying run at the plate and pitcher Burleigh Grimes due to bat. Should he send up a pinch hitter? Old Stubblebeard was obviously tired: he'd given up eight runs and 17 hits. And he'd be a right-handed batter facing a right-handed pitcher. But he was also a very good hitter (he finished the year at .298). So Robinson stuck with him. Grimes rewarded him with a single that scored Brown and brought the Robins within two.

Up came little Andy High. He doubled and Stock scored. Now the Robins were just one run down with Grimes, the tying run, at third and High, the winning run, at second. A base hit by switch-hitting Johnny Mitchell would give the Robins their most sensational win since clinching the pennant four years earlier. But here Robinson made another unorthodox move: he sent pitcher Dutch Ruether to pinch-hit for Mitchell. Ruether had hit .351 for the Robins in 1921, but was 100 points lower than that in 1924.

McQuillan whiffed him on three pitches and the Robins lost, falling a game and a half back.

The rivals moved to the Polo Grounds the next day. Forty thousand fans showed up on a Monday, remarkable in itself. The *Times* described the scene: "The old animosities that used to be directed at Chance's Cubs and Clarke's Pirates awoke again yesterday. And, on the other side, the ancient hatred of Brooklyn for all things baseball across the bridges came to life for the first time since 1921."

Giant fans expected to see the Robins all but eliminated, even with Dazzy Vance pitching. He'd already won 24 games—the last 12 in a row—and broken his own National League strikeout record, but New York had beaten him three times that season. Robin fans hoped their ace would bring them back to half a game from the top. After that they would have to be just one game better than the Giants over the last 15 to capture the flag.

"It was a tautly played game, with every move fought for and the players under a nervous tension," reported the *Times*. The Giants drew first blood when Travis Jackson's third-inning shot to the fence caromed by Wheat for a triple and backup catcher Hank Gowdy singled him home. Wheat got even in the top of the fourth by doubling and scoring on Eddie Brown's single. The Giants reclaimed the lead in the bottom of the fourth, Youngs crossing home on a Hack Wilson sacrifice fly. In the top of the fifth the Robins' backup catcher, Hank DeBerry, clapped a two-run homer to put Brooklyn in front again.

Gradually the Robins pulled away, scoring two in the seventh and one in the eighth while Vance smothered the Giants. Of course there had to be a controversy: with DeBerry on first and Milt Stock on third with two gone in the eighth, Uncle Robbie flashed the steal sign. DeBerry took off before Giant pitcher Rosy Ryan went into his delivery. The right-handed Ryan turned to first, then saw Stock dashing for the plate and threw home instead. Omnipresent Bill Klem called Stock out. The Robins and their fans went nuts, arguing that Ryan had balked. Klem consulted fellow umpire Frank Wilson, who confirmed the balk, and reversed the call. Whereupon the Giants and their fans went nuts.

Not that it mattered. The Robins scored again in the top of the ninth and won 7–2. That gave them four wins in their last five games against the Giants. But it also finished the season series, meaning the Robins would have to depend on other clubs to knock out their rival.

Over the last three weeks the Giants and Robins hosted every other National League team. Both won three of the four games they played against bottom dwellers Boston and Philadelphia. Both split with Cincinnati and took two of three from St. Louis. The Robins did better against Chicago, winning two of three to the Giants' one of three. The difference came down to Pittsburgh, the third contender in this three-horse race. In a brilliant series, the Robins suffered a pair of close defeats and fell out of second place before taking the last game, 2–1, in 10 innings. When the Pirates moved over to the Polo Grounds for three against the Giants they expected an easier time, because Frankie Frisch and third baseman Heinie Groh had injured themselves and couldn't play.

But McGraw threw them off balance. It rained the morning of Monday, September 22, and though the downpour ceased by game time, he used the wet grounds as an excuse to postpone the opener, giving Frisch and Groh an extra day to recuperate. Then he rescheduled the game for Thursday, an open date for the Giants but not for the Pirates, who had planned on making up a rainout with the Cubs back in Pittsburgh. The Pirates protested to league president John Heydler. For once McGraw won a battle with baseball's hierarchs, as Heydler decreed that Pittsburgh make up the Cub game as part of a Friday doubleheader.

Thus disrupted, the Pirates lost 5–1 on September 23 and 4–2 on September 24 to fall out of contention. On September 25 they had a backer in the stands in Zack Wheat (it was an off day for the Robins), but the Giants completed the sweep with a 5–4 squeaker that put them a game and a half ahead of Brooklyn with just three to play. The Giants won again over Philadelphia on September 27 while the Robins lost a 3–2 heartbreaker to Boston, and that was that: the Giants had an unprecedented fourth consecutive National League championship. It was McGraw's 10th pennant in 23 years, the pinnacle of managerial success until Casey Stengel, who played for McGraw from 1921 through 1923, enjoyed an even better run with the Yankees in the 1950s. The Little Napoleon wouldn't have won it, though, had Brooklyn played his team a little tougher early in the season.

In a neater universe, John McGraw and Wilbert Robinson would have retired after the 1924 pennant race. Instead they stuck around past their usefulness, and the rivalry suffered for it.

Over the years McGraw had grown as corpulent as Robinson, aggravating his myriad ailments. As the Roaring '20s sped toward the Depression, he missed more and more games, and when he did sit in the dugout he usually wore street clothes, disqualifying him from going onfield to berate umpires or to coach. Despite their talent, his Giants finished a distant second in 1925 and sank below .500 in 1926. McGraw feuded with cornerstone player Frankie Frisch over a missed sign — Uncle Robbie fans, does this sound familiar? — and traded him to St. Louis for Rogers Hornsby. The Giants came within two games of the pennant in 1927 and 1928 but finished behind Frisch's Cardinals both times. For the next three years the Giants played good ball, but not the great ball necessary to win

McGraw an 11th flag. They were mired in last place on June 3, 1932, when the 59-year-old Little Napoleon, their manager for three decades, called it quits.

For New Yorkers it was like the death of a long-sick relative: not a surprise, in some ways a relief, but still a shock. "It seems strange to think of the Giants under any other leadership than that of John J. McGraw," said John Kieran of the *Times.* "The ownership changed, the players changed, the rules changed and even the scenery changed. But John J. McGraw remained the outstanding and dominant figure through it all."

If McGraw's last years were sad, Robinson's were pitiful. The worst blow ever dealt the Dodger franchise struck at 6:05 a.m. on April 18, 1925, when Charles Ebbets, just four years older than Uncle Robbie, died of heart disease. (Certain that Charlie would have wanted it that way, the Robins went ahead with their season opener against the Giants that afternoon and lost 7–1.) Ebbets was there when the franchise began. He saved it from original owner Charles Byrne's misjudgments, from the National League's contraction, from Ned Hanlon's grubbiness, and from proximity to the fetid Gowanus Canal. Perhaps his partner Ed McKeever would have proved just as staunch a protector, but while standing in the cold and rain as Ebbets was laid to rest he contracted a virulent flu and died 11 days later.

Ebbets's son-in-law Joe Gilleaudeau and McKeever's older brother Steve, baseball novices, each inherited half the team. Neither trusted the other, so they turned the ballclub over to Uncle Robbie. But Robinson had never run anything larger than the Diamond Café, and he'd done that decades before. He finished sixth five years in a row, looking so inept at times that only the loyalty of Ebbets's heirs kept him in his job. It helped that Brooklyn fans chose to adore rather than scorn him and his Daffiness Boys.

Before Casey Stengel and Yogi Berra became managers, their niche in baseball lore belonged to Wilbert Robinson. In one story, Zack Wheat was batting with the winning run on first and nobody out in the ninth. He looked to Robinson for instructions. Uncle Robbie searched his mind for what seemed an eon, then finally put his hands in front of his body and mimicked a bunt. He'd forgotten his own signs! Veteran catcher Val Picinich came to the Dodgers in 1929. Robinson told Picinich he was going to start, but when the time came to fill out the lineup card, he couldn't spell the new receiver's name. "Aw, the hell with it, I'll put DeBerry in to catch," said Uncle Robbie. When the game began, Picinich and DeBerry both trotted out to home plate, and a long session of "I thought I —" "No, I thought I —" commenced.

No player exemplified the spirit of Robinson's Daffiness Boys more than outfielder Babe Herman. A tremendous hitter but indifferent fielder, Herman once reproached reporters for perpetrating the myth that he'd been hit on the head by a fly ball. "If I ever get hit on the head by a fly ball, I'll walk out of here and never come back," he vowed. A puckish scribe asked whether that extended to getting hit on the shoulders. Herman mulled it over, then said, "On the shoulder don't count." On August 15, 1926, he instigated the most infamous Robin gaffe of all time. With DeBerry on third, Vance on second, Chick Fewster on first, and one out, Herman roped one to the right field wall. DeBerry waltzed home. Vance was well past third when he heard someone shout "Back, back!" and stopped dead in his tracks. He retreated to third — where he found Fewster. And who should come sliding in just ahead of the ball? Herman. Three men on third! All were tagged, Fewster and Herman were declared out, and the rally was strangled. The Robins won anyway, but for years afterward the standing joke around Brooklyn had Fan Number One asking how the team was doing, Fan Number Two saying they had three men on base, and Fan Number One asking, "Which base?"

It wasn't all laughs with Robinson, though. When a *New York Sun* cartoonist offended him in 1926, he had the bad form to call the managing editor and complain. Thereafter the *Sun* refused to print his name and referred to his ballclub as the Dodgers, a protocol that gradually spread until other nicknames for the team were relegated to history (although for years the *Brooklyn Eagle* persisted in referring to the team as The Flock, a derivative of Robins).

The row with the *Sun* exacerbated tensions between Robinson and Steve McKeever, who succeeded at having Robinson ousted as team president after 1929. Robbie stayed on as manager and guided the Dodgers to a strong fourth-place finish in 1930, but there was nothing he could do to placate the McKeever half of ownership. After his contract expired in 1931, the Ebbets and McKeever estate holders, along with a mediator from the National League, met to plan the team's future. They agreed to send Wilbert Robinson a check for $10,000 and fire him.

Robinson and John McGraw ended their feud at the 1930 winter meetings. Their handshake ratified the unnatural truce between Giant and Dodger partisans that had been going on since the pennant race of 1924 (and even before — recall the *Times'* remark that Brooklyn rooters "came to life" in September that year for the first time since 1921). If the rivalry was going to remain baseball's best, it needed new blood and fresh controversies.

PART III

1932–1945: Jints and Bums

	Giants	Dodgers
Where They Played	Polo Grounds IV	Ebbets Field
Owners	Charles Stoneham, 1932–36 Horace Stoneham, 1936–45	The Ebbets and McKeever Estates, 1932–45 Branch Rickey, Walter O'Malley, and John Smith, 1945
Managers	John McGraw, 1932 Bill Terry, 1932–41 Mel Ott, 1942–45	Max Carey, 1932–33 Casey Stengel, 1934–36 Burleigh Grimes, 1937–38 Leo Durocher, 1939–45
Best Players	Bill Terry, Mel Ott, Carl Hubbell	Van Lingle Mungo, Dolph Camilli, Dixie Walker
Wore Both Uniforms but Shouldn't Have	Fred Lindstrom	Watty Clark
League Championships, **World Championships**	**1933,** 1936, 1937	1941
Won-Lost vs. Each Other	149–158 (.485)	158–149 (.515)
Won-Lost vs. Rest of League	976–852 (.534)	934–902 (.509)

Robert Joyce had every reason to feel good the night of July 12, 1938. At 33 he was slender and handsome, with thick black locks and dark, piercing eyes. He'd held his job as a post office clerk all through the Depression and was considered a model employee, trusted with the keys and assigned to open shop at 6 o'clock each morning. But the biggest reason Robert Joyce had to feel good was that earlier in the day his beloved Dodgers had thumped the Giants 13–5 at Ebbets Field, knocking Bill Terry's detested overdogs out of first place.

That called for celebration. Joyce headed to his usual hangout, Pat Diamond's Bar and Grill, near the corner of Seventh Avenue and Ninth Street. It was 9 p.m. and the place was packed with a couple dozen people, all familiar except for a few strangers, which was fine as long as they weren't women or Giant fans. He motioned to William Diamond, the owner's son, for a cold one.

How about those Dodgers? he asked. Did you see what they did to them Giants today? Knocked 'em right out of first place.

By three percentage points. They'll lose tomorrow and the Giants'll be right back on top, sneered someone at another stool.

Says who? We got somethin' goin' here. I can feel it. You see who pitched? Posedel, the rookie. And the new third baseman, what's his name? Just came up today.

Packy Rogers.

Yeah. Three hits in four tries. I hear he really creamed that triple to right center. And now we got that outfielder comin' from the Cubbies. Tuck Stainback.

His fellow patrons rose to the bait. Oh yeah, move over, Mel Ott, here comes Tuck Stainback, smirked one. If Stainback's so great, how come this is the second time he's been traded since April? challenged another.

As the beers kept coming, Robert Joyce grew combative. They were mere blocks from the site of old Washington Park, where the *real* William Terry—the one known as Adonis—had battled the Giants half a century ago, yet these so-called Dodger fans showed less pride than a stray dog with a scrap of butcher paper. The more he stood up for his team, the more like Giant fans they responded.

He appealed to William Diamond for support. That was the bartender's job, to settle arguments. Diamond was five years younger than Joyce, married with two kids. His father ran the Democratic Party in the local assembly district and was deputy warden of the civil prison. Bill, tell 'em the Dodgers are turnin' around! Robert Joyce implored.

William Diamond regarded his friend and good customer skeptically. Have you looked at the calendar lately? he asked. It's the middle of July, and the Dodgers just beat the Giants for the first time *all year*. Ten straight they lost to them before today. When we were kids Babe Herman was gonna turn it around. Then Del Bissonette. Joe Hutcheson. Len Koenecke. Nick Tremark. Now you're tellin' me Tuck Stainback? Listen. The Dodgers were a sixth-place team in Uncle Robbie's day, they're a sixth-place team today, and they'll be a sixth-place team the day we die. They're a bunch of miserable bums!

No one took Robert Joyce seriously when, shaking with betrayal, he shouted, "I'm going out to get two guns and shoot up the place," and ran out of the bar.

Though he later claimed he'd drunk 18 glasses of beer and gone out of his mind, his actions over the next two hours displayed cold, sober cunning. He went to the post office where he worked and waited until 12:30 for the night man to close up. Then, using his keys, he slipped inside, found another key to a locked bin containing handguns, and stuffed two of the sidearms in his pockets. He returned to the bar, walked up to William Diamond, and shot him in the left side.

Frank Harvey Krug of Albany, in town visiting relatives, joined waiter Charles Miller in wresting the gun away. But then Joyce pulled his second gun. Krug and another man, Robert Eagan, scrambled for cover. They had no place to hide. Taking deliberate aim, Joyce shot Krug through the heart, killing him instantly.

After deciding to spare Eagan, Joyce strolled out of the bar. Miller, the waiter, notified the police, who collared Joyce a few blocks away. "I guess I went haywire," the killer said. "I was only fooling when I shot them." A jury found him guilty of second-degree murder in Diamond's death, and he plea-bargained another second-degree conviction in Krug's demise, thus becoming the only man known to have been driven to homicide by the Giant-Dodger rivalry.

A few weeks later 26-year-old mental patient John Warde perched for 11 hours on the 17th-floor ledge of the Gotham Hotel in midtown Manhattan while thousands of people gawked below. Police officer Charles Glasco, disguised as a bellboy, tried to coax Warde inside by talking baseball. Glasco thought the Dodgers had a chance at fourth place. Warde disagreed. Hey, I tell ya what, if you come down I'll get us tickets to the game at Ebbets Field today, Glasco offered, to which Warde said, "I'd rather jump than watch those Dodgers," and did.

From the '20s to the '30s, National League baseball in New York City went from languid to life-and-death. The immediate cause was an offhand remark by Giant manager Bill Terry. At a press conference in January 1934, reporters asked him which N.L. teams had the best chance to displace his as world champion. The normally abrupt Terry accommodated the quote-parched scribes with evaluations of the Pirates, Cubs, Cardinals, and even the woebegone Braves. Roscoe McGowen, the *New York Times* man for the Dodgers, asked "What about Brooklyn?" To which Terry replied,

"Brooklyn? I haven't heard anything from them lately. Are they still in the league?"

He said it kiddingly, and his meaning was that the sixth-place Dodgers hadn't made any moves to improve themselves over the winter. But it didn't read with that nuance the next day. Brooklyn Dodger fans, the rivalry's sleeping dogs, howled piteously, then took to assaulting Terry and his players whenever the Giants came to Ebbets Field, not just with jeering chants of *Beat the Giants!* but with bottles, firecrackers, and anything else at hand. When Dick Bartell was hit in the chest with that tomato in 1937, he probably counted himself lucky it wasn't anything worse.

Although it manifested itself most graphically at Ebbets Field and the Polo Grounds, the grudge between Brooklyn and New York went well beyond baseball. The 1930 census showed that Brooklyn had become New York City's largest borough, at 2.6 million a whopping 40 percent more populous than Manhattan. But Brooklynites remained second-class citizens. The Port Authority of New York and New Jersey, a government agency created to improve the region's boat, rail, and vehicle transit, had proposed construction of a freight tunnel from railroad terminuses in New Jersey to docks in Brooklyn. But aided by the railroad industry, Tammany mayor John Hylan thwarted the plan, and eventually new ports were built in Newark and Elizabeth, New Jersey, depriving Brooklynites of thousands of jobs. By 1931, Brooklyn's working stiffs had only to look across the East River at the gleaming new Empire State Building to realize that the future belonged to Gotham's magnates and fixers, not the outer borough lunchpail guys whose ambition extended only as far as talking baseball over beer.

Adding insult to injury was the laughingstock image of Brooklynites fostered by the emerging media of radio and film. Noted Roger Kahn, *eminence gris* of Dodger chroniclers:

> What joined all Brooklyn was a sense, when we were young, that everyone outside was laughing at us. If you listened to a radio quiz program and a contestant said he came from Brooklyn, you next heard a clamor of laughter from the studio audience. If you went to a set-piece war movie, there was one soldier out of Brooklyn. He might be heroic, but Gary Cooper never played him. The best we got was William Bendix throwing grenades and bawling, "Dis is for da folks on Flatbush Avenyuh."

Though hardly the exclusive creation of New Yorkers, the stereotype of urban bumpkins from Toity-Toid Street ranting about dese, dem, and dose was too perceptive to have originated much farther away. And like all pernicious generalizations, it was triply poisonous: hard to shake, easy to live down to, and almost impossible to avoid internalizing.

Bill Terry. The player-manager scores ones of his 1,120 runs for the Giants, fifth in franchise annals behind Willie Mays, Mel Ott, Silent Mike Tiernan, and Barry Bonds. (Transcendental Graphics)

Brooklyn's secondary status extended to the diamond. The Giants revived when Bill Terry replaced John McGraw, winning pennants in 1933, 1936, and 1937. But the post-Wilbert Robinson Dodgers were entertaining mostly for the ways they snatched defeat from victory. On April 16, 1936, they had the Giants two runs down with two outs in the ninth. Giant batter Hank Leiber lofted a routine fly to Dodger left fielder Fred Lindstrom, who had spent most of his career with New York. Lindstrom was reaching to snare the game ender when shortstop Jimmy Jordan, going out for the ball, plowed into him. They knocked each other cold, and Leiber and two baserunners scored to give the Giants a 7–6 win. "I've been in the league for 12 years and that never happened to me until I became a Dodger," a woozy Lindstrom rued afterwards. Rather than remain a Dodger, he retired a month later at age 30.

Play of that caliber caused Brooklynites to refer to their club as "Dem Bums." The origin of the term is in dispute. The *New York World-Telegram's* Joe Williams noticed snowbird fans using it during spring training in 1932. But the popular version is that in the late '30s *World-Telegram* sports cartoonist Willard Mullin, hopping a cab after a game at Ebbets Field, was asked by the driver, "How'd dose bums do today?" and was inspired to depict the Dodgers collectively as a bottom-heavy homeless man. However it started, the nickname appealed to headline writers on the lookout for space-saving shorthand. (The contraction of Giants to Jints had the same motivation.) In time Mullin's Dodger Bum became a beloved icon, but as with so much popular culture shaped by the Brooklyn of this era — think the comedy of Jackie Gleason and Mel Brooks— the undertow of bitterness was unmistakable.

Some blamed the rivalry for the Dodgers' haplessness. If all that mattered to Dodger fans was beating the Giants when it counted, what incentive did ownership have to build a contender? And without a contender to root for, what reason did fans have to watch teams *other* than the Giants? From 1934 through 1937, attendance at Ebbets Field tumbled below half a million, depriving management of the capital needed to purchase good players. Opined Joe Williams in March 1936: "Until recently the Brooklyn owners were able to make the season a financial success out of the Giant-Dodger games alone. These were always so profitable the owners exploited the situation to the neglect of the more general picture. The result has been a gradual disintegration and lessening interest. What Flatbush needs is a new deal, or at least a better deal."

When Robert Joyce argued in July 1938 that Dodger fans' new deal had come, he was actually right. No thanks to Tuck Stainback, of course, but to the brilliant, mercurial Leland Stanford "Larry" MacPhail. "There is that thin line between genius and insanity, and in Larry's case it was sometimes so thin that you could see him drifting back and forth," observed Leo Durocher, the Dodger manager through most of MacPhail's tenure. The son of a Michigan banker, MacPhail had a round, ruddy face with red hair and freckles, but in case that didn't attract enough attention he also spoke in a booming voice and wore expensive, garish clothes. He loved to tell about the night shortly after World War I when he and seven fellow merry men drove deep into Holland to kidnap Kaiser Wilhelm. If they'd only clubbed a guard who subsequently raised alarms, he claimed, they'd have succeeded.

After the war MacPhail settled in Columbus, Ohio, where he made and lost a fortune hawking real estate and used cars. He purchased the local minor league franchise in 1930, sold it to the Cardinals, but continued to run it, developing a bond with St. Louis's Branch Rickey. MacPhail's outstanding performance at Columbus earned him a job as vice president of the Reds. He improved the team on the field and doubled attendance, but left in 1937 and went into the investment business. A year later the Brooklyn Trust Company, which loaned money to the Ebbets and McKeever estates and operated the Dodgers on their behalf, tried to lure Rickey from the Cardinals. Rickey declined, but mentioned an old associate, bored with the investment business, who might be interested in running a ballclub again. And so in 1938 the 49-year-old MacPhail came to Brooklyn.

MacPhail believed in spending money to make money, and in the baseball business that meant spending money on promotion and good players. His innovations transformed the Dodgers. They also shifted the rivalry's balance. Since 1902 the Giants had acted and the Dodgers had reacted. MacPhail reversed the dynamic, and his successors kept it that way for half a century.

But MacPhail could not have changed the rivalry without weak Giant ownership. Charles Stoneham had purchased the team from Harry Hempstead, John Brush's son-in-law, for more than a million dollars in 1919, a record deal. (John McGraw and Tammany judge Francis McQuade bought in as minority partners, but in the late '20s McQuade was ousted in a vicious squabble.) Jersey City native Stoneham was a professional swindler who attracted lawsuits like rotten fruit draws flies. He made his fortune running a bucket shop, a brokerage firm peddling dubious investments without connection to any legitimate stock exchange. After his death in January 1936, ownership passed to his son Horace.

Stocky Horace Stoneham had only one genuine talent — boozing. "To say Horace can drink is like saying that Sinatra can sing," vouched Leo Durocher. And it got worse over time. Marvin Miller, former head of the Major League Players Association (also a Brooklyn native and Dodger fan), first met Stoneham in 1965. "I was floored ... by Stoneham's breath — it had to be at least 80 proof." That was at 11 o'clock in the morning.

Perhaps because of the drinking, Stoneham's intellectual growth stopped around the time Babe Ruth and Lou Gehrig vaulted the Yankees ahead of the Giants in the hearts of New Yorkers. For the rest of his life he believed that if two or three sluggers were good, five or six were better. Between 1936 and 1945 the Giants led the league in home runs six times. But every other dimension of their game suffered, and after their 1937 championship they didn't come close to a pennant for 14 years.

Although Stoneham heeded Bill Terry's entreaties to build a farm system, he lagged behind St. Louis's Rickey, who hatched the idea, and Brooklyn's MacPhail, who bought six minor league clubs and signed working agreements with six others within three years of taking over the Dodgers. As Terry, Mel Ott, and Carl Hubbell, the stars of McGraw's winter seasons, passed their prime, the Giants found no one to replace them. They began to suffer at the gate, trailing the resurgent Dodgers in attendance almost every year after 1939. There's no telling how red Stoneham's bottom line might have blushed had Dodger fans not packed the despised "Polio Grounds" to cheer on their Bums against the Jints. Recollected Dodger pitcher Kirby Higbe, "In the Polo Grounds there always seemed to be as many Dodger fans as Giant fans, or more. There were more fights at our games there than in all the boxing arenas in the country."

By 1939 the Giants had deteriorated into an average team. The slide didn't stop there. On May 23, 1944, they took a 2–1 lead into the bottom of the ninth against the Dodgers. There were two on and two out when Lloyd Waner, in one of his 14 career at-bats for Brooklyn, hit what should have been a routine, game-ending fly ball. Giant right fielder Johnny Rucker was reaching to snare it when center fielder Charley Mead plowed into him. They both collapsed, the ball trickled out of Rucker's glove, and the Dodger baserunners, moving on contact, scored to give Brooklyn a 3–2 win.

As Freddie Lindstrom and Jimmy Jordan would have attested, the rivalry had come full circle.

6. 1934: "Are They Still in the League?"

Bill Terry had three choices after his "Are they still in the league?" line outraged Brooklyn. He could claim it was taken out of context and apologize. He could remain silent and hope it blew over. Or he could dump fuel on the fire.

No one would ever mistake the heir to John McGraw's legacy for a diplomat. At the annual dinner of the Baseball Writers' Association's New York chapter a few days later, he offered a loud, unflattering analysis of Brooklyn's chances. Rebutted Dodger manager Max Carey, "You don't know anything about our ballclub. You don't even know what we're going to have this season!" "Neither do you," Terry replied, "or you wouldn't be sitting there laughing." Carey countered that the pennant-winning 1933 Giants were "the luckiest team I ever saw" and bet the aging Terry wouldn't play 125 games at first base. Terry, the last National Leaguer to hit over .400, accepted the wager, saying he not only would play that many games but would lead N.L. first basemen in hitting and guide the Giants to another pennant. The ante: a new suit of clothes. "It's about time I got a new suit," snapped Carey. To which Terry retorted, "Make it two suits. Don't be a piker." The posturing ceased only after the writers reminded them that Commissioner Landis looked harshly upon betting talk.

The confrontation promised a peppery summer. But on the eve of spring training, Dodger management caught the real point of Terry's remark and made a major move: it fired Carey and replaced him with Casey Stengel. "The first thing I want to say is, the Dodgers are still in the league," Stengel announced, but his anxieties bloomed as one player after another succumbed to injury. He didn't know how hazardous his new job really was, however, until May 29, 1934, when the Giants visited Ebbets Field for the first time that season. More than 7,500 Dodger fans turned out despite dank, drizzling weather, and they so begrudged Stengel's sportsmanly willingness to pose for photos with Terry that they hurled firecrackers at both of them. His players were the ones who needed gunpowder going off at their feet: they loaded the bases with one out in the seventh but failed to score and lost, 4–3.

The rivals played a Memorial Day doubleheader the next afternoon, attracting a record paid crowd of 40,993 (over 42,000 total). Eight thousand seatless Dodger fans squatted in the aisles, stood in the runways, and climbed support posts. They bellowed not only at Terry but at his players, including congenial Mel Ott, who had previously escaped Brooklyn's wrath. The abuse just sharpened the Giants, who took both ends of the twin bill. After the Dodgers made off with the series finale, their first win in seven tries against New York, a grateful Joe Gilleaudeau, Charles Ebbets' son-in-law and team vice president, bought each player a hat.

The Giants took two out of three when the teams next met at the Polo Grounds. They might have swept if not for Carl Hubbell. A smart southpaw with a windmill windup and devastating screwball, "King Carl" was the Giants' best pitcher since Christy Mathewson and had a winning record against every team in the National League — except Brooklyn. For some reason none of his magic worked against the Dodgers. On June 30, 1934, just 10 days before he electrified the baseball universe by striking out Babe Ruth, Lou Gehrig, Jimmie Foxx, Al Simmons, and Joe Cronin consecutively at the second All-Star game, Hubbell was blasted all over the yard by the likes of Joe Stripp, Danny Taylor, and Johnny Frederick. The 8–4 loss was the 21st of his career to Brooklyn, against only nine wins.

But sweet moments like that were too few to sustain Brooklyn's rage against Bill Terry. On July 4 the Giants were in first place, three ahead of Chicago, four ahead of St. Louis … and 17 ahead of Brooklyn, mired, as usual, in sixth place. And there the matter might have ended, except for two things: the Giants stumbled down the stretch, and the Cardinals got hot.

On September 6 the Giants led St. Louis by seven games. Wise heads expected them to clinch the pennant during a long upcoming homestand. Instead they lost 11 of 19. At the same time Frankie Frisch's Cardinals won 16 of 21, including a doubleheader sweep by the Dean brothers, Dizzy and Paul, in front of a record 62,573 fans at the Polo Grounds on September 16. The Dean brothers hurled a double shutout against the Dodgers five

Carl Hubbell. Also nicknamed "The Meal Ticket" for his dependability, he threw so many screwballs that his left palm permanently faced outward. (Transcendental Graphics)

days later. Paul's effort in the nightcap was a no-hitter, prompting Dizzy to scold, "Why didn't you tell me what you were going to do? I'd have pitched one too." On September 28 the Cardinals tied the Giants for first place. Each team had only two games left, the Cards against the last-place Reds, the Giants against the Dodgers.

Throughout Brooklyn, talk of the sensational trial in which Bruno Hauptmann stood accused of kidnapping and killing Charles Lindbergh's baby stopped amid palm-rubbing anticipation of the Dodgers denying the Giants the pennant. Should Stengel start a sick Van Lingle Mungo, or go with a lesser pitcher who was healthy? Whoever got the ball would take the hopes and dreams of the entire borough with him. "Dodgers Set to Show They Are in League," blared the *Brooklyn Eagle's* front page headline the morning of September 29.

Thousands of Brooklynites boarded the subway and traveled to the Polo Grounds that afternoon. They made up most of the crowd of 13,774, which would have been three times larger had a morning downpour not caused most fans to believe the game would be canceled. While Giant management pondered whether to postpone, keeping the gates closed until after two o'clock for a scheduled three o'clock start, the Flatbush faithful huddled under umbrellas or the elevated subway line.

Once Terry decided the game was on, the Brooklynites "literally knocked each other down in the wild scramble to get through the turnstiles," reported the *Times.* They raised an ear-splitting din with cowbells, whistles, horns, rattles, and leather lungs. They waved signs reading "Bill Who," "We Wish You Were in Dixie" (a reference to Terry's Memphis, Tennessee, roots), and countless variations on "Yes, We're Still in the League." Startled Giant fans barely mustered a response. The result, as the *Eagle's* Tommy Holmes put it, was that "Bill Terry's band was in the strange position of battling for a pennant in their home park but before a crowd largely hostile."

Stengel went with the afflicted Mungo. He had no choice, for as Ed Hughes of the *Eagle* put it, "Anything less than Mungo is liable to make talk of a none too palatable nature. Just a suspicion that the Dodgers might not be putting out all they had to pulverize the Giants' chances of winning the pennant would about ruin Flatbush." Terry had a tougher choice. His big three, Carl Hubbell, 23-game winner Hal Schumacher, and Freddie Fitzsimmons (who had beaten the Dodgers five times already in 1934) were worn out, so he settled on Roy "Tarzan" Parmelee. The 27-year-old fastballer had missed the first half of the season with appendicitis, but had compiled the league's lowest hits-per-innings ratio since.

Through the first four frames only the clouds threatened. But Mungo, batting .239, started the fifth with a single, lumbered to second on a passed ball, and splashed his way home on shortstop Lonnie Frey's base hit up the middle. After retiring the side in order in the bottom of the fifth, Mungo again stunned the Giants with his bat, slapping a two-out, full-count single to knock in the Dodgers' second run. "The racket of the previous inning was now doubled in volume," the *Times* reported. That was nothing compared to the reaction when the scoreboard put up three first inning runs for the Cardinals against the Reds.

As the rain began to fall once more, Lonnie Frey led off the top of the seventh with another single. He was sacrificed to second, then scored on first baseman Sam Leslie's shot past the slick-fielding Terry to give the Dodgers a 3–0 lead. But in the home half of the seventh the Giants struck back: center fielder George Watkins walloped a solo shot into the right field upper deck. Brooklynites feared the homer would prove a Giant wake-up call, but an unperturbed Mungo struck out Gus Mancuso and induced Blondy Ryan to ground out to end the inning.

The eighth sped by, both teams going down one-two-three. For the ninth, Terry sent rookie Al Smith to the mound. In seven years Smith would gain notoriety as one of the pitchers who stopped Joe DiMaggio's 56-game hitting streak, but on this day he heard catcalls of Hey, who ya gonna put in there next, Herbert Hoover? from Brooklynites amused that his name was identical to the Democratic candidate for president in 1928 (and New York's former governor). The rattled Smith faced four batters and yielded three hits to put the Giants another big run behind.

Terry called upon Dolf Luque, a wily 19-year veteran, to get out of the jam. The Havana-born Luque was one of the first Latinos in the big leagues, and the first of renown, winning 194 games. Like several other players in this era (Lefty O'Doul, Freddie Fitzsimmons, and even Van Lingle Mungo) he performed for both the Giants and Dodgers and made significant contributions to each. But this time his 44-year-old arm failed him: with the bases loaded, he walked Dodger catcher Al Lopez to put his team behind 5–1.

Terry led off the bottom of the ninth. He chopped a grounder down the third base line for an infield hit. Mel Ott followed. Mungo, prone to lapses in control, walked him on four pitches. That brought Hall of Famer Travis Jackson to the plate. Anxious Dodger hearts thumped.

Just when Mungo looked finished, however, he found his last reserves. He struck out Jackson looking. Next up: George Watkins, who had clanged him for that homer. He fanned Watkins looking, too. With one out to go, Terry announced a pinch hitter: San Francisco native Lefty O'Doul, ending a stellar career that included a .349 lifetime batting average.

Mungo zipped strike one, strike two, strike three past O'Doul to end the game.

"Under a leaden sky as dark and as dismal as the pennant hopes of the New York Giants, the champions of the baseball world were dealt a staggering blow," crowed Tommy Holmes under a banner headline on the

Eagle's front page. Reminisced Mungo some time later, "Knocking the Giants out of the World Series that year was probably the highlight of my career."

But the Giants hadn't been knocked out. True, Paul Dean and the Gas House Gang had beaten the Reds 6–1 to take sole possession of first place. But if the Giants beat the Dodgers on the last day of the season, and the Cardinals lost to Cincinnati, New York and St. Louis would finish tied and meet in a playoff to determine the champion. So there was still a chance for the Giants to reach the World Series.

More than 45,000 fans poured into the Polo Grounds for the all-important final game, including another vast contingent of "demented Flatbushers inconsiderate of the rotting Giants' feelings" who, reported the *Eagle*, "stampeded through the grandstands bearing huge placards 'Is Brooklyn in the National League?'"

The Giants bombed veteran Dodger pitcher Ray Benge for four first-inning runs, and with Fitzsimmons going for them, they had every reason to believe they would win. But this wasn't the usual Dodger-killing Fitzsimmons. With one out in the second he gave up a triple to Tony Cuccinello and a bloop single to Danny Taylor, and Brooklyn was on the board. In the fourth he yielded a leadoff double to Len Koenecke and a single to Sam Leslie, bringing the Dodgers within two. Frustrated, Fitzsimmons did a Mungo and went at the Dodgers with his bat, slamming a solo homer in the bottom of the fourth to increase New York's lead to 5–2.

But then came news from St. Louis that the Cardinals, with Dizzy Dean going for his 30th win, had scored two runs in the first.

The Giants went hollow. An error and a wild pitch contributed to a Dodger run in the sixth. In the eighth Fitzsimmons gave up an RBI double to Koenecke that brought Brooklyn within one. Terry relieved his chunky knuckleballer with Hal Schumacher. As Schumacher warmed up, the scoreboard flashed news that St. Louis had scored three more runs. Dodger fans erupted. At first base, Terry hung his head.

Schumacher got Sam Leslie to ground to shortstop Blondy Ryan, who trapped Koenecke in a rundown. Koenecke scrambled back and forth long enough for Leslie to take second, which was crucial: a moment later Schumacher threw a wild pitch, and Leslie, determined to prove that *Dodger hustle* wasn't an oxymoron, flew past third and gunned for home. He scored, tying the game.

In St. Louis, the Gas House Gang also scored, giving Dizzy Dean a 6–0 lead.

Back at the Polo Grounds, the Giants and Dodgers went into extra innings. When Schumacher put runners on second and third to start the

10th, Terry brought in Carl Hubbell, who struck out the first man he faced. Then Hubbell intentionally walked Joe Stripp to set up an inning-ending double play. He had the perfect DP candidate in Al Lopez, slow afoot and average with the bat. Lopez obligingly hit a hard ground ball to Ryan at short.

But Ryan muffed it, and the Dodgers went ahead, 6–5.

They scored twice more, but it hardly mattered. Hughie Critz, Terry, and Ott went quietly in the bottom of the 10th, and the New York team took a long, dejected walk to the center field clubhouse while Brooklynites partied at the Polo Grounds.

Bill Terry played every game in 1934 and led all National League first basemen in hitting. But he owed Max Carey two new suits. There's no evidence he ever paid off.

7. 1939: "All Tangled Up in the Spirit of the Thing"

In 1939 New York City staged a World's Fair. Built in undeveloped Flushing Meadow, Queens, and subtitled "The World of Tomorrow," the proto-theme park bolstered tourism while giving government and industry an opportunity to present themselves in a flattering light. One lavish pavilion after another depicted a happy future, all gee-whiz technology and material comfort. President Roosevelt's opening speech on April 30 was the first publicly televised broadcast in New York.

After a decade of deprivation, New Yorkers desperately wanted to believe better times were ahead. But it was hard to overlook that the Germans, Italians, and Japanese were on the march. Maybe there wouldn't be war, but if there was, only head-in-the-sand isolationists—most of whom hailed from the middle of the country, not the East Coast—believed America could stay out of it. All over New York, people barely a generation removed from Europe's political roiling worried about relatives in the Old Country—and their own teenage sons. As always in frightening times, they retreated into the familiar. And from April through September in New York nothing was more familiar than the rivalry between the Giants and Dodgers.

But that too was changing.

Given wide latitude to run the Dodgers, Larry MacPhail first spruced up Ebbets Field with a paint job, uniforms for the ushers, and a press club (with free drinks) for reporters. Then he demanded $50,000 to purchase Dolph Camilli, the Phillies' slugging first baseman. The Brooklyn Trust

Company had already loaned the Ebbets and McKeever families more than half a million dollars and had given MacPhail another $200,000 to fix the ballpark. George V. McLaughlin, president of the company, was a former police commissioner fabled for his parsimony. But MacPhail blustered until McLaughlin relented, and the Dodgers had their first star hitter in years.

The Giants ignored the hubbub in Brooklyn until MacPhail announced his intention to play night games at Ebbets Field. He had introduced night ball to the majors while running the Reds in 1935, and the innovation had contributed substantially to Cincinnati's rise in attendance. But opposition remained from traditionalists, players worried about visibility, and owners worried about utility bills. Bill Terry belonged to the first two categories, Horace Stoneham to the third. When MacPhail asked each National League team for permission to reschedule one of its games in Brooklyn to the evening, the Giants were the only foe to refuse.

Undaunted, MacPhail planned the first night game in New York City for June 15, 1938, against the Reds. He invited scores of celebrities, from Commissioner Landis and Mayor Fiorello LaGuardia to Babe Ruth (whom he hired a few days later as a coach). He signed sprinter Jesse Owens, hero of the 1936 Olympics, to compete with ballplayers in the 100-yard dash, low hurdles, and broad jump. He even put on a fireworks display. One last drawing card fell in his lap: 22-year-old Johnny Vander Meer, who had thrown a no-hitter in his previous start, was assigned to pitch for Cincinnati.

Asked if he would be attending the historic game, Bill Terry facetiously replied, "Yes. I've always wanted to see Jesse Owens run."

When the lights went on at 8:35 p.m., more than 40,000 fans (38,748 paid) erupted in applause. Pregame ceremonies delayed the first pitch until 9:45. Then Dodger fans got more history than they bargained for when Vander Meer pitched his second consecutive no-hitter.

The seven night games in Brooklyn that year averaged more than 25,000 customers, as opposed to fewer than 10,000 for day games. But despite a 14 percent drop in their own attendance, the Giants announced they would continue playing day games only in 1939.

By then MacPhail had opened a second front, breaking the gentlemen's agreement among the Giants, Dodgers, and Yankees against radio broadcasts. The conventional wisdom was that if fans could hear the game for free, they wouldn't pay to watch it at the ballpark. MacPhail had proven that false in Cincinnati. He had also discovered that radio could be lucrative. He arranged to broadcast over 50,000-watt WOR, signed advertising contracts worth a combined thousand dollars a game, and brought in Mississippi-born Walter Lanier "Red" Barber to call the action.

Larry MacPhail with reporters. In 1939 he took the Dodger press on a cruise, only to have the yacht run aground and the pilot quit. Brooklyn Eagle writer (and later Dodger executive) Harold Parrott steered the ship home. (Transcendental Graphics)

MacPhail claimed he first heard fellow redhead Barber on a college radio station in Florida reading a paper on bovine obstetrics. Probably apocryphal, but MacPhail's Reds *did* hire Barber to broadcast their games in 1934. The people of southern Ohio, familiar with southern accents and expressions, took to Barber readily. But to Brooklynites his intonations and expressions were initially strange, as borough native (and later, *San Francisco Chronicle* sports columnist) Lowell Cohn explained: "He spoke with a folksy southern accent, which suggested to us generations of culture, plantations with flowing wisteria trees and people with inherited wealth who went out Sunday mornings on fox hunts or something like that. This image was quite a contrast to what we had around us—shriveled oak trees, and in terms of fauna, well, if our borough had had an official bird, it would have been the sparrow or that moocher, the pigeon begging for peanuts in the park."

Before long, however, Barber became a civic treasure. As he put it, "I didn't broadcast with a Brooklyn accent, but I did broadcast with a Brooklyn heart."

Forced to play catch-up, Horace Stoneham collaborated with the Yankees on a radio deal, arranging for WABC to broadcast weekday and Saturday home games. Mel Allen and Arch McDonald did the announcing.

On opening day 1939 Barber called New York City's first baseball broadcast in years. Before 25,496 fans at frigid Ebbets Field, the Giants beat the Dodgers, 7–3. Zeke Bonura, a slugger Stoneham bought from the Washington Senators, belted his first National League homer. Leo Durocher, the Dodger shortstop, played with a 102-degree fever and committed two errors. By the seventh inning Dodger fans, convinced that for all MacPhail's hurly-burly nothing had changed, sat on their hands, while a delegation of Giant fans in the left field

Red Barber. "If a million people went to Ebbets Field to see the Dodgers play, ten million listened to Red broadcast the games," wrote Robert Creamer. (Transcendental Graphics)

seats, also convinced nothing had changed, stood for the visiting side's seventh-inning stretch.

It was the feisty, fast-living Durocher's first game as Dodger manager. Never much of a hitter — when he came up with the Yankees, Babe Ruth labeled him "The All-American Out" — he depended on a sure glove and quick mind for survival. He made his name as a member of St. Louis's raucous Gas House Gang, where he and manager Frankie Frisch, a similar personality, forged an uneasy alliance. After Durocher's average slipped to .203 in 1937, Frisch and his boss, Branch Rickey, deemed Durocher more trouble than he was worth and peddled him to the Dodgers.

A couple of months later MacPhail arrived and figured out how to turn the deal for the fading shortstop to Brooklyn's advantage. Durocher had the makings of a superb manager, probing for an opponent's weakness and exploiting it ruthlessly. MacPhail regarded him as warily as Frisch and Rickey did, but after 1938, the Dodgers' sixth losing season in a row, he named Durocher his manager. "He fired me 60 times if he fired me once," Durocher remembered. "If Leo would drop that zero off the end, he would be closer to being right," MacPhail countered, which nonetheless betrayed how often they clashed.

Durocher restored the spirit of John McGraw to the rivalry. Like the Little Napoleon, he grew up in the Northeast (West Springfield, Massachusetts) the son of impoverished immigrant parents, and he learned early to fend for himself. He too made up for lack of size with ready fists. He had the same love of gambling. And he also bedeviled umpires, hence the nickname Leo the Lip. McGraw and Durocher shared a preference for the one-run strategies nearly forgotten in the lively ball era, and both would do anything — cheating included — to win. "If I were playing third base and my mother was rounding third with the run that was going to beat us, I would trip her. Oh, I'd pick her up and brush her off, and then I'd say, 'Sorry, Mom.' But nobody beats me," Durocher said, and he meant it. The one difference between them was that where McGraw drank, Durocher womanized. (His fourth wife, Lynne Walker Goldblatt, is no relation to the author.)

At June's end Durocher had his team close to .500, but it was still too early to know whether this was an aberration or the beginning of a new phase in Dodger history. On the second of July, 51,435 curious fans paid their way into the Polo Grounds for a Sunday doubleheader between the Giants and Dodgers. The Dodgers won the first game 3–2, but quickly fell behind 4–0 in the nightcap thanks to another Bonura homer. The Dodgers rallied for three runs in the fourth, though, and had the tying run on first with one out when Durocher himself came to bat.

The Lip badly wanted a sweep, because it would put the Dodgers over the .500 mark. When Giant starter Hal Schumacher brushed him back he fumed, even though Schumacher was routinely wild — he holds the post-1900 Giant record for most walks allowed — and Durocher, a zealous proponent of the beanball, had instructed his own starter, Whitlow Wyatt, to throw at the Giants. Durocher swung hard at a Schumacher pitch. He grounded into a double play. Out of frustration and rage, he stepped on Bonura's foot as he crossed first base.

Bonura was an indifferent fielder, so he might have had his foot on the middle of the bag, as Durocher alleged. But then again, he might not have. Whichever, Bonura demonstrated why he was nicknamed "Bananas," firing the ball at Durocher in retaliation. Then Bonura chased the Dodger manager into right field, caught him, knocked him down, and landed a number of solid blows. Even the proud Durocher didn't claim he won that fight: "I took a lunge at him and held on for dear life so that all those calmer heads which are supposed to prevail could get a chance to do their job."

A week later fans were still talking about the fight, having paused briefly to honor Lou Gehrig, who gave his famous farewell speech on July 4. Both sides stoked the controversy. "Looks like Terry's team can't take it when Wyatt threw a few inside pitches at them. They will get more of them when we see them next weekend," Durocher vowed. Responded Terry, "He went out of his way to spike Zeke. Only a beaten team starts throwing beanballs." And when somebody commented that it hadn't been much of a fight, the Giant manager added, "How could it be with Durocher in it?"

The following Friday, Saturday, and Sunday the Giants played at Ebbets Field. The *Brooklyn Eagle* trumpeted the series with a special "Beat the Giants!" section celebrating the history of the rivalry. Invited to comment on the host team, Horace Stoneham said, "If Durocher keeps them hustling, I feel they have a great chance for sixth place," thereby justifying Tommy Holmes's assessment that "The greatest natural rivalry in major league baseball isn't likely to get much hotter than it is right now with fans, officials and the players themselves all tangled up in the spirit of the thing."

The Giants — and the extra detachment of police on hand — caught a break when the first game fell on a Ladies Day. The presence of 15,000 women restrained the 21,000 men in attendance. Zeke Bonura was booed heartily his first two times at bat, but his third time up he lashed a single that put the Giants on the board. Despite that, the Dodgers pulled out a 3–2 win to close within a game and a half of the Giants, who fell six behind front-running Cincinnati.

Another sellout crowd filled Ebbets Field for the Saturday doubleheader. It roared as Durocher was presented with the 2,500 pennies Brooklyn fans contributed to pay the $25 fine the league had assessed him for fighting, and it roared again when someone threw a banana at Bonura, but the Giants took the opener, 8–3. In the second game Van Lingle Mungo carried a 3–0 shutout into the eighth before he ran out of steam, giving up two runs and loading the bases with two outs for ... yep, Zeke Bonura.

Durocher brought in Freddie Fitzsimmons, who'd pitched so effectively *against* the Dodgers for the Giants back in 1934. Terry had traded Fat Freddie to Brooklyn in 1937 for pitching prospect Tom Baker, the worst deal of his career. Fitzsimmons wound and threw. Bonura mashed the ball. But it went right into the glove of third baseman Cookie Lavagetto, killing the rally, and Fitzsimmons held on in the ninth to save the 3–2 victory.

The next day Bonura hit into a pair of double plays, but the Giants won anyway to go into the All-Star break in second place. Durocher's surprising Dodgers were hot on their heels in third.

When the rivals hooked up again in mid August, they had both fallen out of contention. But they were only two games apart, the Giants on top. The Dodgers romped for six first-inning runs and held on to win the opener, 8–5. With Horace Stoneham, nearly 11,000 ladies, and 6,000 boys from the Knothole Club at Ebbets Field for the second game, the Giants amassed an early 7–0 lead and cruised to victory. But the Dodgers won the rubber match 5–1 to pull within one game of the Giants. Four days later they accomplished the unthinkable: they passed the Giants in the standings.

As if that wasn't sign enough of a changing rivalry, on August 26 the Dodgers presented the first telecast of a major league game. "This is Red Barber speaking. Let me say hello to you all," the mellifluous voice welcomed crowds watching primitive screens at the RCA Building in Manhattan and the RCA exhibit at the World's Fair. Baseball was more than a decade from becoming a TV staple, but MacPhail was giving Stoneham — and his colleagues — yet another foretaste of the future. (Thirty years later Stoneham was still suspicious of TV, limiting local broadcasts almost exclusively to road games against the Dodgers.)

The Giants had five more games against the Dodgers in September. But the rivalry was overshadowed by developments in Europe, where the Germans invaded Poland, provoking declarations of war from France and England. On September 9 and 10, playing to crowds under 20,000, the Dodgers swept a pair at Ebbets Field to put the Giants behind them once and for all. They got hot and climbed past Chicago into third place, finishing the season 15 games over .500 for the first time since 1930.

The Giants fell to 77–74, their worst record since 1932. Their declining performance cost Horace Stoneham almost 100,000 paying customers. Attendance was now only three-quarters what it had been just two years earlier. Belatedly, Stoneham rigged the Polo Grounds for night play. On May 24, 1940, the Giants became the last team in the National League to play after dark. Some Dodger fans who crossed the East River for the occasion conceded that the 200-million-candlepower system was 10 percent better than the one at Ebbets Field, but snickered that it made the Giants look 10 percent worse than usual.

The Giants and Dodgers played their first night game against each other on August 5, 1940, at Ebbets Field. Dixie Walker stroked four hits and Whitlow Wyatt hurled a shutout as the Dodgers prevailed, 6–0. Two days later 53,997 fans gathered at the Polo Grounds for the first night game between the rivals there. It was also Mel Ott Night. Giants and Dodgers together honored Master Melvin, the affable Louisianan who had come to the big leagues as a 17-year-old and had led the Giants in home runs every year since 1928. Then Dixie Walker lashed another four hits as Brooklyn stomped Hubbell, 8–4.

In 1941 the Dodgers ended — at 21 years — their longest stretch between pennants. It was also their first 100-win season. They played even better in 1942, winning 104 games, but Branch Rickey's Cardinals nosed them out of first place. There was no longer any question that the rivalry had tilted decisively in favor of Brooklyn. But by then America was involved in World War II, and sports rivalries took a back seat to the larger cause. On opening day 1942 at the Polo Grounds, Mayor LaGuardia summoned Leo Durocher and new Giant manager Mel Ott to home plate and handed them war bonds they'd purchased. "I see you brought your friends with you," LaGuardia joked as Giant partisans hooted Durocher.

At the urging of Larry MacPhail, every major league team donated the proceeds from one home game to the war effort. The Dodgers hosted the first such contest on May 8, 1942, against the Giants. It was also the first twilight game, MacPhail's solution to the wartime ban on night ball. The Dodgers sold 42,822 tickets, raising nearly $60,000 for the Navy Relief Society. Mayor LaGuardia threw out the first pitch, and everybody sang "God Bless America." The *Times* called it "perhaps the best-natured gathering that ever played host to the Giants in Flatbush." It might not have been so good-natured had the Dodgers not triumphed, 7–6.

Three months later the Giants hosted the Dodgers in a twilight benefit for the Army Emergency Relief fund that drew 57,305 and raised nearly $80,000. Ahead 7–4 in the bottom of the ninth, the Dodgers' Whit Wyatt gave up a single to Bill Werber and walked Ott. The bashing Giants had three chances to tie the score. But in a move hearkening back to the 1889 World Series, umpire George Magerkurth called the game. His logic was sound — under the wartime curfew, lights had to be out an hour after sunset, and the official time of sunset had been exactly one hour earlier — but it wasn't communicated to the crowd, which threatened mayhem. Management momentarily quieted things by shining a spotlight on the American flag in center field. When that lost its pacifying power, a band broke into "The Star-Spangled Banner." Eventually singing drowned out the boos, and the crowd dispersed.

On June 25, 1944, with the Normandy invasion well underway, the Giants and Dodgers joined the Yankees in a unique three-way exhibition

Mel Ott. Just how much did the short right field fence at the Polo Grounds help him? Only 188 of his 511 homers were hit on the road. (Transcendental Graphics)

at the Polo Grounds. More than 50,000 fans purchased $25 or more in war bonds to attend. Milton Berle presided over the pregame festivities, which included introductions of rivalry emeriti Roger Bresnahan, Hooks Wiltse, Nap Rucker, and Zack Wheat. (Fittingly, Bill Klem was there too.) Then the teams rotated six times between batting, fielding, and watching. The Dodgers won, 5–1–0, over the Yankees and Giants, respectively.

It sounded like the kind of stunt Larry MacPhail would dream up. But it wasn't. After the 1942 season Brooklyn's flamboyant impresario, nostalgic for the glory days of the Great War and under pressure from Dodger ownership over his free spending, reenlisted as a colonel in charge of public relations for the Army's Service and Supplies unit. The idea for the three-sided game came from the sports division of the Treasury Department's War Finance Committee. MacPhail's successor, old mentor Branch Rickey, canceled a Dodger exhibition in Buffalo to make it possible.

MacPhail returned to New York after the war, buying into the Yankees. His antics set in motion one of the rivalry's most shocking surprises. But he also got a surprise of his own when the innovative tradition he'd established in Brooklyn was taken farther than he'd have ever dared.

PART IV

1946–1957: Reality Strangles Invention

	Giants	Dodgers
Where They Played	Polo Grounds IV	Ebbets Field, 1946–57 Roosevelt Stadium, 1956–57
Owners	Horace Stoneham	Branch Rickey, Walter O'Malley, and John Smith, 1945–50 Walter O'Malley, 1950–57
Managers	Mel Ott, 1946–48 Leo Durocher, 1948–55 Bill Rigney, 1956–57	Leo Durocher, 1946 Clyde Sukeforth, 1947 Burt Shotton, 1947 Leo Durocher, 1948 Burt Shotton, 1948–50 Charlie Dressen, 1951–53 Walter Alston, 1954–57
Best Players	Bobby Thomson, Monte Irvin, Willie Mays, Hoyt Wilhelm	Pee Wee Reese, Carl Furillo, Jackie Robinson, Gil Hodges, Roy Campanella, Duke Snider, Don Newcombe
Wore Both Uniforms but Shouldn't Have	Daryl Spencer	Clem Labine
League Championships, **World Championships**	1951, **1954**	1947, 1949, 1952, 1953, **1955,** 1956
Won-Lost vs. Each Other	116–151 (.434)	151–116 (.566)
Won-Lost vs. Rest of League	836–748 (.528)	974–610 (.615)

For many fans, the rivalry between the Giants and Dodgers reached its peak in the dozen years after World War II. Only once in the previous 56 seasons had both teams finished within five games of first place, but between 1946 and 1957 they did it four times—and their 1951 pennant race produced the most thrilling moment in baseball history. New York and Brooklyn dominated the National League, the Giants winning two pennants, the Dodgers an incredible *six*. "The rivalry between the Dodgers and the Giants was very intense," recollected Vin Scully, a Manhattan native and Giant fan who began broadcasting for the Dodgers in 1950. "At Ebbets Field there was a door separating the two clubhouses. In the early '50s they nailed that door shut, because it was like the mongoose and the cobra."

Even so, memories of this era revolve chiefly around the Dodgers. For good reason: no team has ever come as close to the ideal as the Boys of Summer, a collection of colorful characters who stayed together year after year, requited the love of their fans, and *won*.

They made history, too.

The National and American Leagues had always excluded African American players. Occasionally someone like John McGraw attempted to break the color line, but never more than half-heartedly. In 1947 Dodger president Branch Rickey resolved to accomplish what three generations of baseball executives had resisted: the racial integration of the major leagues.

He received vital support from his manager, Leo Durocher, who as early as 1943 accused ownership of a gentlemen's agreement that kept blacks out of the game. He also got a lift from Albert "Happy" Chandler, successor to the racist Kenesaw Mountain Landis as commissioner and, though from Kentucky, a firm believer that "if a black boy can make it at Okinawa and go to Guadalcanal, he can make it in baseball."

But Rickey and his allies were heavily outnumbered. The otherwise innovative Larry MacPhail turned tail when confronted by integration. In 1942 he wrote Raymond Campion, an African American church leader from Brooklyn, that the exclusion of blacks from the major leagues had nothing to do with discrimination, but with concern for the survival of the Negro Leagues! "It is very questionable in my mind whether many of the colored people understand the practical baseball problems which are involved," he condescended. Appointed to the Major League Committee on Baseball Integration in 1945, he never attended a single meeting.

According to Chandler, Horace Stoneham warned fellow major league owners in January 1947 that if the Dodgers brought up African American Jackie Robinson, blacks in Harlem would burn down the Polo Grounds, and the owners subsequently voted 15–1 against allowing Robinson to play in the majors, Rickey being the sole dissenter. Though Chandler's account has been disputed, there's no question Rickey put his career and reputation on the line by bringing Robinson to Brooklyn.

When the 28-year-old, California-bred Robinson stepped onto Ebbets Field on April 15, 1947, for a game against the Braves, he too had a career and reputation at stake — as well as his safety, sanity, and the fate of millions of African Americans. Every bit as combative as Durocher — after a remarkable rise to Army lieutenant, he was court-martialed (and acquitted) in 1944 for refusing to sit in the back of a bus — he re-

Jackie Robinson. Though plagued by injury late in his career, he always got healthy for the Giants, playing more games against them than against any other opponent. (Transcendental Graphics)

sponded with supernatural restraint to the stream of indignities heaped upon him. Shaking off death threats and daily acts of discrimination, he stole twice as many bases as anyone else in the league, finished second in runs scored, and led the Dodgers to a pennant, making him one of the few baseball players worthy of the term *hero*.

He was the third key member of the Dodger dynasty to arrive in Brooklyn. Pee Wee Reese came first, in 1940, and replaced Durocher at shortstop. From a peach-fuzzed 21-year-old he matured into the steadfast team captain, fondly remembered for putting his arm around Robinson in the face of abuse from racist fans. Also preceding Robinson was outfielder Carl Furillo, a moody Pennsylvanian with a strong bat, stronger arm, and visceral hatred of Durocher. Gil Hodges and Duke Snider arrived for good the same year as Robinson, although they didn't become regulars until later. Roy Campanella established himself as the Dodgers' second black star in 1948, more easygoing than Robinson but an equally formidable presence on the field. Third baseman Billy Cox and pitchers Preacher Roe and Carl Erskine also joined the Dodgers that year. Starter

Don Newcombe (1949), reliever Clem Labine (1951), and super-utility-man Jim Gilliam (1953) rounded out the core.

Except for Cox and Roe, every one of these players was still on the Dodger roster in 1956, Robinson's final season. Six (Reese, Furillo, Robinson, Campanella, Erskine, and Gilliam) played their entire career for the Dodgers, and four (Reese, Robinson, Campanella, and Snider) were elected to the Hall of Fame.

There were stars among the fans, too. The best-known was Hilda Chester, a foghorn-voiced, heavyset single mother besaddled by poverty and illness. She came to MacPhail's first Ladies Day, got hooked, and became a regular in the center field bleachers, developing an act that included a "Hilda Is Here" sign, a cheap hula skirt, and a clanging cowbell. She parlayed her notoriety into a job with ballpark vendor Harry M. Stevens at Yankee Stadium and Aqueduct Raceway, where she once told a Giant fan, "Like Mae West sez, to hell wit yez an' a boost for meself."

Another source of entertainment was the Dodger Sym-phony, a group of amateur brass and percussion players dressed in top hats and tattered tuxedoes. They heralded the umpires' arrival with a rendition of "Three Blind Mice" (before the days of four-man crews) and banged a bass drum whenever an opposing player struck out and sat on the bench. They marched through the aisles playing loudly and enthusiastically, but not always in sync.

There were celebrity fans, too, most prominently General Douglas MacArthur. Fired in 1951 for defying civilian command during the Korean War, MacArthur received a tickertape parade up Manhattan that brought out more celebrants than Dwight Eisenhower's 1945 return from Europe. He took in a game at Ebbets Field, where the fans gave him a rousing reception (Brooklynites were staunch New Dealers but fierce anticommunists) and management offered him free box seats whenever he wanted them. Not surprisingly, he decided to stay, and spent his fading-away years watching the Dodgers. (His teenage son Arthur, however, was a Giant fan who saw his first major league game at the Polo Grounds, where he received VIP treatment.)

The historic achievement, the success on the field, and the devotion of the fans are the main part of the Dodger story in this era, but not the *whole* story. Behind the scenes—and sometimes out in the open—the Dodger organization was consumed by strife.

Take Robinson's arrival. During spring training in Havana, Cuba, players from the South, led by the aptly nicknamed Dixie Walker, started a petition to keep him off the team. Durocher got wind of it late one eve-

Hilda Chester. With working-class pride typical of Brooklyn, she refused Leo Durocher's offer of a grandstand pass and rooted from the bleachers. (Transcendental Graphics.)

ning and called a midnight meeting. Wearing a yellow bathrobe, he stared down his groggy players. "You know what you can do with that petition. You can wipe your ass with it," he said. But he didn't stop there. "I'll play an elephant if he can do the job, and to make room for him I'll send my own brother home. So make up your mind to it. This fellow is a real great ballplayer. He's going to win pennants for us. He's going to put money in your pockets and money in mine. And here's something else to think about when you put your head back on the pillow. From everything I hear, he's only the first. *Only the first, boys!*"

It was probably the noblest moment of Durocher's life. Branch Rickey flew down to lend his support, pleading with the petition signers to transcend their Jim Crow values. Those who didn't, like Walker, he eventually traded.

The deal for Walker brought Preacher Roe and Billy Cox to Brooklyn. The latter was at the center of another race-based controversy in 1953 when Jim Gilliam came along. Cox was a World War II veteran afflicted with what we'd today call post-traumatic stress syndrome. He wasn't much of a hitter, but he was the best fielding third baseman of his day. When word came that Robinson was taking over third to make room for the African American Gilliam at second, Cox reacted badly, and the white players verged on rebellion until management vowed to trade any malcontents—a potent threat, inasmuch as the Dodgers figured to finish first again, and in those days a World Series share could double a player's income.

Durocher himself was a constant source of turmoil. Rickey was well acquainted with him from their days in St. Louis. "He has the most fertile talent in the world for making a bad situation infinitely worse," he quipped. Nonetheless, he virtually adopted the dandyish, profligate Lip, monitoring his behavior and garnisheeing his salary to pay off debts. "I was always afraid to lie to Branch Rickey because I was always sure he knew the answer before he asked the question," Durocher admitted.

When Rickey came to Brooklyn in late 1942 he found Durocher back to old habits, engaging in high-stakes card games with his players and rolling out the clubhouse carpet for gamblers, bookies, and other lowlifes. He also heard complaints from baseball executives about Durocher's foul mouth and dirty tactics. So he brought Durocher into his office, lectured him interminably, and held off signing him to a new contract. When he finally did re-sign Durocher, it was to a player-only deal, which back then was less secure than a management contract. And just to show Durocher he wasn't kidding, he fired coach Charlie Dressen, an even bigger gambler. (Although Dressen was soon brought back.)

All that did was make Durocher more discreet: he had the gamblers in his home instead of the clubhouse. In March 1945 his best friend, actor George Raft, used Durocher's apartment and a pair of loaded dice to bilk a star-struck mark out of $18,500 in a game of craps. Although Durocher knew nothing of the swindle, the ensuing court case embarrassed him, baseball, and new commissioner Chandler. So did an ugly incident at Ebbets Field on June 8, 1945, when Durocher used brass knuckles to break the jaw of a heckler just back from military service. That one went to court also, with a criminal acquittal but a $6,750 civil judgment against Durocher.

When Durocher persisted in palling around with Raft and other shady types, Chandler summoned him for a round of golf in November 1946. He ordered Durocher to move out of Raft's Southern California home and to cease consorting with gamblers and crooks. Durocher complied, but a month later he scandalized baseball again by marrying actress Laraine Day, whose divorce from her previous husband had yet to be finalized. Many in the Borough of Churches were offended by Durocher's disregard for traditional values. The Reverend Vincent Powell, head of the Catholic Youth Organization, withdrew over 100,000 kids from the Dodger Knothole Club because "the CYO could not continue to have our youngsters

Branch Rickey and Leo Durocher. How many baseball men would let themselves be photographed in this pose today? (Transcendental Graphics)

officially associated with a man who represents to them an example in complete contradiction of our moral teachings."

All this was fresh in Happy Chandler's mind in spring training 1947 when the Dodgers hosted the Yankees in Havana for some exhibitions. Durocher strolled onto the field and saw in the other team's box Larry MacPhail, now part-owner of the Bronx Bombers. And who was that with

MacPhail? None other than Memphis Engleberg and Connie Immerman — two of the gamblers Durocher had been warned against talking to. "Where does MacPhail come off flaunting his company with known gamblers?" Durocher fumed. "If I even say hello to one of these guys, I'd be called up before Commissioner Chandler and probably barred."

When Branch Rickey also condemned MacPhail, the Yankee boss blusteringly denied any association with the gamblers and accused Durocher and Rickey of slander. The hullabaloo led to a series of closed-door hearings — after which Chandler suspended Durocher for the entire season "as a result of the accumulation of unpleasant incidents ... which the Commissioner construes as detrimental to baseball." Even MacPhail was stunned.

Chandler's draconian edict reflected badly on Rickey, Durocher's patron and protector. Dodger co-owner Walter O'Malley was quick to exploit the embarrassment. The Bronx-born, plutocratic O'Malley was a bankruptcy attorney hired by the Brooklyn Trust Company to watch over its investment in the Dodgers. Much as Charles Ebbets worked his way to the top as Charles Byrne's right-hand man, so O'Malley gained influence by catering to the whims of the Brooklyn Trust's George V. McLaughlin. With McLaughlin's blessing, in 1944 he joined as an equal partner with Rickey and John Smith, head of the Pfizer Company, in the purchase of half the McKeever estate's Dodger holdings. A year later the Ebbets estate put up all its stock for sale, and the threesome bought that too. Collectively they became majority owners, but in reality Rickey owned 25 percent, Smith owned 25 percent, and O'Malley owned 25 percent. (Dearie Mulvey, daughter of Steve McKeever, held on to the last 25 percent.) Smith was the fulcrum. He threw his support behind fellow pious Protestant Rickey.

O'Malley, who considered Rickey a "psalm-singing fake," wasn't willing to settle for a silent partnership. As a prominent member of Brooklyn's conservative Catholic establishment, he could have quelled the ecclesiastical condemnations of Durocher, but he preferred that Rickey squirm. The strategy paid off. For John Smith, the Durocher scandals were too much. He switched allegiance to O'Malley, and after he died in July 1950 his wife gave O'Malley control of his stock. O'Malley used the leverage to oust Rickey less than four months later. Over the next few years O'Malley sedulously purged the Dodger organization of Rickey loyalists. Anyone who uttered Rickey's name he fined a dollar.

So where were the Giants while all this was going on? Leo Durocher had the ultimate answer. He was sitting in the visitors' dugout at the Polo

Grounds before a game on July 5, 1946, shooting the bull with Red Barber and reporters Frank Graham and Milton Richman. Accounts differ as to how he got on the topic. According to Durocher himself, he was explaining why he liked Eddie Stanky so much. "He can't do a goddamn thing but beat you. Sure, they call him the Brat and the Mobile Muskrat and all of that. Take a look at that number four [Mel Ott] out there. A nicer guy never drew breath than that man there. Walker Cooper, Mize, Marshall, Kerr, Gordon, Thomson. Take a look at them. All nice guys. They'll finish last. Nice guys. Finish last."

In Graham's version, Barber was teasing Durocher about all the home runs the Giants hit against the Dodgers in a doubleheader the day before. Durocher snorted that the homers were cheap shots, Polo Grounds specials to the corners. "Why don't you admit they were real home runs? Why don't you be a nice guy for a change?" Barber persisted. "Nice guys!" Durocher spat. "Look over there. Do you know a nicer guy than Mel Ott? Or any of the other Giants? Why, they're the nicest guys in the world! And where are they? In last place!"

According to Richman, Durocher was complaining about fair-weather friends. Barber urged him to be a nice guy and take a more forgiving view of human nature. "Nice guy?" responded Durocher. "Being a nice guy gets you nowhere. Absolutely nowhere. Look over there," he said, pointing to Ott. "There's one of the nicest guys in the world. Is it doing him any good? He's in last place. That's where nice guys finish. Last."

Whichever version you choose, two things are clear: Durocher meant no offense (Ott took none), and he never literally said *Nice guys finish last,* one of baseball's most famous contributions to American parlance. The epigram was the invention of headline writers the next day. And though Durocher acknowledged that he never said such a thing, he never hesitated to exploit it either, using it for the title of his autobiography.

Ott's Giants *did* finish last that year. The next year, 1947, they delighted owner Horace Stoneham by setting a record for homers with 221, but they improved only to fourth, 13 games behind the pennant-winning Dodgers, who even with sleepy Burt Shotton standing in for Durocher played headsup ball, leading the league in walks and stolen bases. After six seasons spent mostly in the second division, it became clear to Stoneham that Ott couldn't handle pitchers; the Giants never had an ERA below the league average during Ott's tenure. But Stoneham loved Ott, and so did the fans, so when the 1948 season rolled around, Master Melvin was still in charge.

The Giants started strongly that year, but they couldn't sustain the momentum. By the All-Star break Stoneham decided once and for all to make a move. He came up with a radical — some would say insane — idea:

hiring Burt Shotton, idled by Durocher's reinstatement. To avoid any hint of tampering, he asked National League president Ford Frick to set up a meeting with Branch Rickey at Frick's Manhattan office. The meeting took place the afternoon of July 15. When Stoneham asked permission to speak to Shotton, Rickey came back with a shocker: "No, I may need him at any moment myself." Swallowing his surprise, the Giant owner asked if that meant Durocher would soon be available.

Durocher had been under tremendous pressure since his return. Scandalmongers scrutinized his every move. Fans and pundits agreed that if Shotton, who got lost going to the Polo Grounds, could win a pennant with the Dodgers, then Durocher ought to conquer the universe with them. Meanwhile, Rickey wanted Jackie Robinson moved to his best position, second base, and traded Eddie Stanky to do it, depriving Durocher of his favorite player and creating a hole at first base. And Robinson, after a winter on the banquet circuit, reported to spring training 20 pounds overweight.

Though more caustic than usual, Durocher kept his nose (and everything else) clean. And in a moment of serendipity, he had catcher Gil Hodges try on a first baseman's mitt. But the Dodgers got off to a bad start, attendance fell, and O'Malley, supported by Smith, leaned heavily on Rickey to get rid of the Prodigal Son. On July 4, after Durocher was ejected from a wild game in which the Dodgers beat the Giants 13–12, Rickey sent an intermediary to the clubhouse to request Durocher's resignation. Durocher refused, correctly surmising that Rickey didn't have the heart to fire him outright.

Stoneham hadn't known any of this, of course. But he had long admired Durocher — his Giants had an unsightly 69–118 (.369) record against The Lip's Dodgers — and leaped at the chance to get him. Rickey recalled Durocher from Montreal, where he was scouting Brooklyn's top farm team for pitching help. They met in Rickey's office that night. Rickey revealed Stoneham's interest. Unsure where he stood, Durocher asked, "Am I the manager of this ballclub now?" Yes, Rickey answered, confirming that Durocher hadn't been fired. "Will I be the manager of this ballclub tomorrow, next week, next month, and until the close of the 1948 season?"

That one Rickey couldn't answer.

Loyal as he was to Rickey and Brooklyn, Durocher placed a higher value on survival. He called Stoneham, and they arranged to meet at Durocher's apartment on Manhattan's posh East Side. Before Durocher could get there, Stoneham arrived with Carl Hubbell. Laraine Day, a teetotaling Mormon, turned off the Dodger broadcast she was listening to and fixed them drinks.

The announcement of Durocher's switch from the Dodgers to the Giants was made the next morning. At first there was dead calm, then a gathering realization that something huge and irrevocable had occurred, and finally a tremendous, at times melodramatic, outpouring of emotion. "The only word to describe their reaction is 'dumbfounded,'" wrote the *New York Herald Tribune's* Al Laney of the Giants, who were preparing for a game against the Pirates when the announcement was made. By the time Durocher arrived in Pittsburgh, the press corps was shaking off its dismay. "I loved Mel Ott and I tell you right now I'm gonna knock your brains out," the *New York Mirror's* Kenny Smith promised him. And the Giants returned home to the Polo Grounds to find the fans' attitude hardened. "It took them two years to learn to barely tolerate me," recalled The Lip.

In Brooklyn the reaction was mixed. Jackie Robinson had developed a searing enmity for Durocher due the harsh methods Durocher used to get him in shape. "I sure do like to play for that man," he said of Shotton. "I can hardly wait." But Roy Campanella, a rookie in 1948, missed Durocher. "I thought Leo was a tremendous manager. I never had a bad word for Leo because he lived and died with me." Though some fans were glad to see Durocher go, most venerated him as the leader who turned the Dodgers from laughingstocks to terrors. "That cheapskate Rickey has given the pennant to the Giants," groused the bartender at the Left Field Bar and Grill. Another Durocher supporter called the *Herald Tribune* to confirm the news, then said, "Okay, send a photographer down to the Brooklyn Bridge in 20 minutes. I'm jumping off."

Ten days later the Giants played a single game in Brooklyn. "Tonight's Dodger-Giant game needs only the appearance of Memphis Bill Terry as Brooklyn manager to complete the sense of unreality," mused the *Eagle's* Tommy Holmes. Fans were lining up for bleacher seats by 10:30 in the morning, and Ebbets Field was sold out two hours before game time. The *Eagle* estimated nearly 15,000 fans were turned away. Years later Durocher claimed that "the whole park stood up and booed me" when he first came on the field, but the game account by the *Eagle's* Harold C. Burr contradicted him. "All Brooklyn was still a trifle stunned and wounded to the quick to see their beloved Lippy wearing the uniform of the hated enemy — the feared John McGraw and the despised Bill Terry — but they viewed the sight more in sorrow than in anger." Whatever emotion fans might have vented at the start, they were silent from the cry of "Play ball," as Durocher's Giants scored five first-inning runs and cakewalked to a 13–4 victory.

Leo Durocher proved one thing in 1948: for all his personal failings, he was a managerial genius. Running the Dodgers, he beat the Giants eight times in 12 tries. Then he took over the Giants and beat the Dodgers seven out of 10. (The teams split the season series.) With him as the catalyst, the next seven years of the rivalry were filled with beanballs, taunts, arguments, beanballs, spikings, collisions, beanballs, fights, and retaliations. Oh, and did we mention beanballs? Whenever the Giants played the Dodgers, Durocher's advice to his pitchers, shouted from the dugout so everyone could hear, was "Stick it in his ear!" One hurler in particular, the glowering Sal Maglie, took the words to heart and became the most hated man in Brooklyn. "When I was pitching for the New York Giants in the early 1950s," he recalled, "my friends used to warn me never to walk across the Brooklyn Bridge. If I ever set foot in Flatbush, they told me, I would be committing suicide."

After Durocher left the Giants in 1955 — and Maglie, in the second most startling uniform switch of the era, became a Dodger — a lot of spirit went out of the rivalry. (Jackie Robinson was traded to New York in December 1956, but had already decided to retire and never wore the black and orange.) That slackening passion made it easier for Horace Stoneham and Walter O'Malley to instigate a change far more devastating to Giant and Dodger fans than The Lip's overnight defection.

8. 1951: "The Inexpressibly Fantastic"

Horace Stoneham's first assignment for Leo Durocher was to write an evaluation of the Giants. Durocher begged off, saying he needed to spend time with the team first. Stoneham agreed, but when the 1948 season ended and a report still wasn't on his desk, he demanded one. Durocher wrote him four words: *Back up the truck.*

The Giants were loaded with plodding sluggers. Durocher preferred players who could run and field. He and Stoneham argued into 1949 before Stoneham finally relented. In June the Giant owner traded catcher Walker Cooper and replaced him with defensive whiz Wes Westrum. In July he brought up African Americans Hank Thompson and Monte Irvin, making the Giants the second National League team to integrate. (The first big league confrontation between a black batter and pitcher occurred on July 8, 1949, when Thompson of the Giants faced Don Newcombe of the Dodgers.) A month later he sold Johnny Mize. It was a good start, but the Giants still finished 24 games behind the champion Dodgers in Durocher's first full year at the helm.

That winter Stoneham traded two more boppers, Sid Gordon and Willard Marshall, along with shortstop Buddy Kerr and pitching prospect Red Webb, to the Boston Braves for shortstop Alvin Dark and Durocher's prize pupil from his Dodger days, Eddie Stanky. "From that time on, we had a tight infield — which improved our pitching a hundred percent — and we had two guys who could do things with the bat, could run the bases, and who came to kill you," rejoiced Durocher.

Next, Stoneham refashioned the pitching staff. In 1950 he signed Sal

Maglie, previously blackballed by Commissioner Chandler for jumping to a short-lived Mexican League. Later that year he added another starter, Jim Hearn. The club finished hot, nearly helping the Dodgers win the pennant by sweeping four late-September games from Philadelphia's Whiz Kids. (The Dodgers had a chance to tie for first on the season's final day, but lost a 10-inning heartbreaker to the Phils at Ebbets Field.)

Based on that improvement there were high hopes for 1951, with some writers picking New York to win its first pennant in 14 years. The Giants began the season by splitting four games in Boston, then opened their home schedule with three against the Dodgers. Brooklyn swept, sending the Giants into a tailspin they didn't come out of until they'd lost 11 in a row. They finished April with a record of 3–12, already six games behind Brooklyn. "It would take a miracle for them to win the championship now," moped *New York Times* writer Arthur Daley.

Sal Maglie. When pitcher-author Jim Bouton, a New Jersey native and Giant fan, asked him what he threw to get the Dodgers out, his proud response was "97 snappers." (Transcendental Graphics)

The last two games of the skid came at Ebbets Field. In the Giants' 11th straight defeat starter Larry Jansen, a control artist, beaned Jackie Robinson. When Gil Hodges followed with a homer, Robinson shouted at Jansen all the way around the bases and kept it up after he reached the bench. But that was just a prelude to the next game, when Robinson and Sal Maglie got into it.

Mentored in the Mexican League by rivalry alumnus Dolf Luque, Maglie followed a time-honored pitching philosophy: start with the fastball high and tight, then throw curveballs down and away. So often did he throw at batters that he became known as Sal the Barber, for shaving them close. He saved his keenest brushbacks for the Dodgers. "I really hated that club. If I could've gotten that feeling every time I pitched I'd have been a lot better pitcher," he said. The Giants gave him a six-run lead in the top of the first, which relaxed him. But Brooklyn's Gene Hermanski led off the bottom of the inning with a homer, so Maglie went back to his signature style and spun Carl Furillo around. That angered Robinson — who thrived on anger. He belted a solo homer. Maglie responded by decking Pee Wee Reese the next inning.

Usually it's the pitcher's job to defend his teammates against bean-balls by retaliating in kind. Rookie Clem Labine did just that, low-bridging Bobby Thomson, the Glasgow-born, New York-bred outfielder known as "The Staten Island Scot." But Robinson wanted more, especially after Maglie started his next at-bat with a high and tight fastball. He bunted down the first base line, hoping Maglie would field it. The ball went foul, but Robinson, a star football player at UCLA, bowled into Maglie anyway. The benches emptied and a brawl nearly ensued. Maglie went on to win the game (and break the Giants' losing streak), but he yielded a single to Robinson that at-bat, walked him the next time, and remained wary of him the rest of his career. Grumbled Durocher afterward, "I told Maglie to stick to his pitching, that Robinson was trying a bush league trick to get his goat. And that's all it was."

"If it's a bush play, I learned it from a bush manager. I learned it from Durocher. I remember him standing here in the Brooklyn dressing room telling us, 'if they throw at you, bunt along the first base line and run right up their backs,'" Robinson countered the next day.

The incident renewed a feud between Robinson and Durocher that had been raging since 1949, when Robinson shed the turn-the-other-cheek constrictions imposed by Branch Rickey and had his greatest season, batting .342, knocking in 124 runs, scoring 122 more, leading the league in steals, and winning the Most Valuable Player award. On May 30 that year, Robinson tried to swipe second while Durocher was changing pitchers. The umpires ruled that time was out and returned Robinson to first. Durocher aimed a gesture at Robinson that suggested the Dodger second baseman had a swelled head. Robinson responded in the best possible manner, hitting a homer in the 13th inning to win the game.

But thereafter Robinson answered in the worst possible manner. He would sniff the air, ask whether Durocher was wearing Laraine Day's perfume, and call the Giant manager a pussy. "Fuck you!" Durocher would retort, to which Robinson would say, "Give it to Laraine, she needs it more than I do." Durocher would come unglued. Once he even got racial. "I found myself calling him things that would have shamed the worst bigot," he contritely disclosed.

Their latest spat reached the ears of National League president Ford Frick. "I'm tired of hearing what's going on with him [Robinson] over there," he snapped. No word whether he was tired of Durocher and his head-hunting pitchers.

Although the Giants went 14–7 after leaving Brooklyn, they were still under .500 and in fifth place. To get back in the race they needed more talent. As luck would have it, they happened to have the most talented player in baseball on their top farm team in Minneapolis.

Willie Mays had just turned 20 and was hitting an astounding .477 with 29 extra-base hits in 149 at-bats when the Giants called him up. He didn't want to go. He didn't think he was ready. "What are you hitting now?" Durocher asked. Mays told him. "Do you think you can hit two fucking fifty for me?" Mays thought he could. "Then get down here on the next plane," the manager barked.

Mays went hitless in his first 12 major league at-bats. In his fourth game he slammed a prodigious homer against Warren Spahn ("If that's the only home run he ever hits, they'll still talk about it," marveled Giant radio broadcaster Russ Hodges), but then went another 12 trips without a hit. He sat by his locker and cried. Durocher was usually hard on young players, snide and hectoring about every mistake. But he also had a sixth sense about how to get the most from his men. He recognized at once that Mays needed tender loving care. "As long as I'm the manager of the Giants, you're my center fielder," he vowed, then mixed practical advice with further endearments. The next day Mays got two hits. He got two more the day after. By the end of June he was around .300.

Mays was a godsend to the Giants. Durocher loved him for his speed, defense, and heads-up play. Stoneham loved him for his power. His teammates loved him for his life-of-the-party attitude. And the fans loved him for his infectious enthusiasm. At last the Giants had a public relations answer to the Boys of Summer and Casey Stengel's front-running Yankees. So many people pressed themselves on Mays those first few weeks that he couldn't keep their names straight, greeting them with an evasive "say hey." New Yorkers ate that up, too, dubbing him "The Say Hey Kid."

Mays got his first taste of the rivalry on June 26 at the Polo Grounds. Roy Campanella told him, "Wait till you get Don Newcombe tomorrow. He hates colored rookies. He'll blow you down." Mays would be a favorite target of Dodger pitchers for the next 20 years, but this night Sal Maglie was the one throwing knockdowns, nearly decapitating the Dodgers' newly

Willie Mays. When he complained that the chatty Campanella was distracting him at bat, Leo Durocher's advice was, "Pick up a handful of dirt and throw it in his face." (Transcendental Graphics)

acquired left fielder, Andy Pafko. That brought a retaliation pitch from Preacher Roe at the Giants' Whitey Lockman. Lockman dusted himself off and hit an upper deck shot, and the Giants won, 4–0. Pafko got his revenge the next day, pounding a three-run homer to pace the Dodgers to a 10–4 rout of Jim Hearn. Mays, unfazed by Campanella's warning, homered against Newcombe. He also made a somersaulting catch to rob Carl Furillo of a hit, coming up with the ball in one hand and his cap in the other.

A week later the Giants and Dodgers convened for an Independence Day doubleheader at Ebbets Field in front of more than 34,000 fans. In the opener, the Giants were leading 4–0 behind Maglie in the eighth when Campanella and Reese homered to bring the Dodgers within one. Gil Hodges, whom Maglie had beaned earlier in the game, singled in a run in the bottom of the ninth to send the game to extra innings. Bobby Thomson's homer put the Giants ahead in the 11th, but Robinson knocked in Duke Snider, then scored on a squeeze play to win it. In the nightcap, the Giants trailed 4–1 in the ninth but had a rally going when Earl Rapp grounded to Robinson. Umpire Babe Pinelli declared a double play when Giant pinch runner Hank Schenz, a recently acquired utility infielder, strayed beyond the baseline in an attempt to take out Robinson. The call ended the game, but not Durocher's protests.

A crowd of 32,921 attended the third match, in which Newcombe, supported by homers from Pafko, Hodges, and Snider, beat the Giants 8–4. The sweep put Durocher's club seven games behind. Said Dodger manager Charlie Dressen, "The Giants are through. They'll never bother us again."

How much joy it gave Dressen to utter those words! He was an odd choice for Walter O'Malley's first manager, a conceited cuss completely out of place in the corporate environment the new owner was building. Some have speculated that O'Malley hired him to irritate Branch Rickey, who detested Dressen as a dime store Durocher. Acutely aware of the comparisons to Durocher, Dressen yearned to prove himself the better manager, feeling that much of Durocher's Brooklyn success was due to his own efforts as coach. The sweep at Ebbets Field gave him nine wins in his first 12 games against The Lip.

Over the next two weeks the Giants fell another game behind the Dodgers and into third place. Durocher was frustrated. Stoneham had given him the players he wanted. His team was expected to contend after its strong finish in 1950. He'd brought up Willie Mays. But the Giants were sinking, and nothing he tried — juggling the lineup, moving fielders from one position to another — made them better. He was out of answers.

Then one came. The likely source? Hank Schenz, the man who'd killed a rally in Brooklyn by going out of his way to spike Jackie Robinson.

Schenz had spent four years with the Cubs, where one of his duties was hiding in the scoreboard with a telescope and stealing the other team's signs. On July 19 Durocher called a team meeting. "We can't get first, but we got to get second!" he bellowed, and announced a few changes. Bobby Thomson would move from the outfield to third base, replacing the slumping Hank Thompson. Durocher himself would coach third. And, oh yes, the Giants would steal the other team's signs during home games. "He asked each person if he wanted the sign," Monte Irvin recalled. About half of them did.

Durocher had Abraham Chadwick, the Polo Grounds electrician (and a devoted Dodger fan), install a buzzer in the clubhouse behind center field and connect it to the phone in the Giant bullpen. A spy in the clubhouse — Schenz at first, later coach and former catcher Herman Franks — would peer through a telescope, decrypt the opposing catcher's signs, and buzz once for a fastball, twice for anything else. Then someone in the bullpen, usually reserve catcher Sal Yvars, would clue in the batter using prearranged signs like crossed or uncrossed legs.

The Giants won three of four from Cincinnati, scoring 26 runs, before departing on a 17-game road trip.

Despite winning nine of their first 14 away, the Giants fell nine and a half behind the streaking Dodgers. They trooped into Ebbets Field at the end of their long sojourn knowing the three-game set—a rare Wednesday doubleheader followed by a Thursday single game—could make or break them.

Walter O'Malley charged separate admissions for the afternoon and evening halves of the doubleheader. The early crowd watched the Dodgers take apart the Giants, 7–2. The night owls saw a rivalry classic. For the first time all season aces Maglie and Newcombe started against each other. By the end of the third Newcombe had a three-run lead. After seven Brooklyn was in front 6–2.

The 25-year-old Newcombe, a chauffeur's son from nearby Madison, New Jersey, had come to the Dodgers in 1949 and led the staff with 17 victories. The next season he won 19. In those two years he started and completed more games than any Dodger pitcher. He was the first African American staff ace in major league history. But he was unfairly saddled with a reputation for loafing with a big lead and choking in the close ones. He reinforced the image that night by giving up a run in the eighth to make it 6–3, a solo homer to Bobby Thomson in the ninth to bring the Giants within two, and then, with just one out to go, walking Giant second baseman Davey Williams and giving up a single to Al Dark.

Dressen brought in reliever Clyde King, who was enjoying a career year. But King hit Don Mueller with a pitch to load the bases, then surrendered a two-run single to Monte Irvin to tie the game. The Dodgers rescued themselves from an embarrassing loss in the bottom of the 10th when, with two out, Pafko, Campanella, and Hodges singled to load the bases and the usually punchless Billy Cox hit one over the outfielders' heads.

The victory gave the Dodgers an 11½-game lead, the largest in their history to that point. "Maybe the Dodgers wrapped up the pennant last night," mused veteran Dodger chronicler Roscoe McGowen. He must have been even more convinced the next day when, with Douglas MacArthur looking on, Campanella hit two homers to lift Brooklyn to a 6–5 triumph. The game was tarnished by 24 bases on balls, but ended glossily when a Furillo-to-Robinson-to-Campanella relay erased the tying run at the plate and an around-the-horn double play secured the final outs.

Remember the door between clubhouses at Ebbets Field that Vin Scully mentioned? After the sweep, the Dodgers mocked the Giants through it. "Eat your heart out, Leo! So that's your kind of team?" they whooped. Jackie Robinson shouted, "Hey Pee Wee, have a beer. When we win Dressen buys the beer." And then Robinson, Reese, Newcombe, and

Furillo, encouraged by Dressen, started singing, "Roll out the barrels, we've got the Giants on the run." Though outwardly stoic, the Giants seethed. (Durocher complained to the league, which led to the boarding of the door.) "Human beings can only take so much, and we had a bellyful," Alvin Dark stated when he recalled the incident after the season.

The Giants' outrage didn't translate into victories right away; they lost their first game back at the Polo Grounds 4–0 to the Phillies' Robin Roberts. That August 11 defeat, coupled with a Dodger win in the first game of a doubleheader, dropped them 13½ games out of first. (The Dodgers lost the nightcap to end the day 13 ahead.) In major league history only one team had recovered from a larger deficit, the 1914 Braves. But that team began its comeback on July 5. The Giants were five weeks deeper into the season and had just 44 games to go. Even if they won 30, the Dodgers would have to win only 20 of their remaining 47 to claim the flag.

For that reason, few attached any importance to the Dodgers' Polo Grounds visit on August 14, 15, and 16. New Yorkers took more interest in the death of legendary newspaper publisher William Randolph Hearst and in Harry Truman's denunciation of red-baiting Senator Joseph McCarthy ("When even one American who has done nothing wrong is forced by fear to shut his mind and close his mouth, then all Americans are in peril").

They missed the birth of a legend. In his 10 weeks with the Giants Willie Mays had made some flashy plays, but none that suggested he belonged among the greatest center fielders of all time. The Dodgers had Billy Cox on third and Ralph Branca on first with one out in the top of the eighth, score tied one apiece. Furillo hit a long fly into the gap in right center. Mays, shading Furillo to left, raced after it, running, running, running, and defied all probability by stretching out and catching it. But that wasn't the amazing part. Still on a dead run heading away from home plate, he whirled 270 degrees and launched a cannon shot that landed smack in catcher Westrum's mitt to nail Cox, who had tagged up. Said a boggled Charlie Dressen, "He'll have to do it again before I believe it." Mays then led off the bottom of the inning with a single and scored on Westrum's game-winning homer.

Maglie and Newcombe faced off again in the finale, both sporting a 16–5 record. Both gave up only four hits. But one of the hits against Newcombe was a Monte Irvin fly that Furillo misplayed into a triple, scoring a run, and then Newcombe, who let loose only 22 wild pitches in 2,154 big league innings, again lived down to his reputation for choking in tight games by uncorking one with Thomson on third, giving the Giants a 2–1 win and a sweep of the series.

"Leo figured that if we could sweep the Dodgers, we could catch fire," recounted Mays. Leo was right. The Giants emerged from the Dodger series with six straight wins. They rode to Philadelphia for three games and won those. They returned home and took two from the Reds, one from the Cardinals, and four from the Cubs. The 16-game streak was their longest since 1916. More important, it brought them within five and a half games of first place.

The Dodgers didn't panic. By the end of August they restored their lead to seven games. But their moods darkened on September 1 and 2, when they visited the Polo Grounds and were blasted 8–1 and 11–2. In the opener Don Mueller, nicknamed "Mandrake" for his wizard-like bat control, turned slugger and hit three home runs. Bobby Thomson also whaled one. Alvin Dark and Eddie Stanky converted a Pee Wee Reese liner into a triple play, and the Dodgers' only run scored when Sal Maglie beaned Jackie Robinson with the bases loaded. (The two had words but didn't fight, and Dodger pitchers plunked Whitey Lockman twice in retaliation.) The next day Mueller hit two more homers. The ostensible reason for Mueller's power burst? His wife had given birth that weekend. Passing Durocher in the third base coach's box after receiving the news he cried, "It's a boy! It's a boy!"

But the Dodgers suspected something else was behind Mueller's— and the Giants'— torrid hitting. "I said, 'Charlie, you notice when we come here, we never fool anybody? We throw a guy a change of pace, he seems to know what's coming?'" recalled coach Cookie Lavagetto, who pretty much doped out *how* it was happening, too: "He [Durocher] had a message sender in center field in the Polo Grounds. They had a wireless. Then they had word signs from the bench."

In the second game the frustrated Dodgers so caustically argued a strike call against Pee Wee Reese that plate umpire Al Barlick ejected Ralph Branca and Dick Williams. An inning later the Dodgers harassed Barlick again, this time for calling a Newcombe pitch a ball. Barlick tossed Newcombe, Robinson, and Clem Labine. Afraid he might run out of players, Dressen ordered everyone remaining on his bench to the clubhouse — which at the Polo Grounds, remember, was behind center field. The Dodgers dawdled across the grass for five minutes, drawing boos from the crowd and scowls from the umps. Mop-up reliever Phil Haugstad hit Bobby Thomson with a pitch and brushed back Mays, but it was cold comfort. The Dodger lead was down to five.

A week later the Giants traveled to Ebbets Field for the rivals' last scheduled meetings of the season. In the opener, Newcombe shut out the Giants on two hits, 9–0. The next day, before a full house, Maglie hooked up against Branca. Irvin's two-run shot in the fourth was the only scoring until the eighth, when Snider doubled and Robinson tripled him home. Durocher visited the mound to encourage his ace and order his infield in. Dodger fans waved white handkerchiefs at him. They kept it up even after Durocher returned to the dugout, prompting a plea from public address announcer Tex Rickart, best known for such Brooklynisms as "a little boy has been found lost," to stop. Which of course led to even more hankie-waving.

It was another act of hubris that intensified the Giants' resolve. On the next play Andy Pafko smashed one down the third base line. Thomson nearly fell over snaring the ball, but he held on and trapped Jackie Robinson off the bag. After tagging Robinson, he used his outfielder's arm to rifle down Pafko and end the threat. Maglie survived one more scare in the ninth when Gil Hodges hit a long fly down the left field line. It hooked foul, and Irvin, brave soul, reached into the stands amid a swarm of Dodger fans to catch it. The 2–1 win kept the Giants in contention.

Well, theoretically, anyway. They had made up eight games in a month, but were still five and a half behind (seven in the loss column) with 16 to go. Even if they played .750 ball the rest of the way for a record of 12–4, the Dodgers could play a game under .500 and win the pennant. And any Dodger worried that the Giants' sign stealing might be a factor could rest easy: only three of New York's final games were at home.

On September 17 Roy Campanella was hit in the head by a fastball from Chicago's Turk Lown, the latest in a rash of injuries to the indispensable Dodger catcher. A demoralized Newcombe lost that game to let the Giants within four. A Giant win and Dodger loss the next day reduced the lead to three. With Campanella hurt, Snider and Reese slumping, and the pitchers fighting exhaustion, the Dodgers realized they didn't have the pennant wrapped up after all. Over the next two days they pushed the lead back out to four and a half.

Then Charlie Dressen inflicted a wound on himself.

Former paratrooper Clem Labine had rescued the Dodgers' moribund pitching staff by tossing four straight complete-game wins since returning from the minors in late August. But it was cold the night of his fifth start, against the Phillies on September 21, and he couldn't get loose, loading the bases in the first inning. Although the situation allowed him to wind up, he pitched from the stretch because it felt better. Dressen ordered him to throw from the windup. Labine refused. Willie "Puddin' Head" Jones then hit a grand slam, dooming the Dodgers to defeat, and a peevish Dressen consigned his hottest pitcher to the last seat in the bullpen. It was an especially curious decision given that the man Dressen weighed himself against, Leo Durocher, never benched a player who could help him win.

From then on precious little went right for the Dodgers. "During that last week we fought desperately to keep the pennant from slipping through our fingers. Everybody was grim and silent," remembered Campanella. New Yorkers watched with glee — and Brooklynites with horror — as the Giants gained a game and a half on September 25 to close within one, gained another half game with a Dodger loss on September 27, and climbed into a tie for first by virtue of yet another Dodger defeat on September 28. With two games left, it was anybody's pennant.

Both teams won on September 29. On September 30 Larry Jansen won for the 22nd time as the Giants nosed out the Braves in Boston, 3–2. It was their 37th win in 44 games since August 11, an .841 winning percentage. And pending the outcome of the Dodger game in Philadelphia, it put them in first place.

Thousands of Dodger fans took the train to Philadelphia to cheer on their heroes, only to see them fall behind 6–1 after three frames. But with everything at stake, the Boys of Summer showed their character. A procession of hurlers — including Labine — checked the Phillies while the offense climbed back into the game. Robinson, after contributing to the early deficit by grounding into a double play, striking out, and failing to glove what turned into a two-run single, hammered a triple in the fifth to spark a three-run rally and bring the Dodgers within one. The Phils got two back in the bottom of the fifth, however, and an inning later Phillie fans cheered as the scoreboard posted the final from Boston, notice to the Dodgers that even if they won, the best they could do was force a playoff with the Giants.

Still, they didn't quit. In the eighth Hodges beat out an infield single and Cox dumped one just inside the right field line to put the tying run at the plate. With the pitcher's spot due, Dressen sent up reserve catcher Rube Walker, getting more at-bats thanks to Campanella's woes. Walker roped a two-strike double to knock in Hodges and Cox. The Phillies brought in their best pitcher, future Hall of Famer Robin Roberts, but Furillo lined a single to tie the score.

Knowing there was no tomorrow, Dressen sent out that supposed choker Newcombe. Working on *no* days' rest — he'd thrown a shutout the day before — the Dodger ace kept the Phillies off the scoreboard. In the 12th, though, the Whiz Kids loaded the bases with two out. Eddie Waitkus, a left-handed batter, ripped a low line drive just to the right of second base. It looked like the game-winning hit, but from out of nowhere Jackie Robinson made a diving, backhanded catch just inches from the ground. It was the most sensational — and important — defensive play of his career. He nearly knocked himself out, and lay on the dirt for several minutes. But he was sufficiently recovered by the 14th inning to hit a Roberts pitch into the upper left field stands for the game-winning homer. Walter O'Malley and his general manager, Buzzie Bavasi, "became as nearly hysterical as such normally composed people can be," reported the *New York Times*. Dodger fans went them one better, pouring onto the field to congratulate the players.

The Giants, who left Boston thinking the Dodgers were finished, received the news on the train home. "Leo was very calm, almost matter-of-fact about it. He told Hearn he was pitching and tried to keep everything low-key. But I can remember thinking that, hell, we've got to play those Dodgers again and I wasn't looking forward to it."

The speaker of those words: Bobby Thomson.

Only once before had a season ended with a first-place tie. The 1946 deadlock between the Dodgers and Cardinals was broken by a best-of-three playoff. The Dodgers won the coin toss and chose to play game one in St. Louis, hosting game two and, if necessary, game three. The Cards won the opener, then took game two in Brooklyn to claim the pennant.

The Dodgers won the toss again in 1951. This time they opted to play the first game at home and the rest at the Polo Grounds. If it seemed they were trying to change their luck, you couldn't prove it by their choice of pitcher: Ralph Branca had also started the first playoff game in 1946, and was the loser.

Despite the short notice and Monday afternoon start time, the opener at Ebbets Field drew nearly a full house, 30,707. Millions more followed the game on radio. "A stranger riding the subway in the morning might have thought the Board of Transportation had the contract for delivering portable radios, so many riders were carrying sets to offices and shops," remarked the *Times*.

Branca, raised a Giant fan in Mount Vernon, New York — he even tried out for the Giants, but was deemed too skinny — gained a 1–0 lead on an Andy Pafko homer in the second. But Bobby Thomson hit a two-run blast off a high fastball in the fourth, and Monte Irvin belted his fifth round-tripper of the year off Branca in the eighth to put New York up 3–1. The Dodgers had Reese on first and one out in the bottom of the ninth with Snider the tying run at the plate, but the Duke of Flatbush pulled a grounder to Lockman, who stepped on first, then threw to second to trap Reese between bases. The Dodger captain was ignominiously run down to end the game.

The rivals switched to the Polo Grounds for game two. The 38,609 attendees witnessed a 10–0 thrashing of the Giants interrupted only by a 41-minute rain delay in the sixth. Robinson, Hodges, Pafko, and Rube Walker (subbing for Campanella, now hobbled by a leg injury) hit round-trippers while Labine, sprung from the doghouse after Dressen realized he had no one else to pitch, blanked the Giants on five singles and a Bobby Thomson double. The series was even.

Certain their boys had righted themselves, Dodger fans partied. "As dawn broke on Atlantic Avenue and Pleasant Place today passersby were shocked at the sight of a body hanging from a corner lamppost. Closer inspection revealed the 'lynching' was merely an effigy of a baseball player, with the name 'Durocher' thereupon inscribed. No one called the police," reported the *Brooklyn Eagle*.

"But tomorrow Sal the Barber will be shaving. It'll be a different day and a different game," warned the real Leo Durocher.

For Dodger fans, October 3 was a red-letter day. On that day in 1916, Wilbert Robinson's team clinched the pennant against the Giants, driving a humiliated John McGraw from the bench. But on October 3, 1946, the Dodgers lost their playoff against the Cardinals. Which of these historic outcomes would repeat itself on October 3, 1951?

Rain clouds from the previous afternoon lingered over northern Manhattan. The portentous sky held attendance to 34,320. Among the watchers: Blanche McGraw, widow of the great Giant manager. Reverence for her grew the farther her husband's reign receded into the past. She handled her regal role cheerfully, exchanging pleasantries with well-wishers and fulfilling requests for her husband's autograph by cutting his signature from canceled checks. She sat with Laraine Day.

The managers gave their players one last pep talk. "Look, I know it's tough to have to play this game, but remember we did our best all year. So today, let's just go out and do the best we can," Charlie Dressen urged the Dodgers. "We haven't quit all year. We won't quit now. Let's go get 'em," Leo Durocher exhorted the Giants.

Sal Maglie, 34 years old, had already pitched 290 innings in 1951, but he'd had three days' rest and had won five of six decisions from the Dodgers that year. "Stick it in his ear!" Durocher growled as Carl Furillo stepped in to start the game. Pumped with adrenaline, Maglie whiffed Brooklyn's volatile leadoff man. But once the initial rush passed, the strain of a long, wearying season set in, telling most on Maglie's out pitch, the curveball. He walked Pee Wee Reese on five pitches, Duke Snider on four. When

Jackie Robinson laced a single to plate Reese, it looked like the previous day's blowout might be repeated. But Maglie escaped further damage by getting Pafko to ground out and Hodges to pop up.

Don Newcombe took the mound for the Dodgers. He'd had only two days' rest after his back-to-back, pressure-packed appearances in Philadelphia. He also had Leo Durocher in the third base coach's box heckling him from the moment he stepped on the field. On the plus side, he'd beaten the Giants five times that year and was in excellent shape. He blew down New York one-two-three in the bottom of the first.

Maglie breezed through the second, compensating for his flat curve by spotting his pitches and changing speeds. In the bottom of the frame Newcombe gave up a one-out single to Lockman. Bobby Thomson followed with a line drive into the left field corner. Thomson rounded first and cruised into second — only to find Lockman standing there. Pafko had done a magnificent job of fielding the ball and holding Lockman to a one-base advance. Third baseman Billy Cox relayed to Robinson, and the mortified Thomson was tagged to end the budding rally. Next inning, when thickening clouds required that the lights be turned on, wags in the Polo Grounds cracked, "Maybe now Thomson will be able to see what he's doing."

The third and fourth innings passed quickly. With one out in the fifth Thomson socked another liner down the left field line and got his double — no baserunner in front of him. In the Dodger bullpen big number 13, Ralph Branca, began loosening up. But Newcombe struck out Willie Mays and Maglie to squelch the threat.

After an uneventful sixth, Newcombe faced the Giants' power in the bottom of the seventh. Monte Irvin led off with a double to left. Lockman bunted. Rube Walker, in for Campanella again, gunned for Irvin at third. Safe! That put Giants at the corners for Thomson, who had already hit the ball hard twice.

Newcombe put everything he had into the confrontation. "I can't ever remember fighting for my life like I did during that one time at bat," Thomson said. He fell behind 0–2, fouled one off, then hacked at an outside breaking ball, lofting a fly to Snider in center field for an easy out. But he hit it far enough for Irvin to tag up and tie the score at one.

According to some accounts, after Newcombe retired the side and returned to the dugout he said, "I got nothing left, nothing." Jackie Robinson yelled, "You go out there and pitch until your fucking arm falls off." Roy Campanella seconded Robinson, saying, "Roomie, you ain't gonna quit on us now." But Newcombe himself, vouched for by Snider and Pafko, insisted he never complained or asked out of the game.

Maglie was the tired one. In the top of the eighth he yielded crisp one-out singles to Reese and Snider, bringing up Robinson with men on first and third. Fearful of a squeeze play, Sal the Barber tried his curve again. It dived into the dirt and skidded past Westrum. Reese scored to put the Dodgers ahead, and Snider advanced to second. Maglie intentionally walked Robinson to set up the double play. Pafko obligingly grounded to third, but when Thomson tried to backhand the ball on an in-between hop it caromed off the heel of his glove, allowing Snider to score and Robinson to take third. The official scorer gave Pafko a hit.

It was the second boner of the game for Thomson. But the cruel fates hadn't finished with him. After Maglie struck out Hodges, Billy Cox belted a wicked one-hopper down the third base line. Thomson lunged, but not in time, and the ball rolled into left field while Robinson scored to make it 4–1. "In my mind I gave it a good try. Still, there were some who figured it was another screw-up by Thomson. Either way, I began feeling that the pennant was flying away from us," Thomson recalled.

Carl Erskine joined Branca in the Dodger bullpen, but the recharged Newcombe set down the Giants one-two-three in the bottom of the eighth, bringing Charlie Dressen within an inning of definitively besting Durocher. Dressen paced the dugout, called coach Clyde Sukeforth every few minutes to check on his relievers, and aimed a stream of derision at the Giants' Larry Jansen, who replaced Maglie on the mound. Jackie Robinson — neither manager, coach, nor captain, but team leader nonetheless — shouted, "Will someone tell Dressen to sit down? He's making us all nervous."

After Jansen retired Brooklyn in order in the top of the ninth, Durocher told his team, "Let's go out there and give them all we got, and let's leave this ballfield, win or lose, with our heads in the air." But he later admitted, "I felt good when I went out to the coaching line, but that doesn't mean I didn't think we had lost it."

Newcombe threw two quick strikes past leadoff batter Dark. As he'd done with Thomson in the seventh, he went to the outside corner, trying to make Dark fish. The Giant shortstop hit a grounder to the right side. Hodges got the tip of his mitt on the ball, deflecting it away from Robinson, and it trickled into right field for a single.

Left-hand batting Don Mueller followed. He planned to go up the middle, but noticed something anomalous: Hodges was holding Dark at first. What was Charlie Dressen thinking? Dark was the Giants' most frequent base stealer (19 tries, 12 successful), but there was little chance of him going with his team three runs down in the bottom of the ninth, and even if he did and eventually scored, so what? That would only make it

4–2. The crafty Mueller pulled a routine grounder that Hodges would have reached had he been playing off the bag. As it rolled into right field, Dark raced to third, and suddenly the tying run was at the plate in the person of Irvin, the league's leading RBI man.

Amid the full-throated cheering of Giant fans (this was *not* 1934, when Dodger rooters dominated the Polo Grounds), Dressen strode to the mound. He intended to replace not Newcombe, but Walker, the catcher. Roy Campanella knew how to prod Newcombe into throwing harder. But then Dressen had second thoughts. Campy was gimping, and the Polo Grounds had acres of foul territory behind home plate. Better to keep Walker out there. After a hearty go-get-'em, he returned to the dugout.

Irvin tried to even the game with one swing, but popped up. Hodges grabbed it in foul territory for the first out.

That brought up Lockman, a left-handed bat control artist like Mueller. Newk started him off with a fastball outside. Lockman lashed it down the left field line just inches fair. Dark scored easily to make it 4–2. Mueller, an average runner at best, watched the play rather than Durocher in the coach's box and chugged clumsily into third, breaking his ankle as Lockman pulled into second. Everything stopped while Mueller was hauled off the field in a stretcher. Clint Hartung, a once-heralded prospect reduced to benchwarming, pinch ran.

Dressen decided it was time to pull Newcombe, and called Clyde Sukeforth one more time. "Everyone knew that Erskine was troubled by arm problems. Sometimes he was okay, but sometimes he could hardly throw the ball. That day he couldn't even reach the catcher with some of his warmup pitches. Here's Branca popping and Erskine the way he was. Branca was the only one who could come in when that big guy [Newcombe] couldn't go any further," Sukeforth explained years later.

In Brooklyn the groans were audible. Branca had had only one day's rest. He'd lost six of his last seven decisions. The Giants had already beaten him five times in 1951. And the next batter, Bobby Thomson, had dinged him for the decisive homer in the first playoff game. (It is widely believed that Thomson hit five or six homers off Branca in 1951, but his only other clout against the Dodger hurler came on September 1.) In some circles there were whispers of favoritism: in 17 days Branca was to marry Ann Mulvey, daughter of Dodger part-owner Dearie Mulvey.

But the truth was that Dressen had nobody else. Erskine was sore. Top reliever Clyde King had won 14 games and saved six, but developed tendinitis in August. Twenty-two-game winner Preacher Roe, after pitching 258 innings at age 36, was also aching, and was left-handed, a disadvantage against the right-handed Thomson and Willie Mays, who followed in the Giant order. Labine had pitched a complete game the day before. The other pitchers Dressen didn't trust in crucial situations.

With first base open, Dressen had to decide whether the Dodgers should pitch to Thomson or intentionally walk him to set up the force at any base and bring up Mays, whose production had dipped in the second half. "I think I must have been the most scared person in the whole ballpark in the bottom of the ninth inning," Mays confessed. He was just a 20-year-old rookie, well aware he'd gone 0-for-3 with two strikeouts against Branca in the opening game. When Dressen decided that putting the winning run on base was too risky, no one was gladder than Mays. Not that he was off the hook — if Thomson failed, he'd be the Giants' last hope — but it was a momentary reprieve.

As Thomson ambled to the right-hand batter's box, Leo Durocher called time. "I think he'll throw you a fast one. High and tight like they always try to pitch you. Be ready for it, Bobby!"

Branca, concentrating so intently that he didn't hear the braying crowd, threw a hummer down the middle. Thomson watched it for strike one.

"Come on! He'll throw you another one!" Durocher assured his batter.

Branca wanted to make Thomson swing at a bad pitch. It would indeed be a fastball, but up and in, where the Giant third baseman would swing and miss or foul it off. The worst that could happen was Thomson taking it for ball one and setting himself up for the curve down and away. A confident Branca, who had told Newcombe "Don't worry about it, big fella, I'll take care of everything," reared back and fired. The ball went just where he wanted, up and in.

And Thomson pounced.

"There's a long fly … It's gonna be, I believe … The Giants win the pennant! The Giants win the pennant! The Giants win the pennant! The Giants win the pennant! Bobby Thomson hits into the lower deck of the left field stands! The Giants win the pennant and they're going crazy! They're going crazy! Waaah-hoe!" shouted Giant radio announcer Russ Hodges through the pandemonium.

One Dodger — Jackie Robinson — stayed at his post to make sure Thomson touched every base. Then he turned away as a gaggle of Giants greeted the skipping deliverer of their fifth — and winning — run. The Giants hoisted Thomson on their shoulders and began carrying him to the clubhouse. Security struggled valiantly to keep the crowd off the field, but the line broke and the players had to race to safety. A mob a thousand deep lingered outside the clubhouse for hours, demanding curtain calls from Thomson, Durocher, and the team.

Across Manhattan, shouting and dancing fans clogged the streets while office workers above them flung streams of tickertape out windows. A phalanx of police arrived at the Giants' downtown office to hold back waves of World Series ticket buyers. Columnist Red Smith captured the delirium in a piece entitled "Miracle at Coogan's Bluff": "The art of fiction is dead. Reality has strangled invention. Only the utterly impossible, the inexpressibly fantastic, can ever be plausible again."

For the Dodgers and their devout, though, Thomson's blow was the worst civic disaster since consolidation into New York City. "We all felt we had embarrassed the borough of Brooklyn," Carl Erskine said. For Pee Wee Reese, "It was the toughest thing I ever went through in baseball." No Dodger took it harder than Branca. He draped himself over the steps between the clubhouse and trainer's room and wailed "Why me?" as coach Cookie Lavagetto sat protectively by him. While Branca wept, Charlie Dressen ripped off his uniform shirt, popping the buttons. Later he told reporters that he brought in Branca on Clyde Sukeforth's recommendation, a buck-passing that might have saved Dressen from confronting his own failure, but cost Sukeforth his job (which was probably forfeit anyway, given his close relationship with Branch Rickey).

Dodger rooters were equally traumatized. "It was the worst moment in my life as a fan, worse even than any loss to the Yankees in the World Series," recalled historian Doris Kearns Goodwin. Longtime Dodger chronicler Donald Honig said, "My best friend and I left his house, and we just walked in utter silence for miles. I was utterly desolate." Wrote Grace Liechtenstein, an author raised blocks from Ebbets Field, "As I look back, now, at the far more important catastrophic dates during the past 50 years, including September 11, 2001, I think of October 3, 1951 as the day I discovered that in an instant the world could go very, very wrong." Joe Flaherty told of one Dodger fan in his 80s who cursed Branca as a "dago bastard," spit at the TV screen, and died on the spot.

"Let's Not Talk About It Anymore," ran the *Brooklyn Eagle* headline the next day. The normally jaunty Tommy Holmes said, "Don't make mine vanilla on this round. I'll settle for cyanide and there must be thousands of people in our fair and unhappy town who feel about the same." Added Joseph F. Wilkinson: "There are no happy moods in Brooklyn, only various stages of rage, frustration, and sadness." He made note of an effigy hanging from a lamppost at 75th Street (Bay Ridge Parkway) and Third Avenue. Not Leo Durocher, but Charlie Dressen.

Did the Giants win because they cheated?

In January 2001, nearly half a century after the Miracle at Coogan's

Bobby Thomson runs past adoring fans. "The only thought going through my mind was: we beat the Dodgers, we won the pennant, we beat the Dodgers, we beat the Dodgers. Over and over again." (©Bettman/CORBIS)

Bluff, *Wall Street Journal* reporter Joshua Harris Prager confirmed the lingering rumor that starting on July 20, 1951, the Giants used a telescope and buzzer to steal signs at the Polo Grounds. Though Branca gallantly noted that Thomson "still hit the pitch," the revelation tainted not only the Shot Heard 'Round the World, as Thomson's homer came to be called, but the Giants' amazing comeback from 13½ games down.

(Branca was traded to Detroit in 1953, where teammate Ted Gray, who learned of the subterfuge from an anonymous Giant, informed him of it. "I made a decision not to speak about it. I didn't want to look like I was crying over spilled milk," Branca said. He demurred again in March 1962, when the Associated Press distributed a story about the sign stealing quoting only unnamed sources.)

Believe it or not, the Giants' method of sign stealing was *not* illegal in 1951. The use of mechanical devices for that purpose wasn't outlawed for another decade. But legality and honor are two separate things. "When you hide somebody deep in center field in your home ballpark with binoculars [sic], then hook up electric wires to relay the stolen pitches to the batter ... then you have crossed the last frontier into team-wide dishonesty. Almost any club could do it. Almost none ever does," asserted baseball scribe Thomas Boswell.

Boswell's faith in the collective morality of baseball players is laudable, but almost certainly misplaced. He himself acknowledged that mechanical sign stealing had been going on since the 1890s. And if Leo Durocher would trip his own mother to stop her from scoring, he certainly wasn't going to lose any sleep over espionage. Nonetheless, it must be granted that what the Giants did in 1951 was wrong. Before we affix a black mark to their incredible achievement, however, there's one more question we must ask: *did the cheating help them?*

The evidence says it didn't.

If the Giants gained an advantage from knowing the next pitch, it would show as an increase in runs scored at home. From the beginning of the season through July 19 the Giants scored an average of 5.46 runs per game at home. After the sign stealing, the Giants scored an average of 4.57 runs per game, *almost nine-tenths of a run per game less.* Meanwhile, their runs per game average on the road remained even, 4.90 through July 19, 4.77 thereafter. The sign stealing actually may have *hurt* them.

The following table shows how the Giant batting order did before and after July 19. Pre–July 19 numbers come before the slash and were compiled over 88 games, or 56 percent of the schedule. Post–July 19 numbers come after the slash and were compiled over 69 games, or 44 percent of the schedule.

Batter	At-Bats	Home Runs	RBIs	Average
Stanky	305/210	11/3	28/15	.256/.233
Dark	354/292	9/5	45/24	.319/.284
Mueller	189/280	7/9	29/40	.302/.261
Irvin	294/264	12/12	61/60	.303/.322
Lockman	347/267	6/6	35/38	.274/.292
Thomson	274/244	16/16	49/52	.237/.357
Mays	199/265	13/7	39/29	.276/.272
Westrum	211/150	15/5	44/26	.246/.180

Irvin and Lockman slightly improved. The rest of the players did worse, with one exception: Bobby Thomson's average went up 120 points! He was a lifetime .270 hitter (.267 excluding those post–July 19 chances), so from July 19 on he performed way above his norm. At the end of the first playoff game he was asked to explain it. He credited the move to third base. "I realized from the start that I was no third sacker. So I concentrated so much on trying to keep from being killed at third base that I never had time to think about hitting until I was up at the plate. Maybe you could call it a triumph of brawn over brain or muscle over mind."

Or maybe you could call it cheating.

In Thomson's defense, much of his improvement came on the road. Only three of his 16 post-July 19 homers were hit at the Polo Grounds. But when Thomson stood in the box against Branca on October 3 and Durocher told him that fastballs were coming, was it baseball acumen, or something more? Thomson admitted that he "didn't know why I wouldn't have" taken signs earlier in the game, but when it came to Branca's fatal pitch in the bottom of the ninth, he equivocated: "It would take a little away from me in my mind if I felt I got help on the pitch."

"They only had to have one win that came about from cheating in order to make the playoff happen," charged David Smith, Dodger diehard and founder of Retrosheet, an organization dedicated to computerizing the play-by-play action of every major league game. But in a race so close that through the entire regular season and 25 innings of playoff the teams were tied, any one of a thousand variables could have tipped the balance, many of them entirely within the Dodgers' control — starting with Charlie Dressen's behavior and judgment.

It's a baseball axiom that you let sleeping dogs lie, but in early August Dressen encouraged his players to taunt the reeling Giants through the door between locker rooms at Ebbets Field. As late as September 29 he was still inciting the rival club, telling the *Brooklyn Eagle,* "The Giants can't hurt us. They are a flash in the pan.... For a team that has no class, they have been very lucky. But in the long run, you know yourself, class will tell."

Indeed.

Then there was his handling of the pitching staff— and his personal rivalry with Leo Durocher. "If it was the kind of game where Leo used 10 pitchers, Charlie would have to use 11," said Clem Labine. The result? At the moment of truth, Dressen had only Branca to fall back on. Three quality pitchers — Roe, Erskine, and King — were sore from misuse, and the rest he didn't trust. Labine himself was a perfect example of Dressen's poor management, a fresh arm of tremendous utility benched for disobeying an arbitrary command. "I believe it was Charlie Dressen's pique, as much as Thomson's bat, that tipped the 1951 pennant from Brooklyn to New York," concluded *Boys of Summer* author Roger Kahn.

By contrast, Durocher's pitchers got better as the season wore on. Through games of July 19, the Giants allowed an average of 4.69 runs per game. After July 19 they allowed an average of 3.30 per game, a decrease of 1.39! The Giants' runs-against numbers were especially impressive for road games, dropping from 5.15 to 3.26. Durocher made judicious use of young hurlers like George Spencer, Al Corwin, and Roger Bowman. Dressen all but destroyed an injured Erv Palica, sent down Labine for a good part of the summer, and never gave Bud Podbielan a chance to establish himself. Pitching and managing — not cheating — made the difference between New York and Brooklyn in 1951.

Bobby Thomson's scalding liner into the lower left field deck fulfilled the fantasy of every kid who ever carried a mitt to bed and dreamed of hitting the game-winning, bottom-of-the-ninth homer with everything on the line. It was a perfect ending to the most unlikely comeback in baseball history.

But Thomson's homer would never have become the most famous in history had it not also been the defining moment of the rivalry between the Giants and Dodgers. In 1960 Bill Mazeroski hit a more important homer, one that gave Pittsburgh the seventh game of the World Series against the New York Yankees, yet few outside western Pennsylvania recall it with anywhere near the reverence accorded Thomson's. That's because context matters. It's not just that Thomson's homer came at the perfect moment, but that it mattered so much to so many. And for that reason, it will remain at the heart of baseball lore for as long as Americans cherish the game.

9. 1952: "There Will Be a Hundred Thousand Suicides in Brooklyn"

After losing pennants in the final games of 1950 and 1951, the Dodgers had a lot to prove. In the words of the *Brooklyn Eagle's* Tommy Holmes, 1952 became "a grim tale of rehabilitation, a determined season-long drive of the Brooklyn athletes, not only to relieve the fans of that feeling of being kicked around, but to restore their own self-respect."

They had to do it without their best pitcher: Don Newcombe was drafted into the army. Nor did anyone expect 37-year-old Preacher Roe to repeat his 22-win performance of the year before. When Clem Labine and Ralph Branca got hurt, Charlie Dressen had to reconfigure his entire mound staff. He promoted Ben Wade and young Billy Loes (from Astoria, Queens) to the starting rotation and put blazing Joe Black in charge of the bullpen. A generation before the term *closer* entered baseball's vocabulary, the 28-year-old Black, a Negro League alumnus, finished 41 games, allowing Dodger starters to complete fewer assignments than any National League team except last-place Pittsburgh.

The Giants also suffered attrition. Eddie Stanky was traded to St. Louis so he could become the Cards' manager. Monte Irvin, the reigning RBI champ, broke his ankle in spring training and was lost until August. And Willie Mays received a draft notice. He failed the military aptitude test (Leo Durocher claimed the young Mays could barely read and write), but the army made him re-take it and he passed. He started the season knowing that in a matter of weeks he would be gone.

Though no one expected the rivalry to match the heights of 1951, the

121

40th home opener at Ebbets Field on April 18 picked up right where the Thomson-Branca confrontation left off. Labine didn't get a single out as the Giants rampaged for five runs in the first. But the Dodgers roared back, scoring one in the bottom of the first and three more in the second to chase Jim Hearn. Mays preserved a 6–5 Giant lead in the bottom of the seventh with a two-out, bases-loaded catch that he considered among his very best. He nearly knocked himself out diving, and when he got up, Brooklyn fans gave him a generous ovation.

Mays wasn't the only one up to familiar tricks. Clutch as ever, Jackie Robinson smashed a homer in the bottom of the eighth to tie the score. Andy Pafko, who on October 3 had stood at the left field fence and watched helplessly as the Shot Heard 'Round the World sailed into the seats, won the game with a walk-off homer onto Bedford Avenue in the bottom of the 12th.

The Dodgers wound up taking two of three, losing only to Sal Maglie, who shut them out. Ralph Branca pitched the middle game, and though he walked Bobby Thomson the first time they squared off, he set down the Giant slugger on two pop-ups and two grounders thereafter en route to an 11–6 victory.

The Giants and Dodgers were scheduled to play three at the Polo Grounds the following weekend, with crowds of 50,000 expected for each game. But a storm washed out the series, a financial calamity for Horace Stoneham. Still, the Giant owner had to be happy. His team ended April with a 7–4 record and stood just a game and a half behind the first-place Dodgers, a huge improvement over the disastrous 1951 start. If Durocher's men had the same finishing kick they had exhibited the previous two years, they'd leave the Dodgers in the dust by mid September.

In late May it looked as if the finishing kick wouldn't be necessary. The Giants reeled off 10 wins in 11 tries early in the month, and on May 26 took over first with a 4–2 win against the Dodgers at the Polo Grounds. In Brooklyn the next day Maglie pitched a shutout to move the Giants a game and a half in front. Yet another Giant triumph over the Dodgers on May 28 threw the Boys of Summer into a bitter funk.

But the May 28 game was significant for another reason: it was the last Willie Mays played before going into the army. Though he had contributed little offensively — .236 average, four home runs, and four steals in 127 at-bats — he'd become the Giants' linchpin in the field and clubhouse. In a tearful farewell, his teammates gave him a portable radio so he could follow their progress wherever he was posted. "Just hold 'em till I get back, boys," he said.

The Giants wouldn't be the only ones to miss him. Reported Red Smith, "When the batting orders were announced, there was a fine, loud cheer for Willie. This was in Brooklyn, mind you, where 'Giant' is the dirtiest word in the language." The crowd hailed him again after he lined to Pee Wee Reese in his last at-bat. And after some initial begrudging ("No one shed any tears when I went into the service," said Carl Furillo) the Dodger players also expressed admiration. "He will be truly great some day," predicted Jackie Robinson.

The loss of Mays so disheartened the Giants that over the next two weeks they went from two and a half up to five down. Not that they were doing badly. Their 30–17 record on June 10 was the envy of every team except the Dodgers, who were 35–12, an especially remarkable achievement given the patchwork pitching staff. The Giants were the only team capable of beating the Dodgers consistently. When Maglie shut them out for the third time on June 26, it marked the Giants' fifth straight win over their rivals.

A week later Jim Hearn, with ninth-inning help from rookie knuckleballer Hoyt Wilhelm, beat the Dodgers 4–3 to make it six straight. But at the Polo Grounds on July 4 the Dodgers snapped that streak — and Maglie's. The Barber lasted only two innings of the rain-interrupted holiday contest and lost 5–1 in front of 49,443, the biggest National League crowd so far that season. The breakthrough victory propelled the Dodgers to a six-game lead by the end of July. Their pennant prospects brightened further when Maglie and Larry Jansen developed nagging injuries that limited their effectiveness the rest of the way.

For Dodger fans haunted by the previous season, though, six games was no cushion at all. "What happens if the Dodgers zoom into one of their patented nervous breakdowns?" fretted the *Eagle's* Tommy Holmes. On August 11, the anniversary of the Giants' low point in the 1951 race, the New Yorkers lost a twin bill to sixth-place Boston to fall nine behind. But that was four and a half less than they'd had to make up in their miracle season — and they finally had Monte Irvin back.

Still, the Giants continued to lose ground. By August 26 the Dodgers had inflated the lead to 10½, giving the Giants just 33 games to pull off another miracle. Even if Durocher's crew played at the same incredible clip it did down the '51 stretch, the Dodgers would have to go only 19–14 (.576, 100 points below their season-long average) to claim the flag.

The Giants made a move anyway, gaining a game and a half going into to their last visit to Ebbets Field on August 30 and 31. Durocher tapped Maglie to start game one. The Dodgers' biggest crowd of the year turned out to boo the Giant pitcher, but at least one spectator cheered him: Willie Mays, in town on a five-day leave. Maglie scattered 10 hits and second baseman Davey Williams launched a three-run homer to beat the Dodgers, 4–3. The next afternoon, however, the Dodgers overwhelmed the Giants 9–1 to stall the advance and finish August nine games up.

Undiscouraged, the Giants won four of their next five to trim Brooklyn's lead to six. Their next five games, all against the Dodgers at home, would decide the season. If they swept they'd be just one back with 19 to play. If they *were* swept they'd be an insurmountable 11 back. The National League broke up two umpiring crews to assign its best arbiters— Al Barlick, Lee Ballanfant, Jocko Conlan, and Bill Stewart — to the showdown.

And right on cue, Charlie Dressen repeated his mistake of the previous year by taunting the Giants. In a *Saturday Evening Post* article entitled "The Dodgers Won't Blow It Again!" he attributed the humiliation of 1951 to a "lack of reserve strength" and the fact that "the Dodgers were overrated last year." "They weren't good enough to be out in front by 13½ games in August. Practically everyone on the team was in hock to the percentages, and the debts were repaid — with interest — in September." But Dressen omitted two crucial points. One was his own culpability for the Dodgers' downfall. He explained Clyde King's uselessness in September, for example, as a consequence of those darn percentages, neglecting to mention that his overuse of King early in the season ruined the curveballer's arm. And other than to say that the percentages favored the Giants after their disastrous April, he gave the champions no credit for winning 37 of their last 44 regular season games. He concluded: "I don't think I'm sticking my neck out in … predicting that the Dodgers will nail the pennant they missed last year. I'm safe in going out on the limb. I've got the ballclub to support me — and the percentages are all against lightning striking the same tree twice."

The reaction from Manhattan was swift — and blunt. "A smarter or less egotistical man never would have risked it," the *Times*' Arthur Daley snapped. And after the Giants took the first two games of the series in a September 6 doubleheader, Leo Durocher cracked, "If we can pull this one out, there will be a hundred thousand suicides in Brooklyn."

A defensive Dressen claimed he did the article purely for the money ($3,000). "If we win, everything's okay. If we lose, I've blown my job anyway," he shrugged. He pointed to a supportive telegram from Walter O'Malley: "We would not be the daffy Dodgers if it could be done the easy way. We have to beat the Giants. If we don't we don't deserve winning. You have done your job well. We need courageous pitching and free and vicious hitting." The Dodger players, by now accustomed to their manager's special talent for, in the words of Red Smith, "saying and doing graceless things on important occasions," realized the onus was on them. Matched against Sal Maglie in the third game of the series, they made the requisite preparations.

None steeled himself more than Gilbert Raymond Hodges. The embodiment of the strong, silent type, Hodges was raised in Indiana's southwest corner, a million miles from Brooklyn. He came to the Dodgers in 1943 a teenaged catcher but spent the next three years in the Marine Corps, serving in the Pacific theater

Charlie Dressen. When the Dodgers were losing he would tell his players, "You hold 'em, boys, and I'll think of something." (Transcendental Graphics)

and earning a Bronze Star. Upon his return in 1947 he endeared himself to Dodger fans not just with his smooth fielding and consistent production — starting in 1949 he knocked in over 100 runs for seven straight seasons — but by marrying a native and buying a house in prosperous Midwood.

With the Dodgers a run down in the bottom of the first, a visibly worked-up Hodges wheeled on a two-two pitch and sent it arcing into the left field upper deck. Although the homer only tied the game, it showed the Dodgers that the pitcher they feared most was vincible. Next inning Pee Wee Reese clubbed a solo homer. Robinson followed with a long fly that was caught, but George "Shotgun" Shuba blasted one off the right field upper façade to make it 3–1. Billy Cox finished off Maglie in the seventh with yet another solo homer, and the Dodgers skated to victory.

But not before Hodges struck again, this time on the basepaths. Trying to break up a double play in the eighth, he leveled Giant second baseman Davey Williams, who had to be helped off the field and was out of the lineup for days. Combined with Roe's earlier beaning of Monte Irvin, the take-out sent Durocher and the Giants a loud message.

In the first game of the next day's doubleheader, the Giants let Hodges know they'd heard it: Hoyt Wilhelm drilled him with a pitch. Hodges countered by sliding spikes-up into Bill Rigney, who had replaced Williams; Rigney had to leave with a three-inch gash in his calf. Joe Black decked the Giants' George Wilson next inning. New York reliever Monte Kennedy went after Hodges and Black. In keeping with an August 5 directive by new National League president Warren Giles, the umpires warned both benches to stop the beanball war or risk suspensions and fines. But with the Giants trailing by six runs (they eventually lost 10–2), Durocher showed what he thought of the new rule. In the eighth he had Larry Jansen hit Andy Pafko, and in the ninth Jansen hit Cox. Both Jansen and Durocher were ejected.

The Giants rallied to win the nightcap, 3–2. Sal Maglie came on in relief and doused a Dodger rally in the seventh, then with Dodgers on first and second and two out in the top of the ninth got Jackie Robinson to ground out to Bobby Hofman, the Giants' third second baseman of the series. When Hank Thompson opened the bottom of the ninth with a base hit and scored on a Don Mueller opposite-field double, it gave Maglie his sixth win of the campaign over the Dodgers. It also gave the Giants 14 wins against Brooklyn in 22 tries, the first time in eight years they won a season series from their rivals. But they were five out with 19 to play, and had to depend on other teams to bring the Dodgers down.

The next day league president Giles punished the Giants for their gratuitous headhunting. He suspended Durocher for two days and fined him $100. (It was Durocher's third suspension of the season.) Monte Kennedy was fined $50 and Larry Jansen $25, although the latter's penalty was rescinded in recognition of his previously sterling conduct. So what happened? The fired-up Giants won five of their next six, while the Dodgers, letting down after the excitement at the Polo Grounds, split their next six evenly. The lead shrank to three, and remained there through September 17.

But there would be no suicides in Brooklyn—at least not over the Dodgers. New York lost its next three while Brooklyn won three, guaranteeing the Dodgers a tie for first. And on September 23, as the Giants sat idle, the Dodgers clinched the pennant with a 5–4 win over the Phillies. Ecstatic fans at Ebbets Field rang bells provided by the Schaefer Brewing Company, a broadcast sponsor.

"What saved the situation for Dressen this year was that the Dodgers never had any true opposition," alleged Arthur Daley of the *Times.* "Monte Irvin's spring training broken leg finished off the Giants. They made a brave try as long as they had Willie Mays, but once Willie the Wonder departed, the pressure on the pitchers became too heavy. They collapsed."

Not quite. What saved the situation for Dressen was an offense that led the league in on-base percentage, slugging percentage, and runs scored; a defense that committed the fewest errors in either league; Rookie of the Year Joe Black; and the Reds, Braves, and Pirates. The Dodgers scored 172 more runs than their opponents, the biggest spread in the majors. But 157 of those surplus runs were piled up against Cincinnati, Boston, and Pittsburgh, the only teams in the N.L. to finish under .500. The Dodgers posted a lopsided 54–11 (.831) mark against them, compared to the Giants' 44–22 (.667). That 10½ game difference tells the story. The Dodgers' 42–46 record against the league's better ballclubs suggests they had plenty of opposition — and that in 1952 they made up for whatever bad luck they'd had the year before.

10. *1954: "The Giants Is Dead"*

Arthur Daley's claim that Brooklyn won for lack of opposition may have missed the mark in 1952, but it perfectly described 1953, when the Dodgers won a franchise record 105 games and outdistanced their nearest pursuer by a whopping 13 lengths. Their 955 runs (nearly 6.2 per game), the most in the senior circuit since hit-happy 1930, were a product of both power and speed: they led the majors in homers and stolen bases. They also had the league's best defense, and their pitchers struck out more batters than any other mound staff.

The Giants crumpled down the stretch, winning just 18 of 59 in August and September. For his annual taunt, Charlie Dressen declared on August 8 that "the Giants is dead," irking not only Giant fans, but English teachers. At the time the Giants were in fifth place, 15½ games out, so there was little chance of the sneer backfiring. Just to be sure, though, the Boys of Summer swept New York in two consecutive weekend series.

The Giants might have been dead, but the rivalry wasn't. Carl "Skoonj" Furillo had hated Leo Durocher since their days together with the Dodgers. After Durocher switched to the Giants, he ordered his pitchers to throw at the Brooklyn right fielder, knowing it took the thin-skinned Furillo out of his game. On September 6, 1953, the teams' last meeting of the year, Furillo heard Durocher's familiar "Stick it in his ear!" Rookie pitcher Ruben Gomez, afflicted with poor control, hit Furillo on the right wrist instead.

Coming just two days after a vicious beanball war in which Larry Jansen had knocked down Snider and Campanella, the purpose pitch sent

128

Furillo over the edge. He headed toward Gomez. The umpires escorted him to first base and resumed play, but Furillo began exchanging insults with Durocher, whom he considered the real culprit. With the count two-and-two on Billy Cox, Furillo called time — and sprinted into the Giant dugout. "Before anyone could get in his way, he got Durocher in a headlock. Leo's hat fell off, and you could see Durocher's bald head start to turn purple from the pressure," remembered *New York Herald Tribune* writer Harold Rosenthal. Members of both teams pulled them apart, but in the confusion Monte Irvin stepped on Furillo's hand and broke Furillo's finger, ending a season in which Skoonj was leading the league in batting average.

Even without Furillo, the Dodgers clinched first place on September 12, earlier than any previous N.L. team. Dressen became the first manager to lead the franchise to consecutive pennants since Bill McGunnigle in 1889–90. Only the Shot Heard 'Round the World kept him from winning three in a row. In 1953 the also-ran Cardinals gave Eddie Stanky a three-year contract. More gallingly, Horace Stoneham gave Durocher a two-year extension while the Giants plummeted to the second division. If those guys were worth multiyear contracts, Dressen reasoned, surely he merited one as well. Egged on by his wife, he asked Walter O'Malley for a three-year contract. O'Malley offered a healthy raise — which would nonetheless leave Dressen's salary well short of Durocher's — but only a one-year deal. With principle, his wife's esteem, and his dignity at stake, Dressen refused to consider anything less than a two-year pact. So on October 14, 1953, O'Malley shocked the baseball world by bidding Dressen adieu.

Charlie Dressen may have been a bumptious, egomaniacal destroyer of pitchers (in 1953 he ruined Joe Black's arm by forcing the fireballer to learn off-speed deliveries), but he was also funny, generous, and resourceful. His success entitled him to keep his job on favorable terms. In the new Dodger environment, however, nobody got to outshine the owner, and between his pennants and flapping tongue, Dressen — like Red Barber, a Rickey loyalist who left a few weeks later — tempted people to believe that others besides Walter O'Malley were responsible for the Dodgers' emergence as the National League's best team.

Over the next six weeks the press conjectured about a dozen managerial candidates, two of them closely associated with the Giants: Frankie Frisch and Bill Terry. Had Terry gotten the job the riot in Brooklyn would have shaken the earth, but 20 years after asking whether the Dodgers were still in the league, Memphis Bill was a well-to-do Florida businessman with little interest in returning to baseball. Pee Wee Reese, the sentimental favorite, didn't want to quit playing — and O'Malley didn't want a player-manager. So who would get the post? Cookie Lavagetto? Fresco

Thompson? Bucky Harris? Lefty O'Doul? Two days before Thanksgiving, O'Malley put an end to the guessing.

Although Walter Emmons Alston's elevation was hyped as a surprise ("Who He?" asked the *New York Daily News*), it was logical enough to have been predicted the day before by *Times* reporter Louis Effrat: "Alston is in the organization. He managed at St. Paul and Montreal and fared well. Numerous current Dodgers, at one time or another, played under him in the minors." Effrat could have added that Buzzie Bavasi, O'Malley's top lieutenant, had worked with Alston for years in the minors and vouched for his ability. The clincher: though originally hired by Branch Rickey (and, like Rickey, hailing from southern Ohio), Alston unblinkingly obeyed whoever was in charge. The O'Malley, as he was coming to be known, could rest assured that his new manager would never upstage the front office, much less demand more than a one-year contract.

But the Dodger players were disinclined to take orders from a man with minimal big league experience (one at-bat, a strikeout, in 1936) and no knowledge of the teams they had to beat. Jackie Robinson, in particular, flouted Alston's leadership. At first Alston did little — a characteristic tendency — but toward the end of spring training he called Robinson into his office, shut the door, and said, "You have two choices. You can either apologize, or only one of us is going to walk out of here." Robinson was hardly one to back down from a challenge. But Alston stood 6'2", weighed over 200 pounds and, once aroused, had a temper that made Furillo's pale. Robinson apologized. That wasn't the end of it between them — a year later Roy Campanella parted them as fists started to fly — but the confrontation established Alston as the boss.

Alston managed his first big league game at the Polo Grounds. Commissioner Ford Frick baptized him into the rivalry by warning him and Leo Durocher not to get acquainted over beanballs. Frick was concerned by Furillo's threat to "get" Durocher after their fight the previous September, and also knew that Sal Maglie, though 37 and fading, hadn't lost his zeal for denting Dodger flesh. But he needn't have worried. Furillo, Maglie, and their teammates conducted themselves like model citizens.

This was a better Giant ballclub than the year before. On February 1 Horace Stoneham made a sad but necessary trade with the Braves, exchanging fabled Bobby Thomson for John Antonelli, a strong young starting pitcher. Thomson's departure cleared space for Willie Mays, discharged from the army after learning one useful thing — the basket catch — during his hitch. Mays's play and outlook revitalized the Giants. As Arthur Daley noted: "The importance of Willie can't be measured by his batting average, his spectacular catches or his incredible throws. He isn't witty and yet no man stirs up more laughter. His shrill voice bubbles like champagne and imparts the intoxicating qualities of contentment, pleasure, happiness and good nature. Every Giant brightens visibly at the sight of this baseball Peter Pan and every Giant has been touched by the contagion of his personality."

With the angels of each team — Blanche McGraw and Douglas MacArthur — looking on, the Giants and Dodgers played even-steven through five, but in the bottom of the sixth Mays clobbered one 400 feet into the upper deck and the Giants held on to spoil Alston's debut, 4–3. The new Dodger manager notched his first win the next night behind the sharp pitching of his own returned veteran, Don Newcombe. At April's end he had the Dodgers in first place, half a game ahead of the Giants and Reds.

But then Roy Campanella broke his hand so badly he required surgery, and the defending champs sagged. They finished May in second place, a game behind the Braves and half a game ahead of the Giants. Once June rolled around they caught fire, winning 21 of 27. But the Giants burned even hotter, copping 22 victories in 26 tries, and took over first place on June 15.

The Giants held a mere one game edge when the Dodgers came to the Polo Grounds on June 29 for the season's first meaningful series. A paid crowd of 51,464, largest at the Polo Grounds in nearly three years, saw "one of the most thrill-packed clashes the ancient diamond foes have staged since their memorable playoff series of 1951," wrote veteran rivalry watcher John Drebinger in the *Times*.

Except for solo homers by Monte Irvin and Davey Williams, Newcombe throttled the Giants through seven. But Maglie, always saving his best for Brooklyn, pitched even better, blanking the Dodgers through eight. Within a strike of victory in the ninth, though, he hung a curve to Campanella, and the ensuing two-run clout sent the game into extra innings. The Giants loaded the bases in the bottom of the 11th, but couldn't score. The Dodgers put men on first and third in the 12th and couldn't bring anyone across (worse still, Reese pulled a muscle on the basepaths and was lost for several days). In the top of the 13th, Dodger third baseman Don Hoak finally broke the deadlock with a solo homer.

Billy Loes, the Dodger pitcher from Queens whose insolence toward management was portrayed as goofy eccentricity, tried to nail down the win. He got two outs, but also walked the bases loaded. With backup catcher Ray Katt due, Durocher took an audacious gamble, sending the occasionally sober Dusty Rhodes to pinch hit. If Rhodes knocked in just one run, Durocher would have to play the rest of the game without a real catcher. Loes, like Maglie earlier, came within a strike of victory. But the 27-year-old Rhodes, enjoying one of the greatest seasons a pinch hitter ever had, lined a single up the middle to score two and claim the win for New York.

A tight contest the next day was decided by a three-run Giant eighth, and the final game of the series effectively ended when — *déja vu* — Rhodes lined a pinch-hit, bases-loaded single to score two runs. The sweep put the Giants four games ahead in the standings, and even farther ahead psychologically. "Small wonder one sees emerging from under rocks Giant fans no one has seen since the gay days of the '51 playoff," John Drebinger gibed.

A week later the Giants and Dodgers played three at Ebbets Field. Team captain Al Dark joined Willie Mays and Monte Irvin in hitting homers as the Giants took the opener, 5–2, giving Sal Maglie his fourth win of the year over Brooklyn. Rain delayed but did not postpone the next tiff, much to the regret of Don Newcombe, pounded for seven runs in four and one-third innings. Dark, Mays, and Irvin homered again, as did Wes Westrum, and Mays made one of his routinely marvelous catches. A beyond-capacity crowd of 34,456 cheered on the Dodgers in the last game, but the Giants again clapped four homers — Irvin, Lockman, and two by Mays, whose 30 for the season put him ahead of Babe Ruth's record 1927 pace — to massacre Brooklyn, 11–2. After Mays's second homer, hot-headed reliever Russ Meyer hit Irvin on the thigh. The Giants retaliated with a replay of September 6, 1953: Ruben Gomez threw at Carl Furillo. The Dodger right fielder nearly came to blows with catcher Westrum, but umpire Dusty Boggess got between them.

The loss was the Dodgers' sixth in a row to the Giants. Alston closed the clubhouse and chewed out his players for 20 minutes, then sent them on the field for postgame batting practice. In the visitors' clubhouse, Leo Durocher couldn't resist gloating: "They're a great ballclub. We were just a little too much for them." A few days later he pulled a Charlie Dressen, declaring, "They're never going to catch us."

The author of the Miracle at Coogan's Bluff should have known better. The 1954 Dodgers didn't like having dirt rubbed in their faces any more than the 1951 Giants did. Although the Brooklyns didn't come busting back right away, on July 26, a makeup of an earlier rain-out, they beat Sal Maglie at Ebbets Field for the first time ever, by the convincing score of 9–1. It was the Giants' fifth straight loss, and it brought the Dodgers within three. But the Dodgers couldn't capitalize on the momentum. On August 11, the anniversary of their 13½-game lead in 1951, they lagged three and a half behind. They didn't need a miracle to win, but they did need to press when they had the advantage.

On August 13 the Giants and Dodgers commenced a three-game set at Ebbets Field. Maglie and Carl Erskine traded goose eggs until the bottom of the sixth, when Erskine singled, went to third on a base hit by Jim Gilliam, and scored on Reese's sacrifice fly. Mays prevented further damage by catching Dodger left fielder Sandy Amoros's drive to deepest center, then catalyzed a two-run Giant seventh, singling home Don Mueller and scoring on Monte Irvin's double. But in the bottom of the seventh Furillo walloped a two-run homer off Giant reliever Marv Grissom, and Erskine held on for the 3–2 win. Dodgers two and a half back.

The next day Furillo all but erased a 5–0 Giant lead with a grand slam off Ruben Gomez. (How sweet that must have been!) A two-run single by Campanella completed the comeback, and the Dodgers pulled within a game and a half of first place.

More than 29,000 fans poured into Ebbets Field the next day. Dazzy Vance threw out the first ball. The Giants slammed four homers off Billy Loes, including Mays's 37th, but the Dodgers amassed nine runs against Jim Hearn and four relievers to claim victory. One of the Dodger runs came on Gil Hodges' 200th career homer, making him the first man to hit that many in a Brooklyn uniform. Now the Dodgers trailed by only half a game with plenty of time left.

But once again the Dodgers went flat after playing the Giants, ending August exactly where they had been before their sweep, three and a half back. Although the Giants might collapse, realistically the Dodgers' best hope was to sweep a three-game series at the Polo Grounds over the Labor Day weekend and build on the resulting momentum.

"In bars, hotels, taxis, barber shops, offices, a premature World Series atmosphere developed as men argued baseball as heatedly as if the results of the Giants-Dodgers three-game meeting might decide Soviet-American relations," the *Times* reported. The Brooklyn Chamber of Commerce passed a resolution stating, "If we can only whitewash the Giants, or even get two out of three, everything will be okay." The teams handled the pressure in characteristic fashion. "On the Dodger bench manager Walter Alston sat alone, an island of silence in a sea of yakkety-yak ballplayers. On the other bench Leo Durocher sat, an island of yakkety-yak in a sea of silent ballplayers," observed Arthur Daley.

Durocher started Maglie, but the Barber left after six trailing 4–2. The Giants got him off the hook by plating a pair against Loes, and in the seventh reliever Hoyt Wilhelm, a poor hitter even for a pitcher (lifetime average .088) bounced a seeing-eye single up the middle to put the Gothamites ahead. On the mound in the eighth, however, Wilhelm lost control of his knuckler and walked the bases loaded with two out. With the pitcher due to bat, Alston had rookie outfielder Walt Moryn pinch hit. Moryn roped one to right, but Don Mueller just did snag it to end the threat, and the Giants wound up winning, 7–4. "Phew, that was a rough one," Durocher conceded.

Next day the Giants exploded for seven runs in the seventh inning to win 13–4. Although the Dodgers came back in the finale to beat John Antonelli, they left the Polo Grounds in worse shape than they entered. "To be four games down with only 19 to play is not the nicest spot to be. However, the club generally feels we have a hot streak coming," Alston bravely maintained.

The streak never materialized. The Dodgers even sank into third place for a few days. When they hosted the Giants on September 20, they faced elimination. Durocher handed the ball to— guess who?— Sal Maglie, and the aging beanballer stymied the Dodgers on five hits for a 7–1 win and the pennant. Celebrating on rival turf could have gotten ugly, but all parties were gracious. Owner O'Malley, manager Alston, and captain Reese crossed to the visitors' clubhouse to wish the Giants well in the World Series, which would be remembered for "The Catch," Mays's snare of Vic Wertz's drive to the deepest part of the Polo Grounds. Said a magnanimous Durocher, "I never felt at ease at any time. You couldn't feel at ease with a club like Brooklyn on your heels and liable to knock you cold any time."

The Dodgers gained a bit of consolation the following day when Karl Spooner, a hard-throwing lefty, shut out the Giants in his major league debut. His 15 strikeouts broke the record for inaugural appearances, held since 1937 by the Giants' Cliff Melton. Spooner tossed another shutout on the last day of the season, fanning 12, and was acclaimed the Dodgers' next great pitcher. But he hurt his arm in 1955 and never panned out. His place in history was taken by a shy, cerebral Brooklyn native who could throw a ball at the speed of light — and who ended the New York teams' decades-long search for a Jewish superstar.

But Sandy Koufax would win only nine games as a Brooklyn Dodger.

Interlude: The Move

Walter O'Malley's Brooklyn Dodgers were highly profitable, perennially at or near the top in attendance and broadcast revenue. Former Cleveland Indian owner Bill Veeck estimated that only the Yankees made more money. But O'Malley wasn't content with a good return on his investment. He wanted the *maximum* return. And when he looked for drags on his bottom line, he found none bigger than Ebbets Field.

The Dodgers would go to Yankee Stadium for the World Series and perform in front of over 60,000 people. Then they'd come home, sell out, yet play for only half as big a crowd. "Ebbets Field when built was supposed to be too large. Today it is woefully too small," conceded Red Barber in 1953. Another problem: maintaining the dilapidated infrastructure. "We'd patch something up and something else would need our attention," carped O'Malley.

The Dodger ballpark was an anachronism in a larger sense, too. It was built when Brooklyn was the next step up the ladder for immigrants (or their children) with means to escape Manhattan's squalid tenements. But by 1930 the flow of immigrants had ceased and the borough had filled its empty spaces. During the Great Depression and World War II, stagnation set in. Once-vibrant neighborhoods turned dingy, and the collective mood soured. After the war, hundreds of thousands of soldiers from Brooklyn flocked joyously home — and then dreamed of getting out as soon as possible.

Uncle Sam gave them every opportunity. The GI Bill allowed them to go to college, qualify for decent jobs, and obtain mortgages on generous terms. Was it any wonder that as soon as they graduated and found work, they moved their young wives and children from the cramped quarters their families had been stuck in for decades and resettled in the modern, split-level suburbs of Long Island and New Jersey?

Their places were taken by African Americans and Latinos who frightened the European Americans left behind. Half a century ago in Brooklyn, white ethnics stuck with their own, seldom forming meaningful relationships across cultural barriers. For them to have befriended the new arrivals would have required imagination and courage rare everywhere in America back then. White kids rooting for Jackie Robinson was acceptable. White kids inviting black kids home for dinner was not.

It was in this context that Walter O'Malley called Buzzie Bavasi into his office at 215 Montague Street, near Borough Hall, and pointed out the window. "Look down there. What do you see?" he asked. "I see a long, long line of poor Puerto Rican people getting their welfare checks," Bavasi answered. As if that wasn't alarming enough to the Dodger owner, the area north of Ebbets Field, known as Bedford-Stuyvesant, had turned into a desperately poor African American ghetto that was expanding toward Flatbush. O'Malley didn't need a customer survey to know that few white suburbanites would attend a game in a black neighborhood, especially when they could watch it on TV. Nor was it likely that Brooklyn's new residents, often struggling just to cover the rent, would support the team to the extent their predecessors had.

The first hint of Ebbets Field's doom came in March 1952, when O'Malley disclosed that he was having plans drawn for a new park. Few took seriously his vision of a stadium with retractable roof, synthetic turf, heated seats, and massive garage. "New Ebbets Field to Have Hot Dogs and Hot Seats," smirked the *New York Times*, mentioning as an afterthought that the park would be built at a different location. Not that O'Malley was thinking beyond Brooklyn. But two subsequent developments broadened his sense of possibility.

The first was a series of congressional hearings into baseball's monopoly status chaired by longtime Brooklyn representative Emanuel Celler. The investigation probed almost every aspect of the baseball business. One of the toughest lines of inquiry concerned restrictions on franchise transfers and expansion. Why was it that the self-proclaimed guardians of the national pastime operated out of only 10 cities in the Northeast and Midwest? Why were the Braves, Athletics, and Browns languishing in two-team towns when huge cities like Los Angeles had no team at all? Although Congress never acted on its dudgeon, owners fretful about adverse legislation voluntarily relaxed their restrictions on franchise shifts.

The second development grew out of the first. In 1953 the Braves became the first major league team in half a century to relocate, leaving Boston for Milwaukee. They were given the run of County Stadium, a brand-new, 53,000-seat ballpark erected at public expense and surrounded by acres of parking. Their attendance, a piteous 281,000 their final season in Boston, soared to a National League record 1,826,000 in Wisconsin. (It was the Dodgers' record, set in 1947, that they broke.) In 1954 the Braves became the first National League team to draw over 2,000,000. Although O'Malley enjoyed a $600,000-plus advantage over the Braves in broadcast revenue, when he compared their attendance to his—and up-and-coming stars like Henry Aaron and Eddie Mathews to his aging Boys of Summer—he feared that without a quick, massive influx of revenue the Dodgers would lose their dominance.

In the summer of 1955 he proposed a new stadium and 2,500-car garage at the junction of Flatbush and Atlantic Avenues, major arteries between downtown and the central and eastern parts of the borough. Nearby Fourth Avenue connected the intersection to western Brooklyn. Two subway lines into Manhattan ran by the site, and the Long Island Railroad had its terminus there. Thus no matter where Dodger fans lived, they would have easy access to O'Malley's park. One sticking point, though: if he tried to purchase the land himself, the owners would jack up their prices. So he asked the city of New York to condemn the land at its assessed value, clear it, and sell it back to him.

City officials responded with disbelief and, in some quarters, contempt. Did The O'Malley really think the municipal government would move heaven, earth, and the Long Island Railroad for his personal benefit when social welfare costs were zooming and the tax base eroding? (The demographic changes affecting Brooklyn were also bedeviling Manhattan, the Bronx, and Queens.) This while he was making hefty profits and could literally capitalize on his connections with the mighty Brooklyn Trust Company if he needed financing?

The rudest brush-off came from Robert Moses, the city's construction coordinator. For years the all-powerful Moses had been leveling neighborhoods to build highways, bridges, and parks. He looked down his patrician nose at spectator sports and at undertakings that benefitted only one borough, yet here was O'Malley proposing a park for the Dodgers as the centerpiece of a Brooklyn-only urban renewal project. On top of that, O'Malley was advocating renovation of the Long Island Railroad terminal just as Moses was supervising construction of the competing Long Island Expressway. "We have no confidence in Walter O'Malley's scheme to put a Dodger field at the Brooklyn terminal of the Long Island Railroad," Moses curtly pronounced.

Walter O'Malley could instantly size up everyone at a negotiating table and, whether it took flattery or threats, persuade them to see things his way. "Walter, what do I think?" Philip Wrigley, owner of the Cubs, once not-so-kiddingly asked him. In Robert Moses, O'Malley recognized a foe unlikely to be swayed by his best weapons, smooth talk and backroom wheeler-dealing. He needed leverage. Realizing that a threat to move would serve nicely, on August 16, 1955, he announced that in 1956 the Dodgers would play one exhibition and seven regular season home games in Jersey City, New Jersey.

Jersey City was Giant country, ancestral home of the Stoneham dynasty and host to the Giants' top minor league team until 1950, when televised big league games killed attendance. Since then, WPA-built Roosevelt Stadium had been used for stock car racing and was no longer suitable for baseball. It seated 7,000 fewer fans than the supposedly too small Ebbets Field. But the message was what mattered: Walter O'Malley was willing to take the Dodgers out of Brooklyn.

The announcement hit New York City — and the Borough of Churches in particular — harder than Hurricane Diane, then wheeling up the eastern seaboard. Said one Dodger fan, "It's a dirty trick to pull a stunt like this." With characteristic Brooklyn bluntness another asked, "Why doesn't the city give the Dodgers some land down by the waterfront instead of building more parks for the bums to sleep in?" Mayor Robert Wagner said, "I am very anxious to keep the Brooklyn Dodgers in New York City," and scheduled an August 19 meeting with Brooklyn borough president John Cashmore, Robert Moses, and O'Malley.

Horace Stoneham seized that moment to inject the Giants into the controversy. "We could certainly use a new field. But instead of helping us, everything the civic fathers have done in recent years has been pointed at hurting us." Giant vice president Chub Feeney added, "If they're going to build a stadium in Brooklyn, they ought to consider building one for the clubs here as well."

Stoneham, not O'Malley, should have been spearheading the ballpark campaign, because the Giants were in far worse shape than the Dodgers. Harlem, the neighborhood around the Polo Grounds, had turned into a slum that for most white New Yorkers was the ultimate no-go zone. Except for a spike during the 1954 championship season, attendance was plummeting below the league average. (See chart.) The ballpark, built in haste two years before Ebbets Field, reeked of decrepitude. And Stoneham, even keener on automobile access than O'Malley, was peeved at the city for converting an adjacent 400-car parking lot into a playground.

The Giants were still profitable. Their broadcast revenue was second

Attendance Trend, 1946-1957

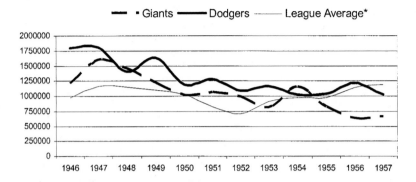

— • Giants ———Dodgers ——— League Average*

*Not including Giants and Dodgers

in the league to the Dodgers' and more than made up for any operating deficit. But like O'Malley, Stoneham was pessimistic about the long term — and had more right to be.

O'Malley responded ambivalently to Stoneham's me-tooism. At the Gracie Mansion meeting with Wagner, Cashmore, and Moses, he was drowned out by a gust from Hurricane Diane. "That must be Horace Stoneham," Wagner quipped, to which O'Malley replied, "Oh no, there's not *that* much wind." But just when he needed to parry arguments that even if the Dodgers left, New York would still have a National League franchise, Stoneham gave him ammunition, and O'Malley made immediate use of it. "This problem is bigger than the Dodgers alone," he warned. "It's unlikely that one club or the other would move. You'll find that the two will move. If one team goes, the other will go."

O'Malley's reasoning? Without the rivalry the Giants faced calamity, because a disproportionate amount of their revenue came from Dodger visits to the Polo Grounds. An average opponent would account for just under 15 percent of the Giants' yearly attendance. Some years the Dodgers approached 40 percent. No matter how remunerative the Giants' media contracts, if the Dodgers moved away and the rivalry died, the drop-off at the turnstiles would imperil the Manhattan franchise.

Still, Stoneham would have been glad to stay in New York if the city constructed a stadium near the Whitestone Bridge, in the eastern Bronx, for both him and the Yankees. George Weiss, the Yankees' general manager, dashed the idea by saying, "We're very happy with Yankee Stadium." Thereafter Stoneham contemplated moving to Minneapolis, where the

Giants had their top farm club. Fans there so loved baseball that after Willie Mays was called up, Stoneham had to take out an ad in the *Minneapolis Tribune* to apologize. Minneapolis was already bigger than Cincinnati, and was building a municipally owned ballpark with plenty of parking.

The wind-blown summit at Gracie Mansion led to the February 1956 formation of the Brooklyn Sports Center Authority, an agency, like those run by Robert Moses, granted broad powers to accomplish its mission. Eager to get going, O'Malley dropped his demand that he own the new park, accepting tenancy in a state facility. But after an initial flurry, the Authority lost momentum. Mayor Wagner took his time appointing commissioners, and then reports emerged that redeveloping the site at Flatbush and Atlantic Avenues would cost more than estimated and shrink the city's declining tax base by another $5 million. The 1956 season ended with the Dodgers no closer to a new home than the year before.

Walter O'Malley wasn't about to wait for politicians and bureaucrats to decide his fate. During the 1956 World Series, which the Dodgers lost to the Yankees, he passed a note to Kenneth Hahn, a Los Angeles county supervisor trying to entice the Washington Senators west. The note expressed O'Malley's own interest in relocating. When the Dodgers stopped in Los Angeles en route to a winter tour of Japan, O'Malley and Hahn met. They tentatively agreed on a Dodger move to Southern California. To demonstrate his sincerity, O'Malley announced the sale of Ebbets Field to a housing developer, with the Dodgers leasing back the park for just three years (although they had an option for two more). O'Malley aide Red Patterson told worried New York reporters that "no serious offer" from another city underlay the Dodgers' first real step out of their antiquated home. Either he didn't know what his boss was up to, or no one asked him to define serious.

Though he kept his Brooklyn options open, O'Malley's restiveness grew increasingly plain. On February 10, 1957, he warned New York officials that "unless something is done within six months, I will have to make other arrangements." Eleven days later he acquired the Los Angeles Angels, Philip Wrigley's Pacific Coast League franchise (along with Wrigley Field in South Central Los Angeles), for the Dodgers' minor league holdings in Fort Worth, Texas, and a payment reckoned at $2 million; under major league rules, that gave him territorial rights to Los Angeles. On March 6 he welcomed Los Angeles mayor Norris Poulson to the Dodgers' spring training facility in Vero Beach, Florida, for private discussions.

With alarms from Brooklyn ringing in his ears, on April 18 Robert Moses finally made O'Malley a substantive offer. The city would build a stadium in Flushing Meadows, Queens, site of the 1939 World's Fair (and, not coincidentally, convenient to the Long Island Expressway) and the

Dodgers could be tenants there. Relishing the reversal of fortunes—now Moses was the one talking ballpark, and he the one with the leverage—the Dodger owner rejected the idea as summarily as Moses had the Flatbush and Atlantic proposal nearly two years earlier.

O'Malley paid Poulson a return visit on April 30. Helicoptering over Los Angeles a couple of days later, he got a good look at Chavez Ravine, a hilly, pastoral tract just a mile from downtown and nestled between the Hollywood, Pasadena, and Golden State freeways. It was a fateful moment. Grasping the site's potential, O'Malley said he wanted to build his own stadium there. Mayor Poulson promised to do everything in his power to accommodate him. The two outlined a deal that, once formalized, would go to the L.A. City Council for approval.

O'Malley also needed approval from National League owners anxious about additional travel expenses. Visiting two teams on the West Coast would be a lot more economical than visiting one. Perhaps Horace Stoneham, who had been useful before, could serve O'Malley's purposes again.

It is widely believed that O'Malley and Stoneham worked in concert—or, in the alternative, that O'Malley duped Stoneham into going to California. In fact, the two owners, while supportive of each other's efforts, worked independently. O'Malley did this much: after his epiphany at Chavez Ravine, he and Poulson invited George Christopher, mayor of San Francisco, to Los Angeles and offered to introduce him to Stoneham, who fondly remembered San Francisco from his footloose youth.

Christopher accepted, and on May 10 was in Manhattan making Stoneham feel wanted, stacking his firm offer against New York's farfetched scheme to build a 110,000-seat coliseum on stilts above a West Side railroad yard. In exchange for a 35-year lease commitment, San Francisco would build Stoneham a new stadium with 10,000 parking spaces. Stoneham would receive concession rights and free office space in the stadium, as well as other lucrative perks, such as the right to sell advertising on the outfield wall. They sealed the deal in Stoneham's Polo Grounds office while the Giants, behind three hits from Willie Mays, beat the Dodgers (and, for the first time, their ex-ace Sal Maglie), 2–1.

The travel objection neutralized, National League owners at the end of May gave the Giants and Dodgers unanimous approval to move to California, so long as Stoneham and O'Malley formally committed themselves by October 1, 1957.

Emanuel Celler, the Brooklyn congressman whose House Anti-Trust Subcommittee previously chided major league owners for not venturing west of St. Louis, was hardly about to let the Giants and Dodgers leave for

California without embarrassment. He had both Stoneham and O'Malley subpoenaed for June 26. O'Malley testified first. Celler made him sit tight while New York City Council president Abe Stark, whose "hit sign, win suit" advertisement adorned the right field wall at Ebbets Field, stated plaintively that "it is my belief a franchise morally belongs to the people of a community. It is not the personal property of any individual to be removed at the slightest whim."

Celler then produced a chart showing team-by-team profits from 1952 through 1956. At $1,860,744 (nearly half a million dollars more than O'Malley spent to purchase the team) the Dodgers had the highest after-tax profit, a bare $3,000 more than Milwaukee but over $400,000 more than the supposedly filthy-rich Yankees. "I believe those figures are accurate, and I'm rather proud of them," an unfazed O'Malley acknowledged before insisting that the numbers represented a "modest" 13 percent annual return and that "if you'd take out the World Series profits, we'd finish in the red."

What Celler really wanted to know was whether the Dodgers were moving to Los Angeles. He posed the question repeatedly, and O'Malley, speaking without notes or documents, proved the ultimate dodger by giving lawyer-like, noncommittal responses. Celler wasn't fooled, concluding "there's really no question about it. I think Mister O'Malley has his mind made up and will go west. It's all cut and dried." But the grilling continued for an hour past Congress's usual adjournment time, forcing Stoneham to come back in July.

The Giant owner got off easily compared to O'Malley, the subcommittee accepting his argument that New York no longer could support three teams because "the baseball population has been moving outside of the city." (The same chart that showed the Dodgers leading all 16 teams in profitability put the Giants seventh, at a genuinely modest $342,602 over five years.) Stoneham also insisted he was acting independently of O'Malley and intended to move to San Francisco even if the Dodgers remained in Brooklyn.

He was true to his word. On August 19, 1957, with no assurance that the L.A. City Council would ratify the O'Malley-Poulson deal — and still needing territorial rights to San Francisco, controlled by the Red Sox — he convened his board of directors and proposed to notify the National League of the Giants' intention to play in California in 1958. There was little drama. The board consisted almost entirely of relatives and cronies, and voted 8–1 in favor. (M. Donald Grant, who later helped found the Mets, cast the sole nay.) Asked by reporters how he would explain the move to young Giant fans, Stoneham said, "We're sorry to disappoint the kids of

New York, but we didn't see many of their parents out there at the Polo Grounds in recent years."

Blanche McGraw spoke for all Giant fans when she lamented, "I can't conceive that I'll never again watch the Giants play at the Polo Grounds. I don't know what I will do with myself. The Giants have been my life." Flanked by Rube Marquard, Carl Hubbell, Hal Schumacher, and Monte Irvin, among others, she saw the Giants play their final game in New York, a 9–1 loss to the Pittsburgh Pirates on September 27, 1957, in front of just 11,606 paying customers. Officially designated the last fan to leave, she watched as thousands of ruffians tore up the park and chanted for Horace Stoneham — in order to hang him.

With the Giants gone, New York desperately sought to keep the Dodgers. But thanks to Robert Moses, chances of reconciling with O'Malley were poor. First Moses called O'Malley's congressional testimony "a smog of controversy, evasion, haggling, and penny-pinching." Then, in a *Sports Illustrated* article, he wrote, "Let me now in my own words give you briefly what I believe will be the conclusions as to the Atlantic terminal site. It won't happen." For good measure he threw in a few *ad hominem* barbs: "For years, Walter and his chums have kept us dizzy and confused," and "Walter honestly believes that he in himself constitutes a public purpose."

O'Malley got another shove out of town from the *New York Daily News'* Dick Young, the most powerful sports columnist in Brooklyn once the *Eagle* folded. For years Young and O'Malley's top man, Buzzie Bavasi, carried on a journalistically unholy relationship wherein Young received scoops from the front office in exchange for kid-glove treatment of the management. But faced with losing his chief subject matter — maybe even his livelihood — Young turned his vitriolic pen on O'Malley (and, by implication, Bavasi):

> There was a time when Brooklyn meant much to O'Malley, when he moved among the high politicos who were part of his family life in his youth. But times have changed, and so has O'Malley. He has shown signs of developing a king complex. The fine organization he once created has, by his own design, become shot through with yes men.

Young claimed that O'Malley's real motive for moving west wasn't money, but "the attention and flattery that Coast sycophants are sure to heap upon him."

Nelson Rockefeller, one of the richest men in the world and an aspiring gubernatorial candidate, proposed that the city spend $8 million to condemn the site at Flatbush and Atlantic Avenues, sell it to him for $2

million, and let him lease it free to the Dodgers for 20 years, allowing
O'Malley to build his own park there. The city balked at subsidizing a
Midas like Rockefeller to the tune of $6 million, and O'Malley didn't trust
him enough to be his tenant. On September 21, this last idea to keep Brooklyn's beloved Bums was declared dead.

Then the Los Angeles City Council failed to approve the O'Malley-
Poulson pact by the National League's October 1 deadline. Before Brooklyn fans could dream of a reprieve, however, the league approved an
extension. The contract was ratified on October 7, and the next day the
Dodgers' Red Patterson read the following statement to reporters at Manhattan's Waldorf-Astoria Hotel:

> In view of the action of the Los Angeles City Council yesterday and in accor-
> dance with the resolution of the National League made October 1, the stock-
> holders and directors of the Brooklyn Baseball Club have today met and
> unanimously agreed that necessary steps be taken to draft the Los Angeles
> territory.

And that was it. Protests of loyal fans notwithstanding, the Dodgers
were gone.

Combined with the postwar demographic shift and the demise of the
Eagle, the loss of the Dodgers killed the old Brooklyn so fondly remembered by its millions of descendants. Because O'Malley's was the final blow,
he often receives blame for the murder. Jack Newfield told of the time he
and fellow Brooklyn scribe Pete Hamill conceived of an article about the
10 worst human beings who ever lived. They each wrote down their worst
three, and when they compared, they found they had put down the same
names in identical order: Hitler, Stalin, and O'Malley.

A different perspective came from Neil Sullivan, a City University of
New York business professor whose 1987 *The Dodgers Move West* remains
the definitive treatment of the subject. Concluded he: "The perception of
Walter O'Malley as a villain not only evades the real causes of the Dodgers'
move; it also obscures the achievements of the franchise in Los Angeles
for which O'Malley merits inclusion in the Hall of Fame."

Yes, O'Malley took a risk to nationalize the national pastime. And no,
he wasn't responsible for the poverty and racial strife that cursed Brooklyn for years until liberalized immigration and spillover from a Manhattan real estate boom began to revitalize it. But as wildly as they overstated
their case, Newfield and Hamill came closer to the truth. The real cause
of the Dodgers' move wasn't Robert Moses' intransigence, the Braves' success in Milwaukee (which curdled so quickly the franchise relocated again

Walter O'Malley (right) receives the key to Los Angeles. A popular joke in Los Angeles had a newly deceased fan asking whether the portly, cigar-toting man by the Pearly Gates was O'Malley, and Saint Peter answering, "No, that's God. He just thinks he's Walter O'Malley!" (Transcendental Graphics)

after 1965), or the complacent belief that the Dodgers would never leave. It was Walter O'Malley's greed. Had he stayed in New York, what's the worst that would have happened? He'd have endured some rough transition years in the late '50s and early '60s, but by 1964 at the latest he'd have moved into a municipally owned stadium in Queens, broadened his fan base to include all of western Long Island, and fared at least as well as the Mets, which is to say very well indeed. But he couldn't wait that long. Nor was he content with a huge pot of gold when he had a chance at a bottomless one.

So he left. In the process he set an example that baseball's oligarchs have followed ever since: warn of fiscal catastrophe even though it isn't true, then threaten a host city with abandonment if it doesn't turn over every last taxpayer nickel. It's a tribute to O'Malley's genius that half a century after he invented it, his colleagues have yet to improve on the formula. But it has cost baseball dearly, bitterly disillusioning fans not just in Brooklyn, but across America. Nowadays everybody assumes the game is about greed — and that's hardly a legacy worth enshrining at Cooperstown.

The rivalry ranked a distant second — maybe a distant tenth — to money as the motive for the shift west. But by moving to San Francisco and Los Angeles, California's competing cultural centers, Stoneham and O'Malley assured its survival. In the words of San Francisco native and Hall of Fame shortstop Joe Cronin, "You can talk all you want about Brooklyn and New York, Minneapolis and St. Paul, Dallas and Fort Worth, but there are no two cities in America where the people want to beat each other's brains out more than in San Francisco and Los Angeles." (As general manager of the Red Sox, Cronin altruistically swapped Boston's Pacific Coast League team, the San Francisco Seals, for Stoneham's Minneapolis farm club to give the Giants territorial rights to the Bay Area.)

The first Europeans to see the hilly, windy peninsula later called San Francisco belonged to a Spanish expedition led by Gaspar de Portola in 1769. A ship captained by Juan Manuel de Ayala sailed into the magnificent bay in 1775, and the next year, just a few months after the Declaration of Independence was signed, the Spanish established a military base (the Presidio) and a religious outpost (Mission Dolores) by the Golden Gate. As elsewhere in California, they "civilized" the docile Native Americans, killing half of them in the process. When Mexico declared its independence from Spain in 1821, the new rulers parceled the surrounding countryside into cattle ranches and tolerated the establishment of a tiny settlement, Yerba Buena, along the shores of San Francisco Bay.

By 1835 word of the bay's potential as a harbor reached the rest of the continent, and the United States made annexation of the region a top priority. On June 3, 1846, less than a month after Congress declared war against Mexico, the warship *Portsmouth* claimed Yerba Buena for America. On January 30, 1847, the village was renamed San Francisco.

A scant 800 people of European descent lived in San Francisco when gold was found in the Sierra foothills. Between January and December 1849 San Francisco grew more than 25-fold, supplying miners with everything they needed. The discovery of silver in western Nevada (the Comstock Lode) led to another boom. San Francisco became the largest city on the West Coast, a freewheeling frontier town bursting with vice, corruption, and wealth.

It was also an early hotbed of the New York Game, source of the term "sandlot" and the first place "Casey at the Bat" saw print. Its first organized team, the Eagle Baseball Club, lost to the Cincinnati Red Stockings during that famous club's 1869 tour. In 1880 San Francisco gave birth to the California League, whose four franchises all operated out of the City by the Bay. Two of the teams moved to Oakland and Sacramento in 1886, and gradually the fledgling circuit evolved into the Pacific Coast League. San Francisco sent a steady stream of players to the majors, including Harry Heilmann, George "Highpockets" Kelly, Dutch Ruether, Lefty O'Doul, Tony Lazzeri, Frank Crosetti, Eddie Joost, the aforementioned Cronin, and the DiMaggio brothers.

With the wharves propelling its economy, by 1900 San Francisco ranked ninth among American cities in population. Six years later an earthquake and fire leveled it, but so indomitable was the local spirit that by 1910 San Franciscans not only had rebuilt, but had staged a World's Fair and added another 75,000 to their number. By 1930, 634,000 souls called the 50-square-mile city their home.

San Francisco was an elegant, sophisticated place, with a European-style civic center, an opera and symphony, and a middle class that dressed up to shop at Union Square. But it was also a thoroughly unionized blue-collar town with tough Irish, Italian, Mexican, and Chinese neighborhoods. In May 1934 the longshoremen went on strike to replace the company union with a real one. The corporations, losing a million dollars a day, tried to break the strike on July 5, touching off a riot that killed two and injured more than 100. That led to a general strike. The unions shut down San Francisco so completely that after four days the corporations capitulated. The Strike of '34 helped establish San Francisco as a choice destination for left-leaning rebels, so that by the time Mayor Christopher concluded negotiations with Horace Stoneham, old-line couples out for dinner in North Beach were routinely rubbing elbows with verse-spouting beatniks.

Not so in Los Angeles. Though many of Europe's serious artists—including Thomas Mann, Bertolt Brecht, Aldous Huxley, Igor Stravinsky, and Arnold Schoenberg—chose it as their refuge from fascism, communism, and war, and many of its resident artists, from Nathanael West to Raymond Chandler to Eric Dolphy, had well-developed dark sides, the City of Angels spurned high culture for popular entertainment.

The desert basin that later became Los Angeles was scouted by Gaspar de Portola during the same 1769 expedition that took him 400 miles up the coast to San Francisco. On September 4, 1781, 44 Mexican emigrants, all but two of Native American, African, or mestizo descent, founded the town of El Pueblo de la Reyna de los Angeles (Town of the Queen of Angels), called El Pueblo for short. It had grown to over a thousand souls but was just another spot on the map when Captain John C. Fremont and Commodore Robert Stockton claimed it for the United States on August 13, 1846. Their heavy-handed rule led to a revolt, but with help from Colonel Stephen Kearny they retook the town for good on January 13, 1847.

In the 1880s Los Angeles began catching up with San Francisco. The Southern Pacific and Santa Fe railroads linked the blossoming burg to markets back east, to which it shipped oranges and other produce. Ambitious real estate barons touted the dry, balmy climate to retirees and invalids, and the population soared nearly five-fold in a decade. A sizable oil deposit was discovered in 1892, leading to another surge. By 1910 Los Angeles topped 300,000 residents, making it the 17th largest city in the nation. It built a port at San Pedro and began competing against San Francisco for shipping.

By 1920 Los Angeles became the largest city on the West Coast. It was San Francisco's polar opposite, sprawling rather than compact, Protestant rather than Catholic, reactionary rather than radical, commercial rather than cosmopolitan. Its exponential growth, fueled by the nascent movie, automobile, and aerospace industries, depended on keeping unions *out*. In 1910, two iron workers firebombed the rabidly right-wing *Los Angeles Times,* setting back the union cause in Southern California for a generation and freeing *Times* owner Otis Chandler to foment hostility toward other scapegoats: Mexicans, African Americans, Jews, and Asians. Whites-only homeowner associations, the Ku Klux Klan, and conspiracy fantasists like the John Birch Society flourished in the craftsman bungalows that typified Southland architecture (and provided yet another contrast to the Bay Area, with its stately Victorians).

To its legion of critics, L.A. was just a soulless conurbation: "19 suburbs in search of a metropolis," according to H. L. Mencken, "the ultimate segregation of the unfit," to Bertrand Russell. But soon, thanks largely to Hollywood films and the relentless publicity behind them, every national cliché about California — beaches, palm trees, sunglassed celebrities— was really about Los Angeles. Its glamorous image, along with the enormous success of its oil, water, land, and entertainment barons, infused its denizens with a blithe self-confidence impervious (even oblivious) to insult, doubt, and smog jokes.

That sunny disposition gave fog-shrouded San Franciscans conniptions. They had a New York sensibility yet a Brooklyn predicament, and thus readily embraced the Giant-Dodger rivalry. If they couldn't dominate Los Angeles in business, politics, or culture anymore, they could at least salvage some self-respect on the diamond.

Angelenos loved baseball, supporting two Pacific Coast League teams, the Angels and Hollywood Stars. They fell hard for the Dodgers. Their connection to the team went back to the '20s and Glendale product Babe Herman. Jackie Robinson grew up in Pasadena and attended UCLA. Two of the Dodgers moving west, Duke Snider and square-jawed, 6'6" Don Drysdale (diligently learning the art of the brushback from Sal Maglie) hailed from Compton and Van Nuys respectively. But in keeping with the attitude that so vexed San Franciscans, Angelenos couldn't be goosed into hating the Giants except at extreme moments. No fan of the *Los Angeles* Dodgers would ever resolve a spat over the rivalry with blazing pistols.

And so baseball's best rivalry moved 3,000 miles west — and got even better.

PART V

1958–1971: Might Versus Mites

	Giants	Dodgers
Where They Played	Seals Stadium, 1958–59 Candlestick Park, 1960–71	Memorial Coliseum, 1958–61 Dodger Stadium, 1962–71
Owners	Horace Stoneham	Walter O'Malley
Managers	Bill Rigney, 1958–60 Tom Sheehan, 1960 Alvin Dark, 1961–64 Herman Franks, 1965–68 Clyde King, 1969–70 Charlie Fox, 1970–71	Walter Alston
Best Players	Willie Mays, Orlando Cepeda, Willie McCovey, Juan Marichal	Sandy Koufax, Don Drysdale, Maury Wills, Don Sutton
Wore Both Uniforms but Shouldn't Have	Juan Marichal	Duke Snider
Division Championships, League Championships, **World Championships**	1962, *1971*	**1959, 1963, 1965,** 1966
Won-Lost vs. Each Other	147–124 (.542)	124–147 (.458)
Won-Lost vs. Rest of League	1,094–873 (.556)	1,089–880 (.553)

Although the postwar period is widely considered the rivalry's best — a perception reinforced by countless nostalgic tomes celebrating the golden age of New York baseball — the 14-year span following the move

151

to California was even better. The teams consistently faced each other with a pennant on the line. They represented not just competing cities, but competing philosophies of baseball. And the fans turned out in droves: in 1966 the 18 games between the Giants and Dodgers drew more than *all* home games for the Chicago Cubs or Cincinnati Reds.

Only if you go by that great intangible, passion, can you argue that the rivalry was better in the late '40s and early '50s. Reminisced Giant outfielder Jackie Brandt, "It was a real rivalry in New York with the Dodgers because of the fans, they made it a rivalry. They hated each other. They fought and threw bottles, and yelled and screamed. They didn't do that in L.A. and San Francisco. They just went out and watched the ballgames. It was just, 'Let's beat 'em.' In New York it was, 'Let's *kill* 'em.'"

Perhaps so. But California's "laid-back" ambiance has often been mistaken for a lack of intensity. The rivalry quickly gripped both cities, especially the first few years. "We learned to hate the Dodgers before we learned to hate the Russians," recalled a Bay Area resident who was in grade school when the teams moved west. Entertainer Danny Kaye, a Brooklyn native and Dodger fan, recorded the "D-o-d-g-e-r-s Song" ("Oh, Really? No, O'Malley"), a patter song describing a made-up game between the teams. It became a novelty hit in Los Angeles *and* San Francisco.

And if you measure intensity by numbers, especially those with dollar signs in front of them, Californians took the rivalry to unprecedented heights. The Giants' home attendance their first dozen years in San Francisco averaged 340,000 more than their last dozen years in New York — which was nothing compared to the Dodgers, who drew an average of 837,000 more fans per season. Nothing did more to swell the gate than games against each other. On a per-game basis, Dodger attendance went up 59 percent overall in Los Angeles, but nearly 74 percent for Giant games. And had the Giants played their first two seasons in a larger venue, their per-game average against the Dodgers in San Francisco would have exceeded their per-game average at the Polo Grounds:

Home Attendance	1946–57 vs. Other Teams	1946–57 vs. Rival	1958–69 vs. Other Teams	1958–69 vs. Rival
Giants	10,808/game	30,486/game	15,788/game	29,296/game
Dodgers	15,643/game	23,326/game	24,877/game	40,474/game

It helped that *five times* over this period the Giants and Dodgers battled for the pennant into the final week of the season. It would have been six, but by knocking each other off over the last two weeks of 1969 they let the Atlanta Braves streak past them both.

The introduction of major league baseball on the West Coast coincided with a growing imbalance between the host cities. In 1960 Los Angeles became the country's third largest metropolis. Culturally it loomed larger still. Long the nation's film capital, it lured to its palm-shaded studios a hefty chunk of the television industry (yet another steal from New York). Its popular music, exemplified by the Beach Boys and folk-rock bands like Crosby Stills & Nash, eclipsed the hit factories of Nashville, New Orleans, and Detroit. Its tacky, freeway-fed sprawl increasingly provided the model for a suburbanizing society, while gaudy new skyscrapers downtown and on Wilshire Boulevard heralded its arrival as a corporate capital. Favorite sons Richard Nixon and Ronald Reagan garnered control of the Republican Party, with profound implications for the country's political zeitgeist. Los Angeles even had the era's first full-scale race riot.

All of this San Franciscans could stand so long as they retained superiority in high culture and trade. Ranking their own town with Paris and Venice, they dismissed L.A. as a Des Moines with movie stars. "How can a city go on growing out and out without ever growing up?" needled the *San Francisco Chronicle's* star columnist, Herb Caen. But in the '60s Los Angeles dealt San Francisco's patrician class a lasting blow by opening a first-class performing arts center on Grand Avenue. This after L.A. set back San Francisco's unionized, well-paid, blue-collar workforce by becoming the largest American port (San Pedro and Long Beach combined) on the West Coast.

The *Los Angeles Times* dispatched columnist Paul Coates to find out why San Francisco reacted so gracelessly to L.A.'s rising fortune — or, as Coates put it, why it had "a tolerant attitude towards almost everything except, of course, us." Noting the City by the Bay's high suicide and alcoholism rates, he concluded that it "has become more a museum than a metropolis. It is living on memories. And wistfully stroking the antimacassars of another era. If it doesn't snap out of it, San Francisco, I fear, is in real danger of becoming the Knott's Berry Farm of the north."

Coates was premature. Over the next few years artists, activists, and hippies revitalized San Francisco, giving early and ample nourishment to the subcultures that brought America environmentalism, feminism, gay rights, and Deadheads. But over the long run he was correct, as tourism gradually became San Francisco's chief industry. Acknowledged a somber Caen a few years later:

> In many ways, this is a city of losers. Maybe that's why we have so many more saloons than churches; we figure our prayers may never be answered, but a couple of stiff shots will get us through the day. The natives have always been kind to panhandling bums; they know if they hadn't got a lucky break

somewhere along the line, they'd be standing there with their hand out, too. They are perversely aware of the cirrhosis and bridge-jumping rate — and of the thin line that constantly separates them from contracting the former and performing the latter.

Caen concluded, "The Giants were the perfect baseball team for San Francisco. They couldn't win for losing in New York, and were going broke. Now they are going broke here."

But the Giants' woes didn't begin until late in this period, when the American League's Athletics moved to Oakland. Until then the team prospered — never as much as the Dodgers, but enough to make Horace Stoneham glad he'd accepted Mayor Christopher's offer. And even as attendance dropped, one team still filled Candlestick Park: the Dodgers, personification of the only West Coast city San Francisco couldn't outshine. The farther behind Los Angeles left them in the real world, the more San Franciscans needed to beat the Dodgers. And the Giants obliged, dominating head-to-head competition.

The teams played brands of ball wholly at odds with their civic stereotypes. Sophisticated San Francisco brought up Orlando Cepeda and Willie McCovey to join Willie Mays in terrorizing the league with the game's crudest weapon, the homer; now that Durocher was gone Stoneham could again indulge his fetish for sluggers. Fans sang along to "Bye-Bye Baby," a chirpy tribute to announcer Russ Hodges' trademark home run call. (It's still played on TV broadcasts after an inning in which a Giant homers.) Meanwhile, shallow Los Angeles formulated a heady, speed-based offense hearkening to the deadball era, a transformation accentuated by the move to pitcher-friendly Dodger Stadium in 1962. "Go, go, go!" fans rhythmically chanted whenever Maury Wills reached base. Their first eight years in California the Dodgers led the league in steals. Over that same stretch the Giants, despite playing in wind-blown venues, never finished lower than fourth in homers.

The Giants were a marvel of consistency, posting a winning record every year, although five consecutive second-place finishes in the late '60s earned them a reputation as perennial bridesmaids. The Dodgers may not have contended every year, but they won four pennants to the Giants' one. And though Dodger fans may not have been as savvy as San Franciscans, their sheer numbers made the Dodgers the richest franchise in baseball and Walter O'Malley the most powerful man in the game.

Still, Jackie Brandt was not alone. Many of his colleagues felt something went out of the rivalry once it moved west. "When people ask me to explain how fierce it was," said Don Drysdale, recalling his years in Brooklyn, "I just tell them to imagine the wildest emotion possible between two ballclubs, and triple it. It's never been like that between the Dodgers and Giants on the West Coast, even at its best." Noted *San Francisco Chronicle* writer Bob Stevens, "I talked to McCovey, Alston, Newcombe, Junior Gilliam on the future of the Dodger and Giant rivalry and my conclusion was clear: it's gone."

There's no arguing that during this period beanball wars diminished and cross-team friendships formed, including one between Willie Mays and John Roseboro that may have averted a riot. But given the teams' extended, high-level parity and the hordes of fans who came to see them play, the sense of loss among players and writers can be seen largely as nostalgia — or an inability to recognize intensity in subtler shades.

11. 1958: "We Had People Picking Up Money with Shovels"

While financing and construction of their promised ballpark crept forward, the Giants took up residence in Seals Stadium, situated between the Mission District and Potrero Hill at 16th Street and Bryant Avenue. Opened in 1931 for the Pacific Coast League's San Francisco Seals and Missions, it seated 18,500 until the capacity was upgraded to 22,900 for the Giants. A single-level grandstand extended to the right field corner and most of the way down the left field line, with bleachers behind the right field fence. A huge Longines clock loomed behind the wall in left center. The wall itself angled around in the shape of a diamond top, 365 feet from home plate to the left field corner, 404 to the diamond's left crown, 415 to the diamond's right crown, and 355 to the right field corner. (These distances were moved in a few feet for 1959.) Advertising lined the left field wall. There was no warning track.

Seats were close to the action, providing an intimate feel not even the steady right-to-left-field breeze could diminish. "It had a warmth and a sense of community not unlike Wrigley Field or Fenway Park," said Orlando Cepeda, whose quick adoption by San Franciscans stemmed in part from his accessibility to fans at first base.

Manager Bill Rigney, a Bay Area native, took advantage of the break with New York to give the team a fresh identity, putting three rookies in the opening-day lineup: outfielder Willie Kirkland, third baseman Jim Davenport, and first baseman Cepeda. Catcher Bob Schmidt debuted in the second game, and Felipe Alou, first of the famous trio of brothers,

156

arrived in early June. "It seemed that a new young player was joining the club all the time," Rigney noted. And not just as a fill-in. Willie Mc-Covey came up in 1959. High-kicking Juan Marichal, the best Giant pitcher since Carl Hubbell, joined the team in 1960.

Much of the young talent hailed from Latin America. The Giants were the first team to system-atically pursue Latino ballplayers, recruiting in Puerto Rico, the Dominican Republic, and Cuba long before other teams, still com-ing to terms with the presence of African Americans, thought to load themselves with talent from south of the border. Back in

Orlando Cepeda. As a nine-year-old in 1947 he shook Jackie Robinson's hand and was told by his father, "If you play in the majors one day, it will be because of him." (Transcendental Graphics)

Manhattan, Horace Stoneham had rented the Polo Grounds to the Negro League's New York Cubans. When the Cubans went out of business, the Giants hired owner Alex Pompez to scout the Caribbean. The well-con-nected Pompez soon had friends steering players into the Giant farm sys-tem. Pedro Zorrilla, owner of Puerto Rico's Santurce Crabbers, signed Cepeda as a 17-year-old in 1955.

Cepeda's hitting and vivaciousness made him San Francisco's first "home-grown" favorite. Herb Caen called him "The Copacabana Kid" for his nightclub hopping. Pitcher Johnny Antonelli dubbed him "Cha-Cha" for his love of dance music. But to the general public he was "The Baby

Bull," son of storied Puerto Rican slugger Perucho "The Bull" Cepeda. The free-swinging first baseman wasn't nearly so popular with the Giant front office. He was more than half the player Willie Mays was, he complained, so why did he make only half the money? His salary holdouts became yearly rituals.

Other than those who lost their jobs to rookies like Cepeda, only one Giant seriously suffered from the move west: Willie Mays. "Mays was the symbol of New York being thrust down San Francisco's throat," was how biographer Charles Einstein explained a reception so chilly that at the end of 1958 a *San Francisco Examiner* poll with 30,000 respondents named Cepeda the team's most valuable player by a landslide despite Mays's .347 average, 29 homers, 96 RBIs, and league-leading 121 runs and 31 steals.

San Franciscans considered hometown product Joe DiMaggio, who had played for the Seals, the greatest center fielder of all time, and could not imagine, let alone admit, that someone played the position better. The new home parks afforded Mays little opportunity to make his case. Center field in the Polo Grounds went on forever, enabling him to flag down long flies and return them with his howitzer arm. At Seals Stadium he ran out of room at 410 feet (400 in 1959) and at Candlestick he never had more than 420 feet. Had Vic Wertz hit his famous 1954 drive in San Francisco we'd never have had that marvelous clip of The Catch, because the ball would have been so far gone Mays would have just turned around to see how far beyond the fence it landed. "I remember many an occasion where balls went over the center field fence, and Willie would come back to me and say, 'I just didn't have any room,'" a sympathetic Rigney recalled.

To the ignominy of a region that considered itself so progressive, Mays was also the victim of racial discrimination. He tried to buy a house in the tony Sherwood Forest district just west of Mount Davidson, but neighbors pressured the seller into refusing the offer. Mayor Christopher was so appalled that he offered Mays space in his own house. When Mays finally did purchase the home, someone threw a brick through his living room window.

"The Dodgers were not a hard sell in Los Angeles. Even before we left Brooklyn we began to sell season tickets. So many checks came in we actually had people picking up money with shovels," gloated general manager Buzzie Bavasi, which would lead one to believe the Dodgers enjoyed a glorious transition west. Not so.

The team owned Wrigley Field in South Central Los Angeles, but Walter O'Malley didn't want to use it. It seated only 23,000, and "Walter was leery of playing in Wrigley Field for fear that people would associate a minor league park with a minor league operation," said Bavasi. It could also be that O'Malley didn't want to play in a neighborhood reminiscent of Flatbush. Instead the Dodgers leased the municipally owned Coliseum, which wasn't in a great neighborhood either but at least was on the other side of the Harbor Freeway from Watts.

Opened in 1923, the 93,000-seat Coliseum was a long, narrow oval configured for track meets and football games. A baseball diamond wouldn't fit at either end, so it was laid along the edge of one side, leading to absurd proportions. (And sight lines: some seats were 700 feet from home plate.) The third base foul area was huge while the first base side had hardly any. Worse still, the fence from center to right, a wire mesh job, stood well over 400 feet from home plate, the left field fence a claustrophobic 251. To keep at least a few fly balls to left in play the Dodgers installed a 42-foot screen, but that hardly mollified the Dodger pitchers. After watching media people slam balls over the screen in an exhibition game, Don Drysdale sputtered, "If a bunch of writers and broadcasters can hit home runs over that thing, how am I supposed to get out major league hitters like Aaron and Banks?" All four years the Dodgers played in the Coliseum they led the league in homers allowed at home, while on the road they ranked among the stingiest. The pitching staff's ERA swelled more than a point in 1958 to a league-worst 4.47, even though it led the majors in strikeouts and double plays.

An even bigger blow to the pitchers—to the whole team—came on January 28, 1958, when catcher Roy Campanella lost control of the car he was driving and skidded into a telephone pole, crushing his fifth and sixth vertebrae. Doctors initially professed optimism, but it soon became clear Campy was paralyzed for life. "It was mind-boggling, learning that this robust guy with all that personality and energy never would be able to walk again," said Drysdale.

Although in John Roseboro the Dodgers had a solid replacement, the young hurlers could have used the easygoing Campy's counsel in dealing with their new park's idiosyncrasies. Instead they let frustration get the better of them. "His best pitch was a fastball that he threw in on a right-handed batter," said manager Walter Alston of the 21-year-old Drysdale. "He'd break half a dozen bats a game with that pitch. But when we first got out there, he didn't want to throw it. So it took him a while to adjust."

Unlike the Giants, the Dodgers stayed with their old lineup. They'd finished first in 1955, first in 1956, and a respectable if distant third in 1957, so they didn't feel as much need to clean house. Another consideration: they had moved to the capital of celebrity culture, and there weren't many names in baseball bigger than the Boys of Summer. "The folks out here, by and large, had never seen our great name players in action and we wanted to give them that opportunity," said O'Malley. Never mind that Reese, Furillo, Newcombe, and Erskine were on their last legs; that Hodges, at 34, was beginning to deteriorate; and that Snider faced in the Coliseum's distant right field fence the end of his days as a prolific slugger. Only after the embarrassment of a seventh-place finish would the Dodgers retool their lineup — and style of play.

As if these tribulations weren't enough, the Dodgers nearly lost the chance to build their own stadium. The deal the City Council approved to bring the Dodgers to Los Angeles gave Walter O'Malley 315 acres in Chavez Ravine, $2 million to level the land, nearly $3 million in access roads to nearby freeways, and a half-interest in any mineral (read that oil) wealth uncovered. In exchange O'Malley gave the city Wrigley Field (nine acres valued at $4 million) and agreed to build and maintain a public recreation area by the new stadium. But opponents launched a successful petition drive to force a referendum on the contract in the June 3, 1958, election.

When the Dodgers first polled the public on Proposition B, which would ratify the Chavez Ravine deal, they found 67 percent support. Then the season began, the aging Dodgers fell into the basement, and support dropped to 37 percent. A dismayed civic establishment beat the drum hard for a yes vote.

Opponents formed the Citizens Committee to Save Chavez Ravine, financed to a considerable degree by John A. Smith, who with his brother C. Arnholt owned the Pacific Coast League's San Diego Padres. Success for major league baseball in Los Angeles would diminish Smith's fan base and, more ominously, lead to more franchises on the West Coast, perhaps even in San Diego. A segment of the real estate industry also resisted the measure, preferring the land be subdivided into housing tracts or (one suggestion) cemetery plots. But the most potent opposition came from fiscal conservatives who saw the deal as a giveaway. Many were especially upset by the clause entitling O'Malley to half the revenue from oil deposits. Their cause was articulated by council members Pat McGee and John Holland, who so outraged the *Los Angeles Times* that it often referred to them not by name but by such smeary epithets as "a minority/splinter group in our City Council." McGee and Holland weren't against the Dodgers; they just wanted more in return for Chavez Ravine.

One element never heard from was the Chicano community living in the Ravine. In those days Mexican Americans were all but invisible to the Los Angeles establishment, which eagerly adopted O'Malley's characterization of the Ravine as a garbage dump with "old dirt roads. Old tin cans and junk." The *Los Angeles Times'* June 1, 1958, endorsement of Proposition

B said the area "requires little displacement of anything except irregularities of terrain."

But 40 years later, under less partisan management, the *Times* admitted that a thousand people lived in three towns in the Ravine until the city condemned the land through eminent domain in 1949. The City Housing Authority, to whom title was transferred, let the tract sit before deeding it back to the city in 1955 — just in time to offer it to O'Malley. The 20 families who never left, denigrated as squatters, had in some cases legally occupied the Ravine for decades.

As the June 3 election neared, Dodger supporters claimed that a no vote would force the team to move again, a perception abetted by National League president Warren Giles's warning on May 22 that "if the vote is refuted by the citizens of Los Angeles, it will be my personal recommendation to our league that we take immediate steps to study ways and means of relocating the franchise in another city." The *Times* editorial board argued that a downtown ballpark would unify the "geographical bundle of self-centered sections each fighting with the others for the lion's share of the revenues and improvements that belong to all." No doubt this argument would have earned raspberries in Brooklyn, whose own distinct neighborhoods had been unified by the Dodgers until Los Angeles spirited the team away.

The last Dodger poll showed the vote too close to call. Buzzie Bavasi and Red Patterson secretly scouted other places to play — secretly because if word got out it could devastate the Dodgers' electoral prospects. "Now Red, don't forget, don't tell anybody who we are. Just say we're looking at the Rose Bowl as a possible site for a concert or something," Bavasi cautioned as the two arrived in Pasadena. Inside the stadium they unfurled a tape measure, and Patterson paced to the grandstand. "Hey, Buzzie, it's 352 feet to right field!" he shouted for all the workers to hear.

On the Sunday before the election, Dodger supporters sponsored a five-hour telethon hosted by Joe E. Brown and featuring, among others, comedians Jack Benny, George Burns, Jerry Lewis, and Danny Thomas; actresses Debbie Reynolds and Laraine Day (Leo Durocher's ex-wife); former Dodgers Chuck Connors and Babe Herman; and retired umpire Beans Reardon.

The stadium would be privately financed and cost taxpayers nothing, they said, in contrast to San Francisco's shelling out millions for the Giants' new digs. Dodger Stadium would generate $300,000 a year in tax revenues. The city would gain nine acres in South Central plus a new recreation area in Chavez Ravine worth $500,000. Giving a bit of rhetorical ground to gain more, actor Ronald Reagan made the boldest argument for ceding government assets to wealthy private interests. "Chavez Ravine has been sitting there in the heart of Los Angeles for years and nothing was done with it. Now that a baseball team is to have it, it's worth a lot of money, we are told. Sure, Walter O'Malley got a good deal when he was offered Chavez Ravine as a site for his ballpark. Any deal to be good must be fair to both sides, not just to one."

"I think we were saved by the power of television," Bavasi admitted, as Proposition B passed by fewer than 25,000 votes (52 percent). Bavasi then crowed that the deal really *was* a giveaway, likening it to the purchase of Manhattan from the Indians. "It was the kind of deal of which legends are built," he boasted. In 1999 the ballpark in Chavez Ravine, constructed for about $15 million, had an assessed value of nearly $200 million.

The Giants and Dodgers inaugurated major league play on the West Coast with three games in San Francisco starting on Tuesday, April 15, 1958, and three in Los Angeles starting on Friday, April 18.

Opening day festivities began with a parade through downtown San Francisco. Inside Seals Stadium the Giants were introduced individually, with Willie Mays drawing the most applause. Then the Dodgers were introduced, and Pee Wee Reese, Duke Snider, and Gil Hodges were also loudly welcomed. After the band played "The Star-Spangled Banner," San Francisco's Mayor Christopher strolled to the mound to throw the ceremonial first pitch to bat-wielding Los Angeles Mayor Poulson. Christopher's first pitch nearly hit Poulson on the head. Poulson hung in there as Christopher threw two behind him and another that bounced to the plate. Finally San Francisco's mayor threw a good one and Poulson hit a dribbler. He sprinted out of the batter's box — toward third base. Before he got there he ran out of breath and stopped, though "not until after he passed the photographers," a *Los Angeles Times* writer drolly observed.

At 1:34 p.m. Ruben Gomez, the Giants' biggest winner the season before, threw the first pitch to Dodger center fielder Gino Cimoli, a San Francisco native. Cimoli ran the count to three and two before striking out. For Gomez that was just the start. He stymied the Dodgers with his screwball, allowing six singles and six walks but only one runner as far as third base. "He had us on our ears all day," commended Duke Snider. Don Drysdale, meanwhile, proved little mystery to the Giants, yielding two runs in the third and four more in the fourth. Daryl Spencer hit the first West Coast homer, for which he received a standing ovation. Mays lashed a single with the bases loaded to bring home a pair. Cepeda hit his first big league homer, a solo shot to right center. The Giants wound up winning 8–0.

WE MURDER THE BUMS roared the headline in the next day's *San Francisco Chronicle.*

Back in New York, the Polo Grounds and Ebbets Field "were ghost ballparks, as deserted as graveyards in the bright sunshine of a beautiful warm baseball day," lamented James L. Kilgallen. About 150 New Yorkers, including Blanche McGraw, witnessed the Giants' debut in San Francisco. "So long as the Giants had to move, this was the only city for them," she said diplomatically, then kidded her host, "Horace, without those New York accents, how are people going to refer to them as the Jints?"

Other rivalry participants tried to be as gracious as Mrs. McGraw but failed. "Before the game I thought to myself, what am I doing in San Francisco?" admitted Pee Wee Reese, who hastily added, "once the action starts, you forget what town you're in." And while praising Ruben Gomez, manager Rigney slipped: "He had them Brooklyns in a hole early." Covering his mouth in embarrassment, he said, "It will take me a century to forget to say Brooklyn instead of Los Angeles, I guess. I can say San Francisco pretty good, though."

The next night the Dodgers got their revenge, clobbering the Giants 13–1 behind Johnny Podres, who struck out 11. Snider blasted a 425-foot homer into the wind's teeth. The only bad moment for the Dodgers came in the seventh, when Gino Cimoli was hit in the head by a pitch. "I thought you were dead," Drysdale later told Cimoli, who lay motionless for several seconds. Cimoli's father Abramo ran onto the field and helped carry him to the clubhouse. The outfielder wasn't seriously hurt; he played in the rubber game and homered in a 7–4 loss.

The teams headed south for the weekend series in Los Angeles. The parade down Broadway was so densely packed that at times the Dodger motorcade barely moved. A comely young woman in Dodger garb was seen riding a golden chariot pulled by a sweaty, grotesque figure in a Giant uniform. Mayor Poulson welcomed the Dodgers on the steps of City Hall, shoving a finger in New York's eye by telling O'Malley, "When you moved the Dodgers out here they said you were going out to the sticks. Well, Cabrillo discovered California before Hudson discovered Manhattan. So you're coming up in the world!" O'Malley compounded the insult by presenting Poulson with home plate from Ebbets Field.

The Giants hit 25 balls over the left field screen in batting practice. "Boy, oh boy, let's start playin' right now," salivated Hank Sauer, who smashed two homers in the game. At first sight of the Coliseum's distant right field fence Willie Mays yelled to Duke Snider, "They took the bat away from you. You're done, man."

The crowd of 78,672 set a record for a regular season National League contest. The fans cheered enthusiastically, especially for local boy Snider, whose single to center in the bottom of the third knocked in Jim Gilliam for the Dodgers' first Los Angeles run. Hodges' leaping snare of a Willie Kirkland liner in the fifth drew a chorus of *ahhs,* and in the bottom of the inning the fans spontaneously egged on a three-run rally with rhythmic clapping. In contrast to later Los Angeles crowds, hardly anyone left early, including those sitting so far away they needed binoculars and descriptions from radio broadcasters Vin Scully and Jerry Doggett to follow the action.

Scully replaced Red Barber as head Dodger broadcaster in 1954, but he didn't emerge from Barber's shadow until the move to Los Angeles, where his velvet tone perfectly suited the local sensibility. His knack for relating action and lore in erudite yet entertaining terms soon made him an institution. Even fans in the good seats brought radios to the ballpark, and Scully's voice could be heard echoing throughout the stands. He "singlehandedly taught our new fans in Southern California all about the Dodgers and the National League," said Drysdale. Dodger rooters voted him the team's most memorable personality in 1976.

Scully wasn't yet a popular icon on opening day of 1958, but the crowd was studded with people who were. California governor Goodwin Knight, running for the Senate, was mistakenly chased off the field by Red Patterson during pregame ceremonies and suffered further indignity when a helicopter buzzed the Coliseum with a streamer that read "Christopher for U.S. Senate," that Christopher being San Francisco's mayor, also in attendance. State attorney general Pat Brown, a San Franciscan vying to replace Knight as governor, proclaimed that if elected he'd fight to rename the Giants the Seals.

And then there were the entertainers: Gene Autry, Ray Bolger, Nat King Cole, John Ford, Tennessee Ernie Ford, Zsa Zsa Gabor, George Jessel, Danny Kaye ("I have priority rights on this whole deal because I was born in Brooklyn"), Burt Lancaster, Jack Lemmon, Groucho Marx, Gregory Peck, Edward G. Robinson, Jimmy Stewart, Danny Thomas. Back east the Giants had been Broadway's team. In California the Dodgers embarked on a similar romance with Hollywood that, unlike most relationships with roots in that town, improved with the years.

The home team went into the top of the ninth with a 6–4 lead, but starter Carl Erskine yielded a double off the screen to Jim Davenport and was replaced by Clem Labine. Kirkland blasted one deep to center over Cimoli's head. For a moment it looked as if Cimoli might catch the ball, so rookie Davenport watched over his shoulder. When the ball hit grass he raced for home — and missed third base. With horror Davenport realized what he'd done and thought to go back, but here came Kirkland steaming in with a triple, so he had no choice except to cross home plate. Hodges took the relay from Cimoli, tossed to third, and Davenport's run was canceled — the difference in a 6–5 Dodger win.

The Giants came back on Saturday to rip the Dodgers, 11–4. Gomez won again and Sauer, a resident of nearby Inglewood, poked his third homer over the left field screen. On Sunday Drysdale pitched for the first time with the screen behind him. "When I saw a Punch-and-Judy hitter stand at that plate with one eye on 'The Thing,' it obviously affected me. They could miss the ball and still get a home run," he scoffed. Second baseman Danny O'Connell missed the ball twice for home runs and shortstop Spencer missed for another as the Giants drubbed the Dodgers, 12–2.

The Giants took 16 of 22 from the Dodgers in 1958, which keyed their third-place finish; they went a blah 64–68 against the rest of the league. Cepeda was unanimously voted Rookie of the Year, and with more kids coming the Giants had reason to feel optimistic. The Dodgers finished seventh, their worst showing since 1944, but how discouraged could O'Malley have been considering they drew 1,845,556 customers, more than they ever did in Brooklyn? If he weren't financing his own ballpark he'd need backhoes, not shovels, to move his money around.

12. 1959: "It Gripped the Players as Well as the Stands"

Imagine if Willie McCovey, the embodiment of Giant power during this stage of the rivalry, had come up with the Dodgers. Imagine further if Maury Wills, poster boy for the Dodger gnat attack, had come up with the Giants. Would Dodger fans have sung themselves hoarse with choruses of "when the Dodgers come to town it's bye-bye baby?" And would Giant fans have set the ballpark reverberating with chants of "go, go, go?"

It could have happened.

The 6'4" McCovey, nicknamed "Stretch," was from Mobile, and like fellow Alabaman Willie Mays played baseball with the grownups by age 13. "Since the Dodgers' AA farm team was in Mobile, most everyone in that area grew up a Dodger fan," recalled McCovey. "The Dodgers used to send scouts down to Mobile at that time and they'd have tryout camps. They would spend a week down there with white guys and the last day of the camp, they'd bring in the black guys and look at them for about two hours. There were guys like Hank Aaron, Billy Williams, Cleon Jones and me at that camp. All those guys, and not one of them got signed."

Enter the Giants. When McCovey was 17 a Mobile bird dog contacted Alex Pompez, who arranged for McCovey to attend the same 1955 tryout at which Orlando Cepeda was signed. McCovey performed poorly, but the Giants took a chance on him. He made them into geniuses, advancing rapidly through the organization. In 1957, though, came a bump. "I was clocked as the fastest guy in the Giants farm system. But at Fort Worth one night I tagged up at third base and slid into home plate and my spikes got turned up and twisted." His knee was operated on in January 1958. His speed disappeared.

But he could still hit. Promoted to Phoenix in the Pacific Coast League, he batted .319. The Giants already had a .300-hitting rookie at first base in Cepeda, so they sent McCovey to Phoenix again in 1959. He was hitting .372 with 29 home runs in 349 at-bats when they decided they couldn't keep him down any longer. He debuted at Seals Stadium against Philadelphia's Robin Roberts and went four-for-four with two triples, three runs, and two RBIs. He finished the season at .354 with 13 homers in 192 at-bats and became the second straight Giant unanimously voted Rookie of the Year.

Maury Wills grew up in Washington, D.C. He didn't care for base-ball until Jackie Robinson broke in, whereupon he took up pitching, averaging 15 strikeouts a game in high school. He attended a cattle-call tryout at Griffith Stadium in 1950, when he was 17, and struck out every batter he faced. That earned him an invitation to a more intensive tryout conducted by the Giants, where again he struck out every batter he faced. (He also won the foot races.) The Giants passed on him because at 5'9" and 150 pounds they considered him too small for a pitcher. But the Dodgers took a flyer on him when he agreed to sign for $500.

He started at the lowest rung of the farm system. Seeing lots of pitchers but hardly any middle infielders, he opportunistically converted to second base. He finally reached AAA Spokane in 1957 but hit a mediocre .267 with no power, then started even worse in 1958. "I had my troubles with the curveball," he admitted. New Spokane manager Bobby Bragan noticed the right-handed Wills goofing off in batting practice, taking left-handed swings. "Have you ever *tried* hitting left-handed before?" he asked without levity, and spent the next three days converting Wills into a switch-hitter. The move saved Wills's career.

Don Zimmer had taken over as Dodger shortstop after waiting years for Reese to retire. In early 1959, just as the job seemed his for years to come, he broke his toe. He told no one, but it showed in his performance, and when his average sank to .202 the Dodgers, realizing they had a chance to go all the way, sat him down. Bragan praised Wills, then hitting .313 at Spokane, to Buzzie Bavasi, and though reluctant to bring up an aging, heretofore mediocre prospect, Bavasi took the gamble. After Wills went one for his first 12, Walter Alston put Zimmer back in the lineup. But Zimmer faded even further, and by default Wills became the regular.

In addition to promoting Wills, the Dodgers traded Gino Cimoli to St. Louis for Wally Moon, a left-handed outfielder whose mastery of the inside-out swing led to bloop flies over the Coliseum's left field screen fondly called "Moon Shots." Alston relegated Carl Furillo to the bench in favor of youngster Don Demeter. Jim Gilliam, a floater in '58, was posted at third base every day. Roger Craig, Danny McDevitt, and Larry Sherry were given meaningful mound work.

The changes gave the rivalry balance and tension. A year before, "synthetic attempts to build their meetings into feuds fell on deaf ears in the stands," the *San Francisco Call-Bulletin's* Jack McDonald wrote. "But things have changed this year. The great pitching duel between Johnny Antonelli and Don Drysdale Friday night was a dramatic thing, and it gripped the players as well as the stands."

McDonald was referring to a 13-inning, 2–1 nail-biter on May 22, 1959, in which Antonelli went from the second to the 10th inning without giving up a hit and Drysdale proved nearly as untouchable, retiring 22 of 23 through one stretch and shutting out the Giants until the ninth, when Cepeda bashed a two-out triple to tie the game. Big D persevered, throwing 172 pitches in all, and got the win when a Hodges single off the screen plated Don Demeter. The rivals were proving themselves worthy not only of each other, but of the defending champion Milwaukee Braves.

With a solid rotation of Antonelli, Sad Sam Jones, Jack Sanford, and Mike McCormick behind their slugging offense, the Giants stormed past Milwaukee in early July. Meanwhile the Dodgers, instead of hovering around .500 as expected, played consistently above it, and though they couldn't overtake the Braves or Giants, they never lost sight of them either. A three-way pennant chase developed.

It was in this context that Sandy Koufax gave his first intimation of greatness. The quiet, dignified left-hander, still just 23, suffered from a cold and couldn't get loose for his start on August 31. Perhaps he was also nervous: an astonishing 82,794 spectators filled the Coliseum. He struck out Jackie Brandt and McCovey in the first, but Mays and Cepeda ripped him for doubles to give the Giants a run. The Dodgers played small ball — it was becoming habitual — to tie the score as Gilliam walked, stole second, took third on a passed ball, and came home on a Snider groundout.

Over the next two innings Koufax struck out only one more batter. But in the fourth he K'd second baseman Danny O'Connell and pitcher Jack Sanford, and in the fifth he whiffed Brandt, Mays, and Cepeda, all swinging, although McCovey homered to put the Giants back in front 2–1.

Koufax struck out the side in the sixth — that made 11. He got Brandt and McCovey (on a high, inside curve; "I debated a long time before I

Walter Alston. "I always imagined him as the type who would ride shotgun on a stagecoach through Indian country," said Vin Scully. (Courtesy Los Angeles Dodgers, Inc.)

threw the pitch," he admitted) in the seventh for 13. Alston decided not to pinch hit for him, and in the eighth Koufax blew down Mays on a called strike three and Cepeda on a swing and miss—15. The Dodgers put a run across to tie the score, and Koufax went out for the ninth.

He struck out the side yet again for 18, breaking the National League record for most in a game and tying the all-time record set by Bob Feller. To put the finishing touch on his masterpiece, he singled and scored the winning run when Wally Moon hit a patented opposite-field homer. With typical modesty Koufax told reporters, "I never saw so many bad pitches swung at in one game."

On September 18 the Giants, holding a two-game lead over both Milwaukee and Los Angeles with eight to play, welcomed the Dodgers for their last confrontation of the year. If the Giants swept the three-game set they'd even the season series and, more importantly, leave the Dodgers an untenable five back with five to go. The tension winched tighter when the first game was postponed by rain, forcing a doubleheader (with separate admissions) on Saturday, September 19.

Johnny Antonelli started the first game for the Giants. He'd been mired at 19 wins, and there were whispers that Rigney had overworked him (and the other starters as well). But Antonelli's arm wasn't the problem. He still stewed over an incident at Seals Stadium two months before, when he and Drysdale took a 2–2 tie into the ninth. The breeze blew stronger than usual that day. Dodger second baseman Charlie Neal hit a pop to shortstop Daryl Spencer, who called for the ball, but "all of a sudden Jackie Brandt comes in from left field and he says *he's* got it," Antonelli remembered, "and now, all of a sudden Jackie Brandt looks up and the ball blows out of the ballpark." Antonelli and the Giants lost, 3–2. After the game *San Francisco Chronicle* reporter Art Rosenbaum asked Antonelli, "Hey, what was that pitch Neal pummelled off you?" "*Pummelled?*" Antonelli shot back, and went on an expletive-laden tirade. Rosenbaum reported the outburst, the front office backed away from Antonelli, and fans began to jeer the stalwart pitcher. His desire to pitch for San Francisco vanished.

He certainly wasn't thinking about Maury Wills. Said Spencer, "We didn't even go over him in meetings. Maury Wills? At that point Maury Wills was *nothing*." The Dodger shortstop's average had bottomed out at .206 in early September. He batted eighth, where his speed was useless (he stole just seven bags his rookie season). Just in time for the final push, though, he came alive.

In the second inning he singled, went to third on another hit, and scored when a return throw from catcher Hobie Landrith sailed over

Antonelli's head. In the fourth he slapped an RBI single that sent Antonelli (who never did win his 20th) to the showers. He singled yet again in the sixth and scored on a suicide squeeze by Dodger pitcher Roger Craig, who held steady over the full nine to claim a 4–1 victory.

Okay, reasoned the Giants, so we won't win the season series and we won't eliminate them from contention, but if we win the nightcap we'll be two ahead of them with only six left. Bill Rigney sent out left-handed bonus baby Mike McCormick to face Drysdale. When Drysdale walked the bases loaded with nobody out in the first, the Giants were sure they had him. Rigney described what happened next. "Cepeda was the hitter and he had a three ball and one strike count on him. And I'm saying, 'Well, I'm not going to take the bat out of my fourth hitter's hand. Because if he throws one dead center we're going to get four.' Well, he threw him ball four and he swung at it. And then he threw him ball five and he swung at that, and struck out. Willie Kirkland was next and he struck out, and then he popped up Daryl Spencer and got out of it."

McCormick preserved a 1–0 lead through six. But with one out in the seventh the Dodgers loaded the bases. Big, slow Chuck Essegian pinch hit for Drysdale. The Giants opted to play their infield back and go for the double play. Essegian obliged by hitting a routine grounder to third. Jim Davenport fielded it cleanly. Spencer, playing despite a hairline fracture of his thumb, took Davvy's chest-high throw to second — and dropped it. Tying run in, all hands safe. "Boy, I saw that play forever," McCormick, just 20 at the time, recalled later. The floodgates opened: the Dodgers scored four more and won 5–3 to gain a share of first place with the Giants.

The devastating loss took the life out of the Giants, who performed like minor leaguers in the third game. Eddie Bressoud, McCovey, and Cepeda struck out in the first against Johnny Podres to set the tone. Snider belted the final homer at Seals Stadium to put the Dodgers ahead. The ubiquitous Wills started a run-producing rally to make it two-zip, and the Angelenos tallied two more in the seventh to take a commanding lead. In the eighth the Giants staged a last-ditch rally, but Koufax, in a relief stint, ended the threat by inducing Felipe Alou to fly out. The 8–2 triumph gave the Dodgers nine wins in 11 tries at Seals Stadium, 14 in 22 overall against the Giants, and sole possession of first place. "It makes up for the humiliation we suffered last year," exulted Duke Snider.

The Giants could have come back — they were only a game out, after all — but they won just one of their last five, a disappointment so profound to Horace Stoneham (he'd printed up World Series tickets and had inquired about opening Candlestick Park early for the Fall Classic) that he mulled firing Rigney.

Dodger third base coach Pee Wee Reese, asked how the Giants could have choked so badly in the clutch, said, "Better clubs than the Giants have done it. I should know. I played on one. I mean the Dodgers of 1951."

The Dodgers ended the year tied for first with the Braves, and in a playoff widely viewed as atonement for '51, swept two games to claim the pennant. They were the weakest National League champ in years, scoring only 35 more runs than their opponents. How had they succeeded? Although their 148 home runs masked it, they won with deadball tactics. Playing in a hitters' park they finished only sixth in slugging percentage, but they led the league in walks received, sacrifice bunts, and stolen bases. They played 55 one-run games and prevailed in 33 of them, a .600 percentage. Once the distorting effects of the Coliseum's left field screen were removed — and Wills fully realized his potential — this new, *Los Angeles* Dodger brand of baseball became obvious.

13. 1960–1962: Harney's Horror and the Taj O'Malley

"If you were to write the definitive history of the San Francisco Giants, long before the mention of Willie Mays, Willie McCovey, Juan Marichal or anyone else, there would be Candlestick," said Hank Greenwald, a Giant broadcaster for 17 seasons. "There's no way of calculating exactly how damaging Candlestick Park was to the Giants franchise, and to the city, but some things are obvious."

What was obvious about Candlestick Park from its first day was wind. And when there was no wind there was fog. But the ballpark had so many faults it wasn't fair to blame it for the weather too. The wind blew just as hard at Seals Stadium; remember Charlie Neal's pop-up homer against Johnny Antonelli. "I can't shed more than one recalcitrant tear over the demise of Seals Stadium. The freezing nights and the blobs of moisture that descended on your score book obliterating all marks are still painful memories," wrote one San Francisco writer a couple of weeks before the old yard met the wrecking ball.

Unconstrained by the rectangularity of city blocks, architect John Bolles designed a pear-shaped ballpark with symmetrical dimensions: 335 feet from home plate to the corners, 397 feet to the power alleys, 420 to dead center. He called for unprecedented amenities: seats 20 inches wide, aisles six or more feet wide, and an electronic scoreboard behind the center field fence that stood 50 feet tall and 160 feet long and could be read 400 yards away. Most remarkably, he designed this double-decked structure in the heart of earthquake country using only 26 support posts, none of which impaired views. (And while double-decked freeways collapsed in the 1989 Loma Prieta quake, Candlestick suffered little damage.)

But there's no getting around the fact that city officials and their chief contractor cut too many corners. The first mistake was choosing Candlestick Cove as the site. Named for trees that stuck from its marsh like candlesticks, the Cove, at the city's southeast edge, was too far from downtown to attract corporate customers or provide a benefit to other businesses. And unless fans took local roads through Hunters Point, a poor African American neighborhood, the only way in and out was the Bayshore Freeway, meaning there would be as many as 9,000 cars (Stoneham finally got the parking he wanted) jockeying for two access ramps. Other sites were considered, but when Charles Harney offered the land for $2.7 million on the condition his construction company build the park, the city couldn't refuse.

Only after the contract was signed did anyone notice that provisions for waterproofing, fireproofing, landscaping, lighting, and other necessities had been omitted. Such gaffes pushed costs from the original $5.1 million to more than $7 million. Harney boasted he'd have the park completed in eight months, but when he learned that a contest to name the stadium didn't go as expected — how could they not name it *Harney Park?* — his crews lost initiative.

Groundskeeper Matty Schwab was especially vexed by the second-rate construction. "They weren't going to put in a sprinkling system when I first came here. And I told Horace then, 'If you don't have a sprinkling system in here, then from what I understand about this weather [dry from April to September] you can just forget this job.' Well, he finally went out there and talked to Harney. And Harney said, 'It's not in the specifications and it's going to cost $35,000 extra. Who's going to pay for it?' And after about two and a half, three weeks we came back and found 34 sprinklers four inches above the ground. I said to Harney, 'Charley, you think you could play ball with 34 pieces of pipe sticking up out of the outfield?'"

The most glaring failure was a radiant heating system installed for the box and reserved seats. Hot water passing through 35,000 feet of pipe in the concrete was supposed to warm the Giants' premium customers, but the system never worked. Attorney and publicity hound Melvin Belli, who bought season tickets, sued for his money back and got it. Another bust: the Bolles-designed wind baffle curling over the top of the stadium. Nor did Candlestick's aesthetics prove pleasing. It was too big, too concrete-and-steel, to be cozy. No more banter with Orlando Cepeda while he played first base.

The Giants first saw the park the day before the 1960 season started.

The wind galed at 25 miles an hour, and neither Mays nor Cepeda hit a homer in batting practice. Two years earlier Mays had teased Duke Snider about the L.A. Coliseum. Had Snider been at Candlestick that afternoon and taunted Mays with the same words, "They took the bat away from you. You're done, man," Mays would have agreed. "Somebody's gonna take some terrible salary cuts around here," he moped.

While the players fretted, the politicians preened. Vice President Richard Nixon and Governor Pat Brown were guests of honor at a dedication dinner at the Sheraton-Palace Hotel. Nixon, a heavy favorite to win the Republican presidential nomination and a hardcore fan who'd toured Candlestick months before, said he wished he lived in San Francisco because he was certain the Giants would win the pennant in their new park. Brown, a back-slapping Democrat, tried to one-up Nixon and missed spectacularly: "I hope I'll be there to see the Giants and the Los Angeles Dodgers meet in the World Series next fall!" Perhaps this was when Nixon decided that if he lost his presidential bid he could run for governor in '62 and knock off Brown without a sweat.

The writers also got carried away. The *San Francisco Examiner's* Curley Grieve, for whom the Candlestick press room was named, wrote, "Mourners of Seals Stadium for sentimental or proximity reasons will dry their tears quickly once they see this modern, beautiful baseball plant, surrounded by acres of parking and catering to the comfort of the viewers." Crowed the *San Francisco Chronicle's* Bill Leiser, "It is one of the finest plants ever constructed. And, if we were slow — our plant is complete and a great crowd will enjoy it today while, down in Los Angeles to which city the Brooklyn Dodgers moved at the same time, the first stone for a major league park is yet to be turned."

In a major league display of shortsightedness, the Dodgers were not the first opponents. Instead the Cardinals flew in from St. Louis. Nixon threw out the first pitch. ("Who's Nixon?" asked Cepeda.) Mayor Christopher also threw out a ceremonial pitch, using a sidearm delivery to reach catcher Bob Schmidt on the first try. He, Nixon, and Brown sat in Horace Stoneham's box. Also in attendance: Blanche McGraw and Ty Cobb. Cepeda knocked in all three runs and Mays scored twice to lead the Giants to a 3–1 victory before a capacity crowd of 42,269. Former Giant Leon Wagner hit the first Candlestick homer. "Now I'm all right," said architect Bolles. "A home run *is* possible."

Not as possible, however, as it had been at Seals Stadium. From 143 for all teams at Seals in 1959 the homer total dwindled to 80 at Candlestick. In subsequent seasons Giant sluggers adapted their swings and these numbers rose significantly, but the power shortage, combined with the team's failure to meet the expectations raised in 1959, prompted Horace Stoneham to fire Rigney. The team was doing fine, in second place at 33–25. "He just made up his mind that he wanted to change managers," Rigney said. For reasons known only to his bottle, Stoneham put his chief scout, roly-poly Tom Sheehan, in charge. Sheehan knew little about managing, and despite the arrival of Juan Marichal in July the Giants tanked, finishing fifth. So much for Nixon's baseball acumen. But then, he didn't fare much better in his own field, losing the presidency that fall and getting crushed by Pat Brown in the governor's race of 1962.

The Dodgers endured nowhere near the Giants' construction problems—once construction started. Even before the vote on Proposition B, opponents of a ballpark in Chavez Ravine filed lawsuits contesting the validity of Walter O'Malley's contract with Los Angeles, and the flurry of restraining orders and injunctions indeed prevented the Dodgers from laying the first stone before Candlestick opened.

They did not, however, prevent the city from leveling the Ravine. In May 1959 deputies forcibly evicted the last people living on the hilly tract. Most of the families went peacefully, but not the Arechigas, who had been there since 1923. They barricaded themselves in their house, and as reporters and photographers watched, 14 lawmen braved a hail of rocks thrown by Mrs. Arechiga to remove her daughters. Bowing to the inevitable, 72-year-old patriarch Manuel Arechiga carried out what belongings he could before bulldozers knocked down his house and rendered his family *desterrados*—uprooted ones—a term the former denizens of Chavez Ravine still use for themselves.

The U.S. Supreme Court put an end to the legal wrangling on October 19, 1959, when it dismissed all suits against ballpark construction. The Dodgers survived another scare when state legislation invalidating the contract between Los Angeles and the Dodgers was vetoed by Governor Brown. The various challenges added at least $3 million to the price of construction and forced O'Malley to renounce any mineral rights (no oil was ever found), blacktop his own parking lot, and pay for removing the Arechigas and other desterrados.

Once free to build, however, O'Malley created a state-of-the-art facility, closely supervising architect Emil Praeger, landscape architect Arthur Barton, and chief contractor Vinnell Construction. Workers poured 40,000 cubic yards of concrete, enough, claimed sportswriter Jim Murray, to build a causeway across Santa Monica Bay. They set 13 million pounds of reinforcing steel in the superstructure, laid 80,000 tons of asphalt for roads and parking lots, and installed 550 tons of iron and 375,000 board feet of

Dodger Stadium. The only privately financed ballpark between Yankee Stadium in 1923 and Pacific Bell Park in 2000, and the best of its generation. (Courtesy Los Angeles Dodgers, Inc.)

elm for 56,000 seats. Gardeners planted 183 trees and 30 varieties of shrubs. It was beautiful. Waxed Murray, "There, by heaven and by Walter O'Malley, just as he said it would, stands a baseball park. Not just any baseball park but the Taj Mahal, Parthenon and Westminster Abbey of baseball."

Dodger Stadium, like Candlestick, was symmetrical, 330 feet to the foul lines, 380 to the power alleys, 410 to center field. With its still air and ample foul territory it favored pitchers as much as the Coliseum had favored hitters. Even with big Frank Howard pounding away, the Dodgers hit 36 fewer homers at home in 1962 than the year before — in six more games. Opponents hit a whopping 70 fewer. Not until 1973 did the Dodgers hit more than 50 homers at home. The total run output in Los Angeles dropped only 5 percent that first year but tumbled thereafter, averaging 6.54 per game over the next decade. The rest of the National League averaged 8.08 runs a game in that span.

Vin Scully emceed the April 10, 1962, opening day ceremonies. Burbled National League president Warren Giles, "When Mister O'Malley first asked to move his team to Los Angeles we never saw anything like this at the end of the rainbow." City Council president Harold Henry and Board

of Supervisors chairman Ernest Debs presented O'Malley a sheaf of ceremonial papers to be embedded in the park's cornerstone. Cracked O'Malley, "I thought they might be subpoenas." Edward McCooey, the national
anthem singer at Ebbets Field, became the first to sing it at Dodger Stadium. O'Malley's wife Kay threw out the first pitch, and then the Dodgers
played the Reds (why not the Giants?) and lost 6–3 in front of 52,564.

Not everybody thought the park a jewel. On opening day Virginia
Pinedo-Bye, 15 years old, advanced through the parking lot toward the
stadium. She lived just beyond the Dodgers' property line, in adjoining
Solano Canyon, and had watched in horror as her Chavez Ravine neighbors became desterrados. With a friend she carried a handful of rotten
tomatoes to the fence behind the outfield. While the politicians speechified
and the fans clamored for the game to begin, she and her friend flung the
tomatoes onto the outfield, where they splattered unnoticed.

14. 1962: "Like Two Drunks Having a Fight in a Saloon"

The Giants played at Dodger Stadium for the first time on May 21, 1962. Though in first place, they weren't happy. Horace Stoneham had hired Alvin Dark as manager, and relations in the racially divided clubhouse went from indifferent to hostile as the Louisiana-bred Dark, a cultural if not conscious racist, demanded the Latino players speak English only. "Can you imagine talking to your own brothers in a foreign language?" asked Felipe Alou.

Dark further disrupted the club by moving players to unfamiliar positions and invoking unorthodox strategies. "The Mad Scientist," San Francisco sportswriters soon dubbed him. Willie McCovey, sent to the outfield for the first time in his big league career in 1962, didn't mind Dark's racial attitudes, but thought his on-field machinations went too far. "When we'd play Philadelphia, he and Gene Mauch would play all these little childish games managing. They'd do things like announce one pitcher and have another guy warming up under the stands."

Dark developed an arbitrary system of pluses and minuses to evaluate players, and in spring training divulged that he rated the 1961 performance of white southerner Jim Davenport (.278, 12 homers, 65 RBIs) higher than Cepeda's (.311 and a league-leading 46 homers and 142 RBIs). In fact, "Cepeda had 40 more minuses than pluses," Dark said.

A furious Cepeda wanted Willie Mays to stand up to Dark, but Mays was a conciliator, and Dark had been the shortstop on his pennant-winning teams. "I never thought I'd say this about anybody, but I actually

179

think more of 'Cap' than I did of Leo," Mays proclaimed. Besides, the superstar center fielder had problems of his own. On April 17, 1962, just before a game against the Dodgers, he appeared at a divorce hearing in San Francisco Superior Court, where it was revealed that despite one of the highest salaries in baseball he owed the Giants $65,000 in advances, the IRS $9,000 in taxes, and others thousands more.

The Dodgers had grown fully into their deadball incarnation. Promoted to leadoff, Maury Wills stole 50 bags in 1960 and 35 in 1961, both league highs. Aging Jim Gilliam was still faster than most men in the league, and he remained versatile afield, playing both second and third base. Then there were the Davises, Willie and Tommy. Willie, from East Los Angeles, was as fast as Wills and in 1962 began a string of 11 seasons in which he stole 20 or more bases. Tommy, a Brooklyn native who as a kid had watched the Dodgers from the Ebbets Field bleachers, knocked in 153 runs in 1962, a total unsurpassed until 1998.

Reveling in Dodger Stadium's spaciousness, the pitchers finally looked as good at home as they did on the road. Drysdale led the league in wins (25), innings pitched (314), and strikeouts (232) to earn the Cy Young Award. Koufax began the string of phenomenal seasons that put him in the Hall of Fame, winning the ERA title and striking out over a batter per inning.

In the first match between the rivals at the Taj O'Malley, the Davises picked up a pair of runs in the fourth (single by Willie, homer by Tommy) and Koufax coasted to an 8–1 victory. The next night the Dodgers won again, 5–1. The Giants, the best-hitting team in baseball, had scored two runs in two games at the new park.

The trip wasn't entirely for naught, however. Shortstop Jose Pagan, among others, noticed the infield was unnaturally hard. Manager Dark discovered why. "I got out there and saw these heavy rollers on the infield rolling down the basepaths. I'd never seen that done on dirt before. Those rollers packed that dirt down like asphalt. I went out there on the infield and dribbled a baseball and said 'Holy smoke, I hope no one catches a spike in this.'" The hard surface gave the Dodger speedsters traction. It gave Dark an urge to retaliate.

Right after the series at Dodger Stadium the rivals played in New York for the first time in four years. Contrary to popular impression, the expansion Mets—whose team colors derived from Dodger blue and Giant orange — were indifferently received at first, drawing little more than 150,000 fans to their first 15 home games. But when the Dodgers and Giants returned, the Polo Grounds filled to the rafters.

The Dodgers came first, for a doubleheader on May 30. Though the Mets had nearly as many Brooklyn players as Los Angeles did — Craig, Hodges, Labine, Neal, and Zimmer (not to mention Casey Stengel) to L.A.'s Drysdale, Gilliam, Koufax, Podres, Roebuck, and Roseboro — the largest crowd at the Polo Grounds since 1942 poured through the gates to see the boys in blue and white. They heartily booed Leo Du-*roach*-er, who had returned to the Dodgers as a third base coach. "Now I feel right at home," he said. But they still loved Duke Snider. "Thrill 'em, baby," coaxed Koufax during batting practice, and Snider obligingly smoked one into the right field seats. "Fine time to learn that trick," the Duke pouted. "My only memory of this park is blasting 450-foot drives and having Willie Mays catch them." The Dodgers took both ends of the doubleheader, then won again the next night to go into June just half a game behind the league-leading Giants.

The Giants had only three holdovers from their last New York club, Mike McCormick, Stu Miller, and the beloved Willie Mays, who had to be directed to the Polo Grounds' visiting clubhouse because he'd never seen it. A week before, in San Francisco, he'd gotten into the first fight of his career when Met shortstop Elio Chacon punched him, retribution for a spike wound Mays had inflicted the year before. How would the New York fans receive him?

Not as Chacon would have hoped. The bleacher fans hung over the rails shouting Willie's name. They followed his every move through fielding practice, then hushed as he took batting practice and smashed three balls into the stands. He posed for pictures for 10 minutes. When he was introduced before the game, Cepeda recalled, "we were stunned by the ovation he received. He was the conquering hero returned." He belted a homer in the fifth to pace a 9–6 victory, and the Giants swept the four-game set.

One more note about the torch New York carried for the rivalry. The first Met old-timers game was held on July 14, 1962, with the Dodgers in town. It featured the 1951 Giants and Dodgers. Ralph Branca came despite misgivings. "Nobody remembers that at 21 I won 21 games. Nobody remembers that at 25 I had 75 wins. All they remember is the homer. It was a good pitch. It was a cheap home run, but the good that men do is oft interred with their bones and the evil lives on. Shakespeare. *Julius Caesar.* I went to college."

Branca didn't want to face Bobby Thomson, but many of the 37,253 in attendance hoped for precisely that. One expectant Dodger fan said, "A psychiatrist would tell Branca to hit Thomson right in the head to purge himself of the trauma." A more fatalistic Bums rooter said, "He can hit one again today for all I care. The damage is done." Thomson himself inclined toward the first fan's opinion. "Go get the hard hat," he told Monte Irvin. "I might get one under the chin today."

The Mets, as baseball's latest version of the Daffiness Boys, had by now connected with old Dodger fans. The crowd mercilessly booed Thomson when he was introduced, and just as loudly cheered Branca. Durocher went to the third base coach's box to re-create his role as Giant manager. Clyde King put the first two Giants away, then yielded to Branca, who had been warming up on the sidelines, throwing *hard*. "I'll go out there and face him," he finally resolved. "If I don't, what will they think of me?" Monte Irvin was scheduled to bat, but Durocher waved him off and called in Thomson.

As Thomson grimly strode to the plate — this wasn't easy for him either, serving as an entire borough's scapegoat — Durocher dug under Branca's skin, whistling and pointing at the left field porch.

Branca's first pitch, a fastball, was in the dirt. He continued to throw fastballs and worked the count to two balls, two strikes. (Since when do they keep counts in old-timers' games?) At last he threw a hittable one, and Thomson swung. The ball soared into the drizzly, humid sky. Branca turned to watch its arc.

Duke Snider, though still an active player, manned center field. He too watched the ball rise in the grayness. And then he loped in, caught it in short center, and held it over his head in triumph. Then he ran to the infield and threw the ball clear over the Polo Grounds roof.

By July Koufax was pitching with a numb index finger. When the affliction spread to the webbing between finger and thumb, doctors discovered that a crushed artery had reduced circulation to the area by 85 percent. Koufax would need two months to recuperate. The team went into a funk. The chronically overspending Leo Durocher, determined not to lose out on a World Series check, pulled one of the most brazen moves of a brazen career.

"Three guys who could run like ring-tailed apes, and we had a manager who sat back and played everything conservatively," he spat. "After Koufax went out, I just thought, *to hell with it*. Alston would give me the take sign, I'd flash the hit sign. Alston would signal to bunt, I'd call for the hit-and-run." It was rebellion, and it divided the team into Alston and Durocher factions. Faced with the biggest crisis of his managerial career, Alston did nothing for nearly a month. Why should he? It wasn't in his nature to react quickly, and besides, the team was winning — 17 of 21 to surge five and a half ahead of the Giants.

Alvin Dark hadn't forgotten those steamrollers hardening the Dodger Stadium infield. The morning before a crucial series began on August 10 he hatched a plan with Candlestick groundskeeper Matty Schwab to slow the Dodger attack. Schwab broke up the dirt around first base and mixed peat moss and three wheelbarrows of sand into it. "Jeez, you couldn't tell anything. It looked great. But as soon as you stepped on it, it would pile up," Schwab proudly recalled. Dark then told the press the Giants needed to win five of their remaining seven games against the Dodgers. "If we do that, and we go into the last nine days no more than two games behind the Dodgers, we have the advantage."

The Dodgers noticed the altered basepath immediately and complained to umpire Jocko Conlan, who ordered Schwab to fix it. Schwab refilled his three wheelbarrows, then instructed his son Jerry to go to first base "and put enough water on it so that you can see it." Jerry obliged. Recalled Schwab, "The Dodgers come out and, 'Oh no! What have you got now, a duck pond?' All kinds of remarks, and they were making quacking noises. So Jocko says, 'You've got to dry this out.'" Whereupon Schwab brought back the three wheelbarrows of dirt, peat moss, and sand, and turned the area around first base into a quagmire that came to be known as Maury's Lake.

The Dodgers lost game one in a blowout, 11–2. Schwab did his thing again the next day. When a seething Maury Wills came to bat in the top of the third he yelled at umpire Al Forman, "You ain't got no fucking guts!" To the delight of the full house at Candlestick, Forman threw Wills out of the game. The demoralized Dodgers held a 3–2 lead until the sixth, when Drysdale broke Jim Davenport's finger with an errant pitch. In a gesture that must have dumbfounded Durocher, Drysdale strode to home plate and apologized. After Big D struck out Jose Pagan, McCovey pinch hit. Willie Mac wore out Drysdale. Alston knew that, and had Ron Perranoski, his left-handed bullpen ace, ready to enter the game. But Drysdale had won 11 in a row, 21 in all, and it seemed like an Al Dark move to lift the best pitcher in baseball in the sixth inning. So Alston let Drysdale pitch — and McCovey blasted one into the right field bleachers. The Giants won 5–4 and cut another game out of the Dodger lead.

The largest crowd of the season jammed Candlestick for the third and final game. It cheered maniacally as the grounds crew flooded first and third base, then booed when the umpires, finding their guts, ordered Schwab to spread sand over the areas. Nothing wrong with the mound, though, at least not for Juan Marichal, who smothered the Dodgers on four hits for a 5–1 victory that lifted the Giants to within two and a half of their rivals. The Dodgers stole just one base in the series, and Alvin Dark had three of the five wins he wanted.

After the debacle, Alston finally dealt with Durocher. He convened a team meeting and told the third base coach, "Any sign that I give and you miss, I will fine you $200 and the player at bat $200." If The Quiet Man was going down, he was going down *his* way.

Clubhouse dissension, key injuries, and unprecedented (thanks to expansion) travel demands *on top* of a fight to the death against their bitter rival — no wonder both teams went into September exhausted. The Giants flew to Los Angeles for a four-game set starting on Labor Day. The Dodgers stood three and a half in first place and hadn't yet lost to the Giants in their new park — in fact, hadn't lost to the Giants at home in more than a year. But it was the fans, not the team, who most looked forward to the series.

They greeted Alvin Dark, dubbed "The Swamp Fox" by Vin Scully, with the largest crowd to date at Dodger Stadium, 54,418. Local sportswriters had suggested all sorts of welcoming gestures, from water pistols to watering cans to a medley from organist Robert Mitchell including "Stormy Weather," "Singin' in the Rain," and "Old Man River," but the fans took most enthusiastically to the several thousand duck calls hawked by a stadium vendor. The Giants were greeted by a cacophony of quacking. According to Bob Stevens of the *San Francisco Chronicle,* however, "the symphony of duck calls and 'Charge' blasts was rarely in evidence" as the Giants broke their Dodger Stadium jinx, 7–3.

The Dodgers reasserted supremacy the next night, Willie Davis flying home from first on a single and catcher (catcher!) John Roseboro stealing home in a 5–4 win. The Giants took game three, but it cost them their ace, as Juan Marichal injured his foot making a putout at first. Dodger fans who claimed the loss of Koufax would cost them the pennant now heard similar laments from their Giant counterparts, as Marichal became virtually useless down the stretch.

The narrow win gave the Giants six of their last seven against the Dodgers, better than Dark had hoped. San Francisco was just one and a half back with three weeks remaining.

On September 12 it looked as if that might not matter. In the third inning of a game at Cincinnati, Mays collapsed and needed several minutes to revive. He was rushed to the hospital and diagnosed with exhaustion. "Every spring, Alvin promised Willie would have periodic days off, but somehow they rarely if ever came about. The next day was the first full day of rest Willie had had in all the 1962 season," recalled Marichal. A chastened Dark held Mays out of the lineup for four games altogether. The Giants lost them all and fell four behind with only 13 left.

But then it was the Dodgers' turn to disintegrate. One thing to be said for sitting around and waiting for the homer: it takes less out of players than a scrambling attack like the Dodgers'. "My leg had turned an ugly purple, completely discolored from knee to hip. Just the thought of sliding on that leg sent pains through my body," said Maury Wills, who switched to head-first slides on occasion while setting a record for stolen bases in a season with 104. Even without Wills the Dodgers would have led the league in thefts, and all that running tuckered them out. By mid September they stopped scoring.

Leo Durocher wanted Alston to loosen up. "He took the bats out of their hands and, brother, their assholes tightened so that you couldn't drive a needle up there." Walter O'Malley came from the opposite direction. "Get tough, Walter. You've got to ride herd on 'em. Warn them that if they blow this pennant, they'll lose more than just the World Series money. It will be reflected in their salaries next year." Typically, Alston stayed the course.

"It was like two drunks having a fight in a saloon and trying to stagger to the safety of the swinging doors," Arthur Daley observed from New York. "Both kept falling down. The Giants, however, could crawl better than the Dodgers." With Mays back they won seven of their last 13. Had the Dodgers won just *four* of their last 13 they would have clinched the pennant. But they managed only three.

On the last day of the season, down by a game, the Giants went to the eighth tied 1–1 against the expansion Houston Colt 45s. But after organist Lloyd Fox played "Bye-Bye Baby," Mays stepped to the plate and smashed his league-leading 47th homer. "That's as long a home run as he's ever hit in his career," announcer Russ Hodges hyperbolized. Whatever the distance, it was enough to give the Giants the win and put the pressure on the Dodgers. Hundreds of thousands of Bay Area fans, including the 41,327 at Candlestick, listened raptly to Hodges' recreation of the Dodger-Cardinal game at Chavez Ravine.

Johnny Podres, pitching on his 30th birthday, was magnificent, but ragged baserunning took the Dodgers out of three scoring opportunities and the game went into the eighth scoreless. Then Podres made his one bad pitch of the afternoon, a lazy curve to Gene Oliver. It landed in the left field seats to put the Cards ahead, 1–0. The Dodgers, who hadn't scored in 20 innings, went down a dispirited one-two-three in the ninth.

So the Giants and Dodgers ended the season in a first-place tie, just as they had in 1951. And just as in 1951, they would play a three-game series for the pennant.

Base stealer Maury Wills. While pursuing the all-time stolen base record in 1962, he hid a budding interracial romance with actress Doris Day. (Transcendental Graphics)

"When they came into Candlestick Park after being tied by the Giants that was the grimmest looking bunch of players you ever saw in your life. Snider, who was one of the mildest mannered men you ever saw in your life, he just walked through that door to the dressing room, just as grim as though it was the surrender of the Japanese on the *Missouri*," recalled Bob Stevens. For good reason. Snider, the only Dodger to play on both the '51 and '62 playoff teams, saw the parallels. Both times the Giants had come from behind to catch the Dodgers. Once again the playoff would start on October 1 and conclude, if a third game proved necessary, on October 3. And once again the winner would face the Yankees in the World Series.

The parallels continued through games one and two. The Giants won the first game, 8–0. Alston started Koufax, who hadn't recovered from his injury. Mays bashed a two-run homer in the first and Jim Davenport hit a solo shot in the second. Billy Pierce extended the punchless Dodgers' scoreless streak to 30 innings.

Then the Dodgers won game two. Said Billy Pierce, "Here we were

5–0 ahead in the sixth inning, and Sanford had won 24 ballgames, and you figure it's all over." But after 35 scoreless innings the Dodger offense finally pulled a Lazarus. Jim Gilliam walked. Dark, overmanaging, yanked Sanford for Stu Miller. Snider doubled and Tommy Davis hit a sacrifice fly, and Los Angeles was on the board at last.

Moon walked. Howard singled to score another run. Dark replaced Miller with lefty Billy O'Dell. Alston responded with three right-handed pinch hitters. Doug Camilli (son of Dolph) singled, Andy Carey (not the son of Max) was hit by a pitch to force in a third run, and Lee Walls hit the fence with a double to clear the bases. "I was fighting back the tears when I saw those guys cross the plate," Walls said.

The Dodgers tacked on another run to give themselves a 7–5 lead, but the Giants rallied for a pair in the top of the eighth to tie. Bob Bolin held the Dodgers in check in the eighth, Stan Williams did the same to the Giants in the top of the ninth, and it looked as if the game was going into extra innings. But Bolin walked Maury Wills to start the bottom of the ninth. The fifth Giant reliever of the day, Dick LeMay, walked Gilliam. On came reliever number six, a gangly rookie from North Carolina named Gaylord Perry.

Perry had appeared in a dozen big league games to that point and hadn't been impressive, but he did have sharp control. Dark, knowing a sacrifice was in order, instructed Perry to allow the bunt and make the play at third. The bunt came, Perry fielded the ball, shortstop Jose Pagan covered third — and Perry went to first. After tearing the dugout phone from the wall, Dark replaced Perry with Mike McCormick. Lefty McCormick walked Tommy Davis intentionally to set up the force at any base and get to lefty Ron Fairly, who had gone one for his last 31.

Fairly lofted a fly to center. Mays caught it. On April 25, 1961, Mays had stunned Maury Wills by throwing him out from 300 feet on a would-be sacrifice fly, hailed as the best play Mays had made since the move. But with the game on the line Wills had no choice except to challenge that cannon arm. Mays uncorked one. His throw was off line, however, and Wills scored to end what was then the longest nine-inning game in league history at four hours and eight minutes.

So everything came down to October 3.

Leo Durocher wore the same T-shirt he'd worn to the climactic game of the '51 playoff. Alvin Dark, asked if he'd brought a talisman from that day, said, "Yeah, Willie Mays." (Mays was the only Giant to participate in both playoffs as a player.) But inwardly Dark wasn't so cool. This time he was the one to push an injured pitcher into action prematurely, tabbing Juan Marichal. "He had no choice," said Marichal. "The rest of our pitching was worn out."

More than 45,000 were on hand for the Wednesday afternoon game at Dodger Stadium. The Giants jumped ahead 2–0 on three Dodger errors, but Marichal's foot began throbbing. The Dodgers scored one in the fourth and two in the sixth to take the lead. They tallied another in the seventh and Ed Roebuck, in relief of Johnny Podres, shut down the Giants in the sixth, seventh, and eighth.

The situation going into the ninth was nearly identical to 1951, the Giants needing two to tie in their last at-bat. Although Roebuck was tired — "The smog was just hanging in the park, it was hot, and I was thinking how happy I was going to be when this thing was over" — Alston stuck with him. Roebuck was a sinkerballer, and a tired arm increased the movement of his pitches.

Matty Alou whistled a single to start the inning.

Don Drysdale had pitched the day before but was ready if Alston needed him. Alston wanted a double-play ball, though, and sinkerballer Roebuck was the man to induce one.

Harvey Kuenn batted next. Suspecting a hit-and-run, Alston moved second baseman Larry Burright four steps into the hole between first and second to cut off an opposite-field grounder. But Kuenn pulled the ball to Wills at short, and though the Dodgers got the force, the extra moment Burright needed to reach second cost them the double play. That proved crucial.

Roebuck walked the next two batters to load the bases with one out for Mays. "This was something I had been waiting for for ... how long, 11 years? I wanted it to be on my shoulders. No scared rookie now. I knew what had to be done," said Mays, who had been kneeling nervously on deck when Bobby Thomson decided the '51 playoff. He hit one so hard up the middle it tore the glove off Roebuck's hand. The ball was still spinning in the grass as Kuenn scored to make it 4–3.

That brought Cepeda to the plate. Alston finally replaced Roebuck — with Stan Williams. It was a curious move. Williams could handle pressure, having won a playoff game against the Braves in 1959, and he'd pitched beautifully the day before. But he was also wild — 96 walks in 185 innings — and therefore not a good choice with the bases loaded, especially with Drysdale raring to come in.

Probably Alston believed Williams *couldn't* walk the free-swinging Cepeda. Perhaps he remembered that bases-loaded situation the last week of the 1959 season when Cepeda swung at ball four, then ball five to kill a Giant rally in its cradle. Williams' first pitch zipped across high, and sure enough Cha-Cha swung and missed for strike one.

The Giant slugger stepped out of the box. "It's now or never, I told myself. At the least I had to get that runner in from third." On the next pitch he smacked a line drive to right field. Ron Fairly caught it, and he wasn't all that deep, but he couldn't throw out the runner tagging from third and the Giants tied it.

Had Burright turned the double play, Cepeda's fly would have ended the game and the Dodgers would have won the pennant.

With left-handed Ed Bailey up next, Williams assumed he'd be relieved by lefty Ron Perranoski. But now Alston stuck with *him*. The flustered Williams let fly a wild pitch to put runners on second and third. Alston ordered Bailey walked to create a force at any base, but Williams wanted to face Bailey because Jim Davenport, due next, hit him better. He and Roseboro looked to the dugout, hoping to discuss the matter with Alston — but couldn't find him. "He might've been up the runway to have a cigarette or something," speculated Williams. So they walked Bailey, and then Williams' penchant for wildness really came into play: he walked Davenport to let the go-ahead run score. The Giants plated one more on an error by Burright and took a 6–4 lead into the bottom of the ninth.

For once it went routinely. Billy Pierce, who had been so impressive in game one, got Wills to ground out and Gilliam to fly out. Lee Walls, hero of game two, pinch hit for Burright and also flied out — to Willie Mays, who opted not to chance a basket catch. "That was $15,000 a man!" he explained.

San Francisco went crazy. Drivers honked their horns. The Grace Cathedral carillon chimed out Handel's Hallelujah Chorus from *The Messiah*. More than 50,000 fans converged on San Francisco Airport, spilling onto the runways and disrupting air traffic. The team plane had to land in a maintenance area. Cepeda, Marichal, Billy Pierce, and Felipe and Matty Alou presciently refused to take the team bus, hitchhiking home instead. "People we'd never met in our lives pulled up, offered us rides, and we jumped in," said Cepeda. Mays found the only taxi in the area and also made a quick escape. The rest of the team panicked as fans surrounded the bus and rocked it back and forth. "That was about as scared as I've ever been," recalled Ed Bailey. "It certainly wasn't this way when we won in 1951," said general manager Chub Feeney, to which writer Art Rosenbaum retorted sarcastically, "But that was back in hysterical New York, not sedate San Francisco."

In Los Angeles, there was recrimination. "The scene immediately became ugly. A couple of our players coming off the field, knowing they had just lost thousands of dollars as their share of the World Series money, screamed at Alston, 'You stole my money!'" revealed Duke Snider. Walter O'Malley considered dismissing Alston in favor of Durocher. "I told

A young crowd swarming to celebrate a Giants victory. The 1962 pennant victory over the Dodgers sparked a wild celebration in San Francisco's North Beach district. "Good God," objected one respectable matron, "people will think we're like Milwaukee or something." (©CORBIS)

Walter that if he was going to fire Alston, he'd have to fire me, too," Bavasi said, and that saved Alston's career. Then Bavasi turned around and fired Durocher after The Lip went public with his criticisms of the manager. O'Malley overruled Bavasi and kept Durocher —curiously enough, with the support of Alston.

Years later, Duke Snider got the phlegmatic Alston to confide, "Out of my whole managerial career, I'd like to have back the last week of the '62 season, and the playoffs. I should have had Don Drysdale warming up in that last game. I made a mistake there. I know about the second base situation with Burright, too."

But before you pity Alston and the rest of the Dodger brain trust, consider that a record 2,755,184 fans passed through the team's turnstiles in 1962, accounting for nearly a quarter of the National League's attendance. In New York, the first-place Yankees (who beat the Giants in a dramatic, seven-game World Series) and lovable-loser Mets *combined* didn't draw as many fans. And just like the disaster of '51, the playoff loss galvanized the Dodgers. The losers of '51 were winners in '52, '53, '55, and '56. The losers of '62 put the infighting behind them to win in '63, '65, and '66. By contrast, after 1962 the Giants didn't win another pennant for a generation.

15. 1965: "I'm Going to Get Him on the Head"

By the end of 1964 Alvin Dark had thoroughly alienated his minority players. He was actually quoted as saying, "You can't make most Negro and Spanish players have the pride in their team that you get from white players. And they just aren't as sharp mentally." Even Willie Mays had had enough of him. Though Dark named Mays team captain — the first African American given that honor — Mays did not speak to him the last two months of the season.

Hoping to fire up his disaffected ballclub, in 1965 Horace Stoneham replaced Dark with Herman Franks, a Giant coach on and off since 1949 and before that a backup catcher with several organizations, including the Dodgers. Franks was the anti–Dark, a drinking, chewing, swearing man of means— he'd made a fortune in real estate in his native Utah — and as such a good match for Stoneham, who rapidly fell under the burly manager's sway.

At first Orlando Cepeda, leader of the Latino contingent, welcomed the bilingual Franks. Cepeda had hurt his knee after the 1962 season and for two years played in pain while Dark accused him of faking an injury. He had the knee operated on after 1964 and expected understanding from Franks, but "when I showed up at spring training with my bad knee and in constant pain, Herman picked up where Dark left off. He never showed signs of bigotry. Yet life with Herman was one big nightmare. He said it was all in my mind and that I should get my ass on the field and earn some money."

Hurt and depressed, Cepeda turned to marijuana, a habit that led to an arrest after his playing days and delayed his election to the Hall of Fame for 20 years. During a game in Los Angeles, Maury Wills stared at Cepeda's swollen knee and asked, "Why are you playing?" Wondering that himself, Cepeda traveled to the Mayo Clinic, where doctors advised him never to play ball again. He batted only 34 times in 1965. Franks gave the first base job to Willie McCovey, and in early 1966 convinced Stoneham to deal Cepeda to St. Louis for pitcher Ray Sadecki, the most unpopular trade in San Francisco Giant history.

Fellow Latino Juan Marichal had too much else on his mind to worry about Franks. Marichal had ties to former Dominican dictator Rafael Trujillo, having pitched for the Dominican Air Force team as an 18-year-old. When Trujillo was assassinated, the junta that replaced him regarded Marichal and his family with suspicion. In April 1965 civil war broke out in the Dominican. The junta persuaded Lyndon Johnson to quell the insurrection with American soldiers. Marichal's nation became a war zone, with his family caught in the middle.

"I do not think it difficult to realize that injury and illness can be brought on by other things besides physical causes. I know that with all of the new trouble in my native country, my own reaction was to have a combination of sinus trouble and asthma — accompanied with violent fits of sneezing, sometimes so bad that if I was in my car I would have to stop and pull over to the side of the road," Marichal said.

As blood ran through the streets of Santo Domingo, Marichal lost a close game to Drysdale at Dodger Stadium. He reacted to Drysdale's brushbacks of Willie Mays with "next time, if he's pitching against me and he comes close, we'll see what happens. He'll get it. And real good, too." Drysdale denied he intended to hit Mays. "I'm leading by one run in the eighth inning and Willie McCovey is coming up next. Over the years McCovey's hit me like he owns me, so am I going to put Mays on base and then let him steal?"

The Dodgers had whittled themselves even further into a deadball team. In 1963 they sold Duke Snider to the Mets — and on opening day 1964 the Mets sold Snider to the Giants. "For years and years I hated the Giants. Well, maybe hate isn't exactly the word, but there wasn't anybody the teams I played with wanted to beat more. And now I'm a Giant. You know something? I like it." Los Angeles didn't. Sportswriter Melvin Durslag summed up local reaction: "Once a princely man, a cavalier above reproach, he has been unfrocked as a cad, a shameless blackguard who will take his bread even in San Francisco." Snider hit just .210 with four homers in 167 at-bats for the Giants and retired.

Further renouncing the long ball, after 1964 the Dodgers traded slugger Frank Howard to Washington for pitcher Claude Osteen. Dodger home run totals sank from 140 in 1962 to 110 in 1963 to 79 in 1964. In 1965 they threatened to go even lower, especially after May 1, when Tommy Davis broke an ankle in a game against the Giants and was lost for the season. Maury Wills (who stole 94 bases despite Franks's strategy of walking the pitcher ahead of him), Jim Gilliam, Wes Parker, and rookie second baseman Jim Lefebvre became the first all-switch-hitting infield in history, but combined for only 24 homers. Lefebvre and Lou Johnson, a 31-year-old journeyman brought up to replace Tommy Davis, paced the team with a paltry 12. Willie Davis, with 10, was the only other man in double figures.

By the end of June the Dodgers clung to first by a hair over the Reds and Giants. Marichal beat Drysdale 5–0 on June 28 to bring the Giants within two and a half. It was his 10th win without a loss to the Dodgers at Candlestick. John Roseboro got in the way of Giant shortstop Hal Lanier in a rundown, leading to a nasty collision that umpire Al Barlick deemed obstruction on Roseboro's part. Team captain Wills argued that Lanier was at fault, but Roseboro admitted, "I just didn't get out of his way."

Skip ahead to August 11. At the intersection of Imperial Highway and Avalon Boulevard in Los Angeles, a white patrolman arrested a youthful black driver on suspicion of driving under the influence. A crowd gathered to protest. The protest became violent. Within days rioting spread to the San Fernando Valley, San Pedro, Compton, and as far as Long Beach, San Bernardino, and San Diego. Just as Juan Marichal and other Dominicans were distracted by the violence in their homeland, so African American Dodgers watched in dread as Southern California descended into race war — among them John Roseboro, who lived near the epicenter, Watts.

Home games went on as scheduled even though smoke hung over the stadium and attendance dropped sharply. Johnny Podres and Don LeJohn, driving on the Pasadena Freeway after the August 14 game, watched a stray bullet rip the hood of a car next to theirs. Arriving home from the same game, African American rookie (and L.A. native) Willie Crawford was surrounded by National Guardsmen. "I didn't say a word and neither did they. I just raised my hands over my head and walked into my house." As soon as games ended the players rushed to the nearest TV to catch up on the news, which could hardly have been worse. Thirty-three people were killed, nearly 900 injured, more than 4,000 arrested. Whole blocks lay smoldering.

Amid the death and destruction, the Dodgers traveled to Candlestick for a key series with the Giants.

Wills started the Friday night game by faking a bunt. Giant catcher

Tom Haller leaped from his crouch. Wills drew back his bat and hit Haller, drawing a catcher's interference call that entitled him to first base. "You know what you're going to do?" Herman Franks asked his own leadoff man, Matty Alou. When Alou pulled back his bat he hit Roseboro hard — and did *not* get a catcher's interference call. Alou apologized, explaining he was just following orders, but according to him, Roseboro whizzed the ball to the mound "right by my head." Fellow Dominican Juan Marichal burst into a tirade, warning, "I'll get you guys when I pitch."

"If Maury Wills bunts one on me I'm going to break his leg," Marichal promised Alou after the game, which the Dodgers won. "If he steals one base on me I'm going to hit him, too, the next time. And anybody that hit me good I'm going to get him on the head!"

The contest scheduled for Sunday, August 22, would be the 10,000th regular season game the Giants played in the 20th century (not counting ties). The teams were one-two in the standings, a game and a half apart. Wills led off against Marichal and bunted for a hit. He stole second. He scored. He came up again in the top of the second and Marichal, the best control pitcher of the decade, made good on his promise: he sent Wills spinning out of the batter's box. For good measure he also decked Ron Fairly.

When Marichal batted in the bottom of the third, Roseboro walked to the mound and asked Koufax to hit the Giant pitcher. Koufax refused. He wouldn't throw at batters. He didn't need it to succeed, and was afraid that with his velocity he might kill someone. Hadn't he thrown a warning pitch at Mays— albeit a foot over Willie's head — after the knockdowns of Wills and Fairly? His first pitch to Marichal came right down the pipe for strike one. But Marichal, knowing what the mound meeting was about, remained vigilant. He decided to take the next pitch and bail out if it curled inside. It did come inside, but not threateningly so.

Roseboro moved far to his left to catch the ball, then returned it to Koufax via Marichal's head — so close, Marichal claimed, that it ticked his ear. Marichal asked Roseboro why he did that, Roseboro stood up and took off his mask, and in the next instant all the pressures of a rivalry and world gone mad exploded on the ballfield as Marichal raised his bat and brought it down on Roseboro's head, the worst act of player-on-player violence in major league history.

Koufax rushed to defend his catcher, only to square in self-defense when he found himself exposed to the next blow. Giant shortstop Tito Fuentes, also wielding a bat, rushed from the on-deck circle. Plate umpire Shag Crawford tackled Marichal. The dugouts and bullpens emptied. For 14 minutes bedlam reigned at Candlestick Park, with a capacity crowd threatening to spill onto the field and start a riot.

It was stopped by the San Francisco police — and Willie Mays. While the cops kept the fans at bay, Mays found his friend Roseboro. "Your eye is cut, man, you're hurt bad. Let's get off the field," Mays urged, getting Roseboro's blood on his uniform while guiding him to the Dodger dugout, where the wound was assessed as ugly but not as severe as Mays feared. Roseboro's eye was fine, although a knot "that it would take your whole hand to cover," trainer Bill Buhler said, was forming under the gash. "I'm so sorry, Johnny," Mays murmured, near tears, before running off to cut down berserker Lou Johnson, who badly wanted a piece of Marichal.

"Let me say if it wasn't for Willie Mays it could have been a lot worse," a calmer Johnson said later. "Willie did a hell of a job stopping the battle." In fact, Mays had reminded the entire nation that civility still had a place, and on the ensuing road trip he received ovations in Pittsburgh, New York, Philadelphia, Chicago — and Los Angeles.

When play finally resumed, Mays batted with two on and two out. Koufax, understandably reluctant to throw inside, put one over the plate, and Mays swatted it for a decisive three-run homer. "It is no exaggeration to say that what Mays did that day, first with Roseboro and then to Koufax, brought him finally, late in his eighth San Francisco season, the true adoration of Bay Area baseball fans," noted Charles Einstein.

It fell to National League president Warren Giles to punish Marichal. "If I'd have been influenced by the calls and the wires I received, I'd have had Marichal shot or banned for life. But you can't penalize the other 24 guys on the club or the team itself," he said, acknowledging that the closeness of the pennant race affected his decision to fine Marichal $1,750 — the most ever by the league office — but suspend him only eight days (nine including an off-day), the equivalent of two starts. "They should have suspended 1,750 days and fined eight dollars," sneered Ron Fairly. Wills invoked his favorite adjective — gutless — to describe Giles's decision, and reliever Bob Miller, perhaps thinking of Watts, said, "If you went out on the street and hit a man with a bat you'd get 20 years."

Watts was very much on Giles's mind when he made his decision. The suspension would keep Marichal inactive through August 31. If he pitched his first day back, September 1, his turn would come up again on September 5, meaning he would miss September 6 and 7, when the Giants visited Los Angeles for the last two games between the teams. Just to be sure, Giles forbade Marichal even *to go* to Los Angeles. "Marichal could, it is feared, touch off a riot by appearing there so soon after the Roseboro incident — and with L.A. already riot-jittery," Charles Einstein wrote in a scoop for the *San Francisco Chronicle*.

What happened when a packed house of 53,581 greeted the Giants at

Coach and players try to break up a fight. Umpire Shag Crawford moves to restrain an enraged Juan Marichal, who stands ready to deliver another blow. His target, catcher Johnny Roseboro, is pulled away by Tito Fuentes as Giant coach Charlie Fox intercepts Sandy Koufax. "I think he was hurt much more than I was by the incident," wrote Roseboro in his autobiography. (©Bettmann/CORBIS)

Dodger Stadium on September 6, with hordes of media people, including Leo Durocher and Jackie Robinson for ABC, anticipating blood on the basepaths? "It turned out to be the most orderly afternoon in the history of Dodger Stadium, inside the park and out," marveled *Los Angeles Times* pundit Sid Ziff. Commented Herman Franks, "Two good ballclubs met out there today and just played baseball. The Marichal-Roseboro thing didn't enter into it. There was no jockeying and no trouble." Drysdale brushed back Orlando Cepeda a couple of times, but that was how Drysdale operated and no one made anything of it. Willie Mays received a prolonged ovation. Score one — a very big one —for Dodger fans.

They were rewarded with a brilliant game. Though still suffering headaches, Roseboro slammed three hits in five trips, including a homer.

For once Drysdale got the better of McCovey, striking him out three times—until the eighth, when Stretch singled in a run to start a game-tying rally. The Dodgers regained the lead in the bottom of the eighth, but on the first pitch of the ninth Tom Haller took the tiring Drysdale deep to re-tie the score. The teams battled into the 12th, when Jim Davenport looped a two-out single to score Matty Alou with the winning run. It brought the Giants within a half-game of first place.

The next night Giant third baseman Jim Ray Hart clapped a two-run homer and pitcher Bob Shaw, with help from the first native Japanese player in the big leagues, Masanori Murakami, held the Dodgers to just one run as the "Bully Boys from the Bay" replaced the Dodgers atop the National League standings. It was their fourth straight win. They reeled off another 10 (their longest winning streak in San Francisco) to inflate their lead to four and a half with only 16 to play. On September 20 a seemingly resigned Walter Alston bemoaned his decision to let Drysdale pitch to Haller on September 6, pronouncing it the turning point of the season.

But Alston was toying with his interviewers. He knew that in the history of the rivalry no lead was safe. He also knew his Dodgers had embarked on a win streak of their own. On September 25 Koufax shut out the Cardinals 2–0, fanning 12 to break Bob Feller's record for strikeouts in a season. It was the Dodgers' eighth straight victory and brought them within half a game of the Giants. Mays responded by hitting his 50th homer (his 52 for the season would be equaled just once—by George Foster in 1977—over the next three decades) to pace San Francisco to a 7–5 triumph over the Braves. The next night Drysdale shut out the Cards 1–0 while the Braves' Gene Oliver, who'd put the Giants and Dodgers into a playoff with a homer on the last day of the 1962 season, blasted a game-winner off Marichal to tie the rivals for first with seven games remaining.

On September 28 those same Cardinals who had been shut out by Koufax and Drysdale rampaged against the Giants, 9–1. Meanwhile Lou Johnson poked a 12th-inning homer to beat the Reds 2–1 at Dodger Stadium. Now it was L.A. on top by a game with five to go.

Another Dodger win and Giant loss on September 29 extended L.A.'s lead to two. Both teams won on September 30, but now the Giants were two games out with only three left, and the Dodgers had won 13 straight (tied for their best in Los Angeles). The streak finally ended on October 1, but the Giants couldn't take advantage, blowing an ugly one in Cincinnati, 17–2. Now the best they could hope for was a tie. They did their part by winning their next game. But while they listened anxiously to the clubhouse radio, Sandy Koufax downed Milwaukee 3–1 to clinch the pennant. (The only run for the Braves: a homer by Gene Oliver.) "We didn't want the Giants to lose. We wanted to win it ourselves," Koufax explained while teammates doused him with champagne.

Win it themselves they did, with the puniest offense for a pennant winner in the modern era. Their 78 home runs were the least in the league by far, and their .335 slugging average was the worst for an N.L. champ since 1914. On the other hand, no National League winner since the 1944 Cardinals gave up fewer runs. Koufax and Drysdale were the most magnificent one-two punch since the days of the two-man rotation, throwing 644 innings (44 percent of the team total) for a combined 2.39 ERA. They accounted for 49 of the Dodgers' 97 victories. Koufax led the majors in wins (26), win percentage (.765), strikeouts (382), innings pitched (335⅔), complete games (27), and ERA (2.04) and was unanimously chosen for the Cy Young Award.

The Giants carped that had Marichal not been suspended they would have won. (They also alleged that Roseboro's $110,000 civil suit was timed to upset the Giant ace.) This was even less credible than the Dodgers' plaint in '62 about Koufax's injury. The Giants had a four game lead with 12 to play and Marichal active. The Dodgers may not have had much offense, but they led the league in desire. Instead of whining about losing two-time batting champ Tommy Davis for the season, they went out and took the pennant from their rivals.

The image of Marichal raising his bat to strike the staggering Roseboro has become the symbol of the Giant-Dodger rivalry on the West Coast. That shameful act forever tarnished Marichal's 243-win career. But he and Roseboro reconciled after their playing days. When Marichal was elected to the Hall of Fame in 1983, he called Roseboro with the news and, according to Roseboro, "We both had a little cry on the telephone."

16. 1966: "The Moon Plus the Rest of the Solar System"

Sandy Koufax and Don Drysdale were bright guys. They knew what the Dodgers were worth, and they knew what they were worth to the Dodgers. Koufax earned $85,000 in 1965, Drysdale $80,000. They both wanted more in 1966, but as Drysdale put it, "In 1965, asking for $100,000 wasn't like asking for the moon. It was like asking for the moon plus the rest of the solar system." An agitated Koufax called Drysdale during the off-season. They met at a restaurant with Drysdale's wife, Ginger, as third wheel. Koufax broached the question of salary. They soon realized Buzzie Bavasi was playing them against each other and lying about the other's demands. "This whole thing is easy to rectify," Ginger said. "If Buzzie is going to compare the two of you, why don't you just walk in there together?"

So they did, demanding three-year contracts worth $500,000 apiece. Once Bavasi regained consciousness he said no. His last offer before spring training was $100,000 for Koufax, $90,000 for Drysdale. The pitchers came down to $450,000 apiece over three years, which to Bavasi was like conceding Pluto. Thus began the most celebrated holdout since Joe DiMaggio's in 1938.

According to Bavasi, he told Walter O'Malley, "We can settle this in five minutes, but we'd lose all those headlines." Oh, right, it was just a publicity stunt! It is true that Dodger management received plenty of favorable ink; then as now, sportswriters overwhelmingly supported the team in contract disputes. "Sandy and I read about how greedy we were, how unfair we were being to the rest of the team, and so on," acknowledged Drysdale. But Bavasi underestimated the resolve of his aces. Two weeks before the season Koufax and Drysdale still hadn't signed. At the behest of Chuck Connors, friend to both sides, negotiations finally began in earnest. Koufax signed for $125,000, Drysdale for $110,000. "Reluctantly, we had to concede to ourselves that their ploy worked. Koufax had gotten a $40,000 raise, Drysdale a $30,000 raise. Had they negotiated alone, neither would have gotten that much," admitted Bavasi.

The Dodger holdout overshadowed one of similar duration involving the Giants. Juan Marichal made $60,000 in 1965, pitching 295 innings, winning 22 times, and leading the league with 10 shutouts. "Over the past four seasons, I had won 86 games—one more than Drysdale and two more than Koufax—and I knew what kind of $100,000-plus salaries they were holding out for," he explained. So he asked for $80,000 while privately deciding to settle for $75,000. The Giants offered him the same $60,000, blaming him for the team's failure to win the pennant. It wasn't just the suspension, but his mediocre pitching down the stretch. (The Giants went 4–4 in his September starts.) Only in late March, after Marichal stayed put in the Dominican Republic and refused to budge from $75,000, did the Giants capitulate.

Marichal made his second appearance of spring training on April 3 against the Dodgers in Phoenix. The teams stayed at the same hotel, and Marichal and Roseboro ate breakfast in the same coffee shop. Not a word between them. Nor were there words at the game, possibly on advice from their attorneys; Roseboro still had that civil suit going. (It settled for $7,500 in February 1970.) In his first at-bat against Marichal, Roseboro roped one to right that bounced over Jesus Alou's head. Roseboro rounded third, bidding for an inside-the-park home run, and scored standing up — then tripped on a TV cable and fell on his face. Marichal batted twice. Said Roseboro, "I was afraid Marichal would make some kind of an overture, a handshake offer or something when he came to bat the first time. If he had, I would have had to turn him down."

The next time they met was at Candlestick Park on May 3, but they were not the story. Willie Mays was. The Say Hey Adult had 511 home runs, tied with Mel Ott for the most in N.L. history. It was only right that he break the record against the Dodgers. "If he does it, all I can say is God bless him," averred Drysdale, who would be pitching that night.

The Giants won handily, 8–1, but it was the other Willie — McCovey — who hit the home run. Mays went a quiet one-for-four. So did Roseboro as Marichal pitched brilliantly, shutting out the Dodgers until Jim Lefebvre hit a solo shot in the ninth. It was the Dominican Dandy's 11th home win without a loss against the Dodgers.

Sandy Koufax (left) and Don Drysdale. They hired attorney Bill Hayes to negotiate for them in defiance of professional baseball's policy against dealing with agents. (Courtesy Los Angeles Dodgers, Inc.)

Claude Osteen took the mound for Los Angeles the next night. He hadn't given up a homer in 97 innings, and struck out Mays the first two times he faced him. "I could see what he was trying to do—move the ball around on me, inside-outside," Mays said. Osteen started their third encounter with a high, outside change-up. Mays loved change-ups. He hit it toward the end of the bat, but it had enough carry to go over the right field fence. The 28,220 fans erupted into a 10-minute standing ovation, chanting, "We want Willie! We want Mays!" Twice Mays emerged from the dugout to tip his cap. He was two days shy of his 35th birthday and, in the opinion of many, playing as well as ever.

Certainly he'd lost nothing in the field. Two weeks later in Los Angeles he notched three assists in one night. In the fourth he nailed the fleet Willie Davis going from first to third on a single. In the sixth, with Drysdale on first, Wills hit a Texas leaguer that Drysdale assumed would drop, but Mays caught it and rifled to first for the double play. Wills was on first in the 11th and running with the pitch when Jim Gilliam slammed a gapper into right center. Mays cut off the ball, whirled, and pegged to

McCovey, whose relay arrived at the plate in time for a tag on the aston-
ished Wills.

All for naught. The Giants lost in the 12th, 2–1, on a throwing error
by rookie outfielder Ollie Brown. Two other fine performances were
wasted. Marichal, making his first appearance in Los Angeles since clanging Roseboro, yielded only one earned run in 10 innings. (At first he elicited
boos from the crowd of 53,561, but with each inning appreciation for his
skills increased, until by the ninth Angelenos seemed evenly divided in
their opinion of him.) McCovey saw 10 pitches from Drysdale and rapped
four of them for singles.

The Giants and Dodgers had company down the stretch from the
Pittsburgh Pirates. With eight left the Dodgers led the Bucs by a game and
a half and the Giants by four. All of the Giants' remaining games would
be on the road, their last three in Pittsburgh. San Francisco sportswriters
filed postmortems.

But then San Francisco got hot—city and team both. On September
27, with the temperature 94 degrees, two African American teenagers in
Hunters Point jumped out of a stolen car when a police cruiser turned onto
the same street. The officer commanded them to stop, warned that he'd
shoot, then *did* shoot, killing one of the thieves, who was only 16. By his
own admission the officer was never in danger. The city's black community saw it as murder, and by nightfall its reaction threatened to engulf
Hunters Point, the adjoining Bayview District, and the Fillmore in violence.

Governor Pat Brown, in a tight reelection race against Ronald Reagan, called in the National Guard, which used Candlestick Park as a base.
San Francisco mayor John Shelley imposed a curfew but ordered the police
to show restraint, which they did, even after a contentious meeting
between Shelley and demonstrators culminated in a brick whizzing by
Shelley's head.

Members of the city's Human Relations Commission suggested the
September 28 Giant game be televised as a diversion. Although Horace
Stoneham still clung to the notion that television detracted from his gate,
he complied. Mays taped a promotional message for the city's radio sta-
tions: "Root for your team. I know I'll be out there in center field trying
my best." There was violence that night, but shortly after the broadcast
began at 6 p.m. it dwindled. The Giants won, moving within three of the
Dodgers with four left.

On Saturday, October 1, the next to last day of the season, the Giants
played a pair against Pittsburgh. For once in their lives the Dodgers rooted

for the Giants, and their nemeses came through, sweeping the twin bill and eliminating the Bucs. Just one problem: if the streaking Giants won their last two games and the Dodgers lost their last two there would be — yet again — a first-place tie between them at season's end.

The Giants beat the Pirates in 11 innings on the season's final day, then sat in the airport listening to the Dodger doubleheader in Philadelphia. If the Dodgers lost both ends, the Giants would fly to Cincinnati to make up a postponed game, and if they took that contest, they'd have their tie.

Drysdale lasted only two innings as the Dodgers lost the opener. In the second game Koufax had to beat future Hall of Famer Jim Bunning. Giant hopes soared.

They crashed just as quickly. Willie Davis clipped Bunning for a round-tripper in the third and the Dodgers leaped to a 3–0 lead. Los Angeles picked up another in the fourth, and though Koufax's back stiffened, he was at the height of powers that gave him the most extraordinary five-year run any pitcher has ever enjoyed. After the Dodgers made it 6–0 in the top of the ninth, Giant pitcher Ron Herbel resignedly said, "We know where we're going. Superman is not going to give them seven runs in the ninth inning."

Oh no? Before Koufax got an out in the ninth the Phillies plated three, thanks in part to ex-Giants Harvey Kuenn, who singled, and Bill White, who smashed a two-run double. "Sandy would have been taken out if one more man got on base," acknowledged Walter Alston. But Koufax regrouped to strike out catcher Bob Uecker and put away Bobby Wine on a groundout. All that stood between him and his fifth trip to the World Series was another ex-Giant, Jackie Brandt.

He struck him out swinging.

Although few suspected it, that was the last regular season pitch of Koufax's career. After the Dodgers lost the World Series to the Baltimore Orioles, he retired. His brilliant efforts exacted a terrible price in pain, and had he continued, the arthritis in his elbow might have become permanently disabling. He could have become another DiMaggio, creating a mystique about himself through carefully staged public appearances, but he eschewed the attention and hype. Koufax's aloofness has made it easier to forget that, in the words of Don Drysdale, "he was as good a pitcher as I ever saw. Make that the *best* I ever saw."

Koufax was merely the first to depart. Pique prompted the Dodgers to trade Maury Wills to Pittsburgh. He went AWOL from the team's winter tour of Japan on the pretense he was injured, then showed up in Hawaii to play guitar at the Don Ho Show — where a vacationing Buzzie Bavasi caught him. (In 1969, after Bavasi left, the Dodgers brought Wills back, and he ended his career in a Los Angeles uniform.) Tommy Davis was shipped to the Mets. Jim Gilliam retired.

The Dodgers had brought up another Hall of Fame pitcher, Don Sutton, in 1966, and he proved worthy of the rivalry by decking Willie Mays and absorbing a retaliation blow from Gaylord Perry during a key August game. In 1967 they added Bill Singer to the rotation. But the '67 Dodgers slipped to eighth place, and a rash of panic trades ensued. Roseboro, Perranoski, and Bob Miller went to the Minnesota Twins for Mudcat Grant and Zoilo Versalles (who, as the ostensible improvement on Wills, hit .196 in 403 at-bats). The Dodgers traded with the Giants for the first time since the 1956 Jackie Robinson deal, picking up catcher Tom Haller for second baseman Ron Hunt and utilityman Nate Oliver. Early in 1968 Phil Regan, the bullpen ace who had contributed 14 wins, 21 saves, and a 1.62 ERA to the '66 champions, was shipped to the Chicago Cubs for the forgettable Ted Savage.

These mistakes stemmed in part from changes at the helm. Bavasi left in early 1968 to become part owner of the San Diego Padres. Team vice president Fresco Thompson died. Their replacements, Al Campanis and O'Malley's son Peter, needed time to learn the ropes.

The last Dodger player to have worn a Brooklyn uniform, Don Drysdale, retired due to a torn rotator cuff on August 11, 1969, but not before making one last mark on history — and the rivalry. The National League record for consecutive scoreless innings was 46⅓, set by Carl Hubbell in 1933. On May 14, 1968, Drysdale shut out the Cubs. On May 18 he shut out the Astros. On May 22 he shut out the Cardinals. (In these three games the Dodgers scored a total of four runs.) On May 26 he shut out the Astros again. Through eight innings against the Giants on May 31 at Dodger Stadium he had yet another shutout going. But just two and a third innings shy of Hubbell's mark, the Giants threatened to ruin his string.

Willie McCovey walked, Jim Ray Hart singled, and Dave Marshall walked to load the bases with no outs. Up stepped catcher Dick Dietz. According to Drysdale, with the count 2 and 2 he threw a slider that "just sort of grazed Dietz on the left elbow." Dietz headed toward first, and all the Giant runners jogged forward. But plate umpire Harry Wendelstedt declared Dietz hadn't tried to avoid the pitch, as is a batter's obligation, and therefore was not entitled to first base.

Dietz told a different story. "Don Drysdale threw a spitball. All I had time to do was flinch, and the ball hit me on the elbow. I took two steps to first base and Wendelstedt said 'No!' And I said 'No, what?' He said 'No, you didn't try and get out of the way of it.' It was the worst call, without a doubt, that I've ever seen."

The game stopped for 25 minutes while Herman Franks and coach Peanuts Lowery jawed at Wendelstedt. When play resumed Dietz hit a fly too shallow to score the run from third, Ty Cline smashed a one-hopper to first baseman Wes Parker, who threw home for a force-out, and Jack Hiatt popped up. Drysdale was out of the jam, and he cruised through the ninth for his fifth straight shutout. He passed Hubbell by blanking the Pirates on June 4, then bested Walter Johnson's major league mark of 55⅔ consecutive scoreless innings on June 8 against the Phillies, who finally put a stop to the streak at 58⅔ innings, a mark that stood until another Dodger ace, Orel Hershiser, passed it in 1988.

At Drysdale's retirement ceremony, hosted by Vin Scully and featuring Governor Ronald Reagan, the Giants presented Drysdale a bottle of Vitalis and a tube of Vaseline.

17. 1971: "It's Almost Like the Giants and the Dodgers Have a League of Their Own"

Once the Giants and Dodgers established major league baseball in California, the gold rush was on. The American League launched the Los Angeles (later California, later Anaheim) Angels in 1961. Owned by Gene Autry, the Angels played their first season at Wrigley Field, then moved to Chavez Ravine as tenants of the Dodgers until they opened their own park in 1966. They dented Dodger attendance the first year, but thereafter, even though the two teams played in the same place, Dodger attendance *increased*. This gave Walter O'Malley the confidence to approve a National League franchise in San Diego. (He did not hold Padre principal owner C. Arnholt Smith responsible for the sins of his brother John, a key backer of the fight against Proposition B a decade earlier.) In Southern California, anyway, the more the merrier.

Not so in Northern California. The Kansas City Athletics, owned by Charles O. Finley, a carnival barker trapped in an insurance magnate's body, transferred to Oakland in 1968 and cut Giant attendance by a third. From there the fortunes of the Giants and Dodgers diverged, for the Giants, still reluctant to televise and therefore heavily dependent on gate receipts, lost the means to compete with their rivals. There was already evidence Giant fans were getting bored with their perennial bridesmaids in 1967, when attendance dropped 25 percent. But the team still drew 1,242,480 that year, better than any of its last nine years in New York. The killer plummet coincided with the A's arrival, to 837,220 in '68 and below 800,000 in '69 and '70.

More than ever it became imperative that the Giants win. But the Latino connection dried up, and the great Willie Mays started showing his age. In 1969 Clyde King became the first outsider to manage the team since Leo Durocher. From a baseball perspective he made a smart move: noting that Mays's on-base percentage held steady, he converted the 38-year-old into a leadoff man. From a human relations perspective, though, it was a disaster. "From the beginning, I never got along with Clyde King," recalled Mays.

On June 24, 1969, Peacemaker Willie got into the second, and last, fight of his big league career: with King. Slumping and sore-kneed, he reluctantly agreed to sit out a series at the Astrodome. But while taking batting practice he learned he'd been put in the lineup. He went to the locker room to don his game uniform — and when he returned his name had been scratched off the lineup card. It may have been a misunderstanding. As team captain, Mays usually took the lineup card to the umpires, and when King didn't see him before game time, he assumed Willie wasn't feeling well and substituted Ken Henderson. But Mays was eager to play, and said so. Heatedly. Gaylord Perry, Willie McCovey, and pitching coach Larry Jansen had to keep him off King, who banished Mays to the clubhouse.

King won the battle, but with Horace Stoneham firmly in Willie's corner he lost the war; he was fired in May 1970. He was succeeded by Charlie Fox, a native New Yorker who batted seven times for the Giants in 1942 and was a coach under Franks. He regularly sang for the players in his Irish tenor, and perhaps that explained their hot start in 1971. They took the National League West lead on April 12 (the league had split into two divisions with the creation of the Padres and Montreal Expos in 1969) and raced to 10½ games in front by the end of May. Mays did particularly well, smashing 15 homers by the All-Star break. He led the league in walks and on-base percentage that year and — this is a 40-year-old man we're talking about — stole 23 bases in 26 tries. Much of the credit went to Fox, who did everything up to and including a birthday serenade to make Mays happy.

But then, why shouldn't Mays have been happy? By this point he was acclaimed as the greatest all-around player in history. Even Dodger fans revered him. Noticing without any prompting from the Giants that the 20th anniversary of his major league debut fell during a series at Chavez Ravine, the Dodgers staged a classy pregame ceremony for him. The 40,042 in attendance warmly cheered him, then ruthlessly booed Marichal ("It all goes back to 1965," the Dominican Dandy said) and threw souvenir cushions onto the field as the Giants cruised to a 9–1 win.

Despite a knee injury to McCovey and dropoffs from Marichal and Perry, the Giants went into August eight and a half ahead of the Dodgers. But it was way too early to count out the Angelenos, whose rivalrous spirits ran high. "I hate the Giants. If I ever heard I'd been traded to them, I would immediately retire," swore Wes Parker. On August 2 rookie third baseman Steve Garvey, recovering from surgery on his hand five weeks before, hit a dream shot at Candlestick, a three-run dinger with two outs in the ninth to give the Dodgers a 5–4 win. The Dodgers won the next two also, and Maury Wills proclaimed, "It's almost like the Giants and the Dodgers have a league of their own. You can kind of save the whole year by beating the Giants." The Dodgers would take 12 of 18 games from the Giants in 1971. On September 5, though, they still trailed by eight.

But then they snapped off six wins in a row to close within three. "At times, it almost appeared that the Giants were waiting for them," rued San Francisco sportswriter Prescott Sullivan as the Dodgers flew to Candlestick for the final two games between the contenders. On September 13 Walter Alston pitted Bill Singer against Marichal.

Like Mays, Marichal remained a quality player, but not the superstar of old. He'd gone from June 23 to August 10 without a win and had lost to Singer five days earlier at Dodger Stadium. But at Candlestick he utterly dominated the Dodgers, having won 21 of 22 decisions. Imagine his consternation when Dick Allen, a slugger restoring home run might to the Dodger lineup, pounded a two-run shot in the top of the first. And imagine what he thought in the bottom of the inning when Singer hit Mays in the back, causing Willie to collapse. The boos from the 31,081 fans were deafening.

Marichal was older and wiser now, and the same umpire who had put a stop to his assault on Roseboro, Shag Crawford, stood behind the plate this night. That inclined him toward caution. But in the fourth inning Singer struck again, hitting rookie shortstop Chris Speier on the wrist. "Out, out, out!" the fans appealed to Crawford, but the ump kept Singer in the game. So Marichal took matters into his own hands.

Singer was the first batter in the top of the fifth. Marichal threw one at his chin that had the crowd — likened to a mob by the *Los Angeles Times* correspondent — cheering wildly. Singer had beaned two Giants, though, so Marichal threw at him again. This time Crawford issued a warning, and the cheers turned to ominous boos. Something was happening here, and it looked a lot like 1965.

Marichal disposed of Singer and leadoff hitter Maury Wills, but in his mind he still hadn't evened things up, so he hit 21-year-old first baseman Bill Buckner on the elbow. It was a direct challenge: on July 9 he and the hot-tempered Buckner (a Bay Area native and a Giant fan in his youth) were involved in a confrontation that nearly led to fisticuffs. Now, in an eerie — and frightening — twist, Buckner headed toward Marichal with a bat in his hands. About 10 feet shy of the mound Crawford and Giant catcher Russ Gibson stopped him. The benches emptied. Crawford ejected Marichal, sparking the ire of Giant reliever Jerry Johnson, who flew at the ump and set off another round of jostling. Mays — who else? — held Johnson back.

Eventually order was restored and the Dodgers won, 5–4, but not before someone in the crowd threw beer in Singer's face. Walter O'Malley and Al Campanis, in town for the game, protested the fans' unruly behavior (although they hadn't protested their own fans' behavior when someone threw beer at Marichal after his July 9 contretemps with Buckner). Little did they realize they'd witnessed the beginning of an ugly tradition. Ennui and the arrival of the Oakland Athletics had abraded the Giants' fan base to a nucleus with a high quotient of rowdies — the "kill 'em" types Jackie Brandt remembered from New York and Brooklyn — and this element would dominate San Francisco crowds at Dodger games for the next 20 years.

On September 14 the Dodgers won a seesaw battle 6–5 when Manny Mota, discarded by the Giants during the Dark age, hit a three-run double in the top of the ninth. The numbers? Eight wins in a row for the Dodgers, nine losses in 10 games for the Giants, and the Dodgers just one back in the standings. Grumbled *San Francisco Examiner* columnist Wells Twombly, "The damned Dodgers seemed to think that they were in first place and San Francisco had to catch them. They poured beer on each other and said it was only a matter of time before they shampooed with champagne."

Perhaps that hubris undid them. The Dodgers gained another half game the next day when the Giants lost in Cincinnati, but then they tailspinned, falling three behind by September 23. The Giants, still struggling — they lost 16 of their last 24 — couldn't pull away, and the Dodgers closed to within one with three remaining. On September 28 both teams won. On September 29 both teams lost, clinching at least a tie for the Giants. On the last day of the season the Dodgers sent Sutton to face the Astros while the Giants started Marichal against Buzzie Bavasi's Padres. NBC sent camera crews to Candlestick in case the teams needed a *one-game* playoff, a truncation necessitated by the introduction of the League Championship Series.

Willie Mays helps Willie McCovey celebrate his 1969 MVP award. With the Padre infield shifted toward right for McCovey in the last game of 1971, the 40-year-old Mays stole second, then raced to third because no one was covering it — two stolen bases on one play! (Transcendental Graphics)

Sutton pitched valiantly against the 'Stros, beating them 2–1 in front of more than 52,000 fans. But 130 miles south in San Diego, Marichal disposed of the Padres on 81 pitches for a 5–1 win that gave the Giants the division title. "The Dodgers can go to hell!" whooped Dick Dietz during the clubhouse celebration.

Willie Mays reacted with nuanced quiet. "I'm excited that the young kids are having a ball. I hope it continues Saturday and Sunday [in the League Championship Series against Pittsburgh]." As Willie went, so went San Francisco. Drivers didn't lean on their horns as they had in 1962, nor did cathedral bells break into Handel's Hallelujah Chorus or crowds fill the airport runways. The novelty of major league baseball had worn off for Northern California.

The subdued response was warranted. After winning the playoff opener, San Francisco was eliminated in three straight. The loss marked the end of the great teams of Mays, McCovey, Marichal, and Perry, and by extension the heyday of the rivalry. Over the next few years the fortunes of the Giants and Dodgers would diverge so drastically their rivalry would almost die.

PART VI

1972–1992: Bleeding Dodger Blue

	Giants	Dodgers
Where They Played	Candlestick Park	Dodger Stadium
Owners	Horace Stoneham, 1972–76 Bob Lurie, 1976–92 Peter Magowan Group, 1992	Walter O'Malley, 1972–79 Peter O'Malley, 1979–92
Managers	Charlie Fox, 1972–74 Wes Westrum, 1974–75 Bill Rigney, 1976 Joe Altobelli, 1977–79 Dave Bristol, 1979–80 Frank Robinson, 1981–84 Danny Ozark, 1984 Jim Davenport, 1985 Roger Craig, 1985–92	Walter Alston, 1972–76 Tommy Lasorda, 1977–92
Best Players	Darrell Evans, Jack Clark, Will Clark	Don Sutton, Steve Garvey, Ron Cey, Davey Lopes, Fernando Valenzuela, Orel Hershiser
Wore Both Uniforms but Shouldn't Have	Jeffrey Leonard	Dave Anderson
Division Championships, League Championships, **World Championships**	*1987,* 1989	1974, 1977, 1978, **1981,** *1983, 1985,* **1988**
Won-Lost vs. Each Other	167–205 (.449)	205–167 (.551)
Won-Lost vs. Rest of League	1,456–1,514 (.490)	1,596–1,372 (.538)

"On behalf of all the present players, I want to thank you men for creating and continuing the rivalry that we now have a chance to experience," Steve Garvey told former Giants and Dodgers assembled for an old-timers game in 1974. It was the quintessential Garvey statement: perfect for the occasion, but open to scrutiny. For the rivalry Garvey was experiencing had little in common with the clash of equals that had been raging for 25 years. It was more like the imbalanced rivalry of the early 20th century. But in the old days fans could at least count on the Giants and Dodgers being around year after year. In this era the rivalry's survival couldn't be taken for granted: twice San Francisco nearly lost the Giants to cities with no connection to Los Angeles, and there were plenty of rumored sales in between.

From 1972 to 1985 the Dodgers finished ahead (usually *way* ahead) of the Giants in the standings. Financially they were even more dominant. They became the most successful franchise in baseball, reaching 3 million in attendance in 1978 and exceeding that mark regularly thereafter. They always had at least one marketable star: Don Sutton, the throwback to the Koufax-Drysdale days on a steady march to the Hall of Fame; Garvey, the Popeye-armed, indefatigable first baseman who started out as a Vero Beach batboy; Fernando Valenzuela, the campesino with the colorful windup who claimed he was 20, looked 30, and pitched with the wisdom of a 40-year-old; and Orel Hershiser, the bulldogging born-again Christian with the sinker from the devil's workshop. Along with Cincinnati's Big Red Machine and New York's revived Yankees, the Dodgers stood atop the baseball world.

The city of Los Angeles was on top too. Favorite son Ronald Reagan was elected president in 1980, and his charm made him America's most popular leader since Franklin Roosevelt. Regard for him overseas was more mixed, so it was left to another Los Angeles product, popular culture, to conquer the world. From Mickey Mouse to Michael Jackson, Southern California's entertainment icons grew ubiquitous, as did its contribution to the national cuisine, fast food. The City of Angels even ruled baseball: after Peter Ueberroth, head of the committee that staged the 1984 Los Angeles Olympics, turned the first profit in the Games' history, he was hired as commissioner.

For the Giants and San Francisco, by contrast, life soured. From 1972 to 1985 the Giants posted a winning record only four times, and never finished higher than third place. They drew well under a million fans a year from 1972 through 1977. In 1985 they lost a franchise record 100 games. From Willie McCovey's retirement in 1980 until Will Clark's break-out year in 1987 they had no appealing stars. What they did have was a clique of fundamentalist Christians, known as the God Squad, incapable of connecting with the denizens of America's countercultural capital.

And what of San Francisco's countercultural scene? By the mid '70s it had turned bizarre and lethal. In February 1974 a band of radical thugs calling itself the Symbionese Liberation Army kidnapped newspaper heiress Patricia Hearst as part of a murderous crime spree. In 1978 the city was traumatized by the suicide-murder in Guyana of 912 people from the Tenderloin-based People's Temple and, just eight days later, by the assassination of mayor George Moscone and county supervisor Harvey Milk. Then in the early '80s the city was overwhelmed by epidemics of homelessness and a deadly disease identified as Acquired Immune Deficiency Syndrome, or AIDS.

Understandable, then, that Angelenos considered the rivalry over. As early as 1973 a writer for the *Times* pronounced it "a silly game based on largely irrelevant comparisons between the two cities. Today, the rivalry persists as a kind of family joke, an inter-urban name-calling contest between a city lost in self-love and another city lost in smog." In earlier times attendance was larger than normal for Giant games in Los Angeles. Now there were seasons when *fewer* fans than normal showed up. Even in 1982, the best pennant race between the rivals during this period, the Giants attracted crowds only 7 percent larger than average in Los Angeles.

And so, as it had been earlier in the century, it was up to fans of the weaker team to keep the rivalry going. That Giant partisans did, heaping abuse — and then some — on the Dodgers. Remarked *San Francisco Examiner* columnist and New England transplant Rob Morse, "The lower the standing of the Giants and the more pointless the game, the more pointless violence there is. I moved here late in 1977 when the Giants were 23 games behind the Dodgers and watched fans behave worse than anything I ever saw at Fenway when the Yankees were in town."

Why did Giant fans react so passionately? The answer lies in a chant born in this era and spontaneously invoked at every Dodger game in San Francisco since: *Beat L.A.!* Not beat the team, which would echo those old *Beat the Giants!* cries at Ebbets Field, but beat the *city*. To reeling but stubbornly progressive San Franciscans, Los Angeles represented everything smug and superficial about an increasingly conservative society. When they ridiculed Dodger fans for arriving in the third inning, leaving in the seventh, and volleying beachballs at each other in between, they were, by extension, condemning a larger cultural trend toward distraction and indifference.

The Dodgers *were* showing more of their conservative bent, pressuring players to conform to the clean-cut stereotype of the '50s. Those who did, like Garvey, were lionized. Those who didn't, like Glenn Burke, the first major leaguer to publicly acknowledge his homosexuality, were marginalized or banished. The organization still honors Rick Monday for sprinting across the outfield to rescue an American flag from would-be burners in 1976. Monday wasn't even a Dodger then, but the team obtained him the next winter, and in 1993 hired him as an announcer.

That mom-and-apple piety came back to haunt the Dodgers in the '80s as, among other embarrassments, reliever Steve Howe was exposed as a cocaine snorter and Garvey as a cad. San Franciscans relished the hypocrisy. Asked to list the city's most hated Dodgers, Mike Krukow, the Giants' only 20-game winner in the '80s and later a team broadcaster, named Garvey and Orel Hershiser, "because they exemplified the Boy Scout Dodger image."

But they weren't at the top of his list. That honor, "by a lot," went to Dodger manager Tommy Lasorda.

Lasorda combined Wilbert Robinson's rotundity and Leo Durocher's thirst for celebrity with a colorful bluster all his own. He grew up in Norristown, Pennsylvania, idolizing Van Lingle Mungo and developed a curveball that enticed the nearby Phillies to sign him at age 16. Bought by the Dodgers in 1948, he toiled six years in the minors before getting a September call-up in 1954. He stuck with the club the next spring, but was sent down again when the Dodgers signed bonus baby Sandy Koufax. After an unsuccessful stint with the Kansas City Athletics in 1956 and a short sojourn with the Yankees' AAA affiliate, he returned to the Dodger farm system before retiring in 1960. Thanks to his friendship with Al Campanis he got a job as a scout. In 1965 the Dodgers gave him a chance to manage a rookie league team, and he made the most of it.

Lasorda was adept at motivating young players. He drilled two lessons into his charges. The first was loyalty to the Dodgers: "I don't even have red blood flowing in my veins. Cut me open and I will bleed Dodger Blue." The second? "My objective at all times was to prepare my players to play for the Los Angeles Dodgers, and part of that preparation was learning to hate the Giants. I knew that some of my players were eventually going to play in the major leagues and I wanted to give them an early start and a good base for hating the Giants. The first thing they saw when they walked into our locker room was a sign reading 'Love the Dodgers, But Hate the Giants.'"

He practiced what he preached. Returned to the majors in 1973 as Walter Alston's third base coach, he hurled streams of invective at Giant reliever Elias Sosa for throwing at the Dodgers' Andy Messersmith. The next day Giant manager Charlie Fox accosted him behind the batting cage,

Tommy Lasorda. On the first pitch of the first game he managed for the Dodgers, the Giants' Gary Thomasson homered off Don Sutton. (Transcendental Graphics)

and as wide-eyed players watched, the discussion escalated into a full-scale fight.

By the 1980s, Lasorda and Giant fans had established a routine. He would emerge from the visitors' clubhouse in right field and walk down the foul line toward home plate. The fans would lustily boo him. Somewhere between first and home Lasorda would pretend to notice for the first time. He would blow kisses, tip his cap, or both. The ensuing frenzy wouldn't subside until he was settled in the third base dugout.

It was a win-win gambit. By inflaming rivalrous sentiment Lasorda guaranteed big turnouts for Dodger games, which helped keep the San Francisco franchise viable. And by making himself the lightning rod for fan rage, he let his players concentrate on winning. From 1977 to 1992 the Dodgers played .475 ball elsewhere on the road, .518 at Candlestick.

And there the rivalry's evolution could have ended, Los Angeles and the Dodgers on top, glamorous overdogs *à la* Manhattan, San Francisco and the Giants on the bottom, proud but envious losers *a la* Brooklyn. But this was California, where the karmic wheel turns. From 1986 to 1992 parity returned to the rivalry, in the sense that both teams were fitfully good. Trouble was, they were seldom good at the same time:

Year	Giants	Dodgers	Games Apart
1986	83–79 (3rd)	73–89 (5th)	10
1987	90–72 (1st)	73–89 (4th)	17
1988	83–79 (4th)	94–67 (1st)	11½
1989	92–70 (1st)	77–83 (4th)	14
1990	85–77 (3rd)	86–76 (2nd)	1
1991	75–87 (4th)	93–69 (2nd)	18
1992	72–90 (5th)	63–99 (6th)	9

The only year they were evenly matched, 1990, they fought for *second* place, as Cincinnati led the division from opening day.

The Giants' climb to respectability commenced on September 18, 1985, when owner Bob Lurie, finally realizing that if his real estate empire had been run like his ballclub he'd be cadging quarters on Market Street, announced the hiring of a competent general manager, Al Rosen. Rosen's first act was to name former Dodger pitcher Roger Craig the new manager. Giant fans could be forgiven their dismay in the spring of 1986 when Rosen and Craig, after evaluating the worst roster ever to wear the uniform, decided that except at first and second base they already had the talent to win. Even the players were skeptical. "Roger greeted us in camp and told us we were going to win it. But we had made no major trades in the winter and I was discouraged. I figured we had no chance," recalled Mike Krukow.

But Craig had a plan. He filled the hole at first with gabby, gung-ho Louisianan Will Clark and at second with steady Robby Thompson. He taught the pitching staff his specialty, the split-fingered fastball. And he banished negativity with the hokey phrase *humm baby*. The result? In 1986 the Giants improved 21 games and finished ahead of the Dodgers for the first time since 1971. The next year they won the division title, and in 1989 they went to their first World Series in 27 years.

San Francisco's renewal can't be dated as precisely, but its source can: a stretch of towns from the peninsula to San Jose where denim-clad engineers and entrepreneurs unleashed the most sweeping workplace transformation since the Industrial Revolution. By the mid '80s they had developed personal computers and were spinning off countless other high-tech products. The torrent of wealth flowing into this so-called Silicon Valley spread throughout the region, once and for all linking San Francisco, the peninsula, the South Bay, and the East Bay into a sprawling, L.A.-like Bay Area. The Dodgers and Los Angeles, meanwhile, regressed. Lasorda had inherited a team of young veterans, 18 of whom he'd managed in the minors or winter ball, and for four straight seasons, 1979 to 1982, Dodger newcomers garnered Rookie of the Year honors. But after that, one prospect after another fell flat. The Dodgers won 95 games and the division championship in 1985, but won only 73 and slid to fifth in 1986. From then on Lasorda's teams consisted of terrific pitching backed by spotty hitting and a defense that handled the ball as if it were loaded with nerve gas. He pulled off one of the great managerial feats of modern times by goading a slightly better than average club to a world championship in 1988.

The city of Los Angeles was burned — literally — by its own complacency. For decades the police department was the scourge of ethnic minorities and civil libertarians. Commissions appointed to review the 1965 Watts riot called for improved relations between police and citizenry, particularly in less well-off neighborhoods. But as that terrible uprising receded from memory and L.A. reached the pinnacle of world influence, the need for reform was forgotten.

Then, in March 1991, a witness with a video camera documented the brutal police beating of a handcuffed African American suspect named Rodney King. It was hardly an isolated incident. In 1988 Hall of Fame second baseman Joe Morgan (who had played a huge role in the rivalry six years earlier — more on that later) was passing through Los Angeles International Airport on his way to a golf tournament when officers grabbed him by the neck, threw him to the floor, and handcuffed him on the supposition he was smuggling drugs. Morgan sued for violation of his civil rights, and just 17 days before the King incident won a jury verdict of $540,000.

King's tormentors were brought up on criminal charges. On April 29, 1992, a nearly all-white Simi Valley jury found them innocent. Within moments South Central Los Angeles erupted in a riot that made Watts look like a campfire: 55 people killed, 2,300 injured, 1,100 buildings damaged or destroyed. Angelenos had known for years that their African American community remained isolated. They also knew that other minority communities were burgeoning; census data showed the percentage of foreign-born residents soaring from 11.2 in 1970 to 32.7 in 1990. But not until they saw African Americans, Korean Americans, Hispanic Americans, and mostly white police officers battling in the streets did they realize how far their city had devolved into a Brooklynish agglomeration of hostile ethnic enclaves.

With L.A. gripped by strife, San Francisco's misfortunes still fresh, and one team or the other playing badly, the rivalry devolved into mutual eye-poking. In late September 1989 the Giants had a chance to clinch at Dodger Stadium, but Lasorda declared, "They will not celebrate on our turf" and led his team to a three-game sweep. The Giants had to celebrate in the clubhouse after second-place San Diego eliminated itself with a loss. In 1991 the Dodgers went into the last series of the year at Candlestick tied with Atlanta for first. Will Clark, recalling Lasorda's battle cry two years earlier, exhorted the Giants to a sweep that handed the emerging Braves their first division title of the '90s.

In 1992 the rivalry hit bottom: the Dodgers and Giants finished last and next-to-last for the only time in their history. Lasorda bled oceans of blue as the Dodgers lost more than 90 games for the first time in 48 years. That same year Al Rosen turned 68 and Roger Craig 62. They had become graybeards with backaches and heart conditions, and as their attention drifted, so did the Giants. Owner Bob Lurie, frustrated by four failed attempts to secure public funding for a new stadium, sold the franchise to a group from Tampa, Florida.

Which made it reasonable to ask whether any player in the future would thank Steve Garvey and *his* generation for continuing the rivalry.

18. 1976: "Bobby Thomson Still Lives!"

By 1974 the Giants were in trouble. The Oakland Athletics stole headlines — and customers — with three consecutive world championships. Attendance nosedived to little more than half a million, worse than during the final years at the Polo Grounds. To stay in the black, Horace Stoneham traded one exciting young player after another — Bobby Bonds, George Foster, Dave Kingman, Gary Matthews, Garry Maddox — for cash and lesser players, mortgaging the team's competitive future.

Inquiries into the Giants' availability started in 1971, when a Washington, D.C., consortium invited Stoneham to replace the Senators, who had moved to Texas and been renamed the Rangers by maverick owner Bob Short. "Any invitation, or even discussions about our moving elsewhere, would be an utter waste of everybody's time," Stoneham assured the fans. "We couldn't leave the area if we wanted to. We signed a 35-year contract with the city of San Francisco when we moved here in 1958. It still has 22 years to run."

But by May 1975 Stoneham had exhausted his financial reserves and maxed out his $1 million credit line, giving him little choice except to sell. Offers poured in, including one from the Fukuoka Lions Baseball Club of Japan for $18 million. But in September 1975 that offer was rescinded due to economic conditions (rampant inflation had made exchange rates unstable) and the sense that even cosmopolitan San Franciscans would react poorly to foreign ownership. Stoneham took out a $500,000 loan from the National League, repayable by December 1. When he defaulted, the league took over administration of the team.

But baseball owners had bigger headaches than the Giants. On December 23, 1975, arbitrator Peter Seitz ruled that Dodger pitcher Andy Messersmith and retired Expo hurler Dave McNally were correct in their interpretation of the infamous reserve clause, which bound players to their teams in involuntary servitude: it applied for only one year, not perpetuity. The era of free agency had begun. Then there was the $20 million lawsuit filed by the state of Washington for moving the Seattle Pilots, the 1969 expansion franchise chronicled in Jim Bouton's *Ball Four,* to Milwaukee. Rumors surfaced that either the Giants or Athletics would move to Seattle as part of a settlement.

Coincident with the Seattle rumors came another: that the Giants would be bought by Labatt's, a Toronto brewery. Although at first the Giants denied the story, by January 8 word leaked that Labatt's had in fact offered Stoneham $13.25 million, $8 million for the team plus $5.25 million to settle the inevitable litigation with the city of San Francisco.

That same day, San Francisco inaugurated a new mayor, George Moscone. He had barely shaken the confetti off his suit when the Giants announced they had accepted Labatt's offer. "For once, the refrain 'Bye-Bye Baby!' is sad and subdued," eulogized *Examiner* writer Prescott Sullivan. In Canada, by contrast, they were jubilant. "Giants, Expos Rivalry Could Outstrip that Generated by Leafs, Canadiens," the *Toronto Globe and Mail* crowed, referring to Canada's hallowed hockey rivalry.

But the greenhorn mayor had some big talk of his own. "The San Francisco Giants will remain the San Francisco Giants if I have anything to do about it," he vowed, and immediately ordered the city attorney to prepare a restraining order that would halt the sale.

George Moscone was an able man, but there was no way he could save the Giants by himself. He needed an ally within the ranks of baseball. Lo and behold one appeared, as powerful as he could possibly want: Walter O'Malley, owner of the Los Angeles Dodgers.

It would be nice to think O'Malley wanted to keep the Giants in San Francisco for sentimental reasons, but as always it boiled down to business: the Giants drew the biggest crowds to Dodger Stadium. Not only would O'Malley's attendance drop if the rivalry ended, but it would cost him a lot more to send his team to Toronto for road games than to San Francisco.

A franchise sale required approval from three quarters of the league owners. Stoneham could not vote, meaning three of the other 11 owners could block the move. O'Malley had his own vote plus that of the San Diego Padres, run by old ally Buzzie Bavasi. He needed just one more. Reportedly he had more than that, but he never had to show his hand.

Horace Stoneham. His nephew Chub Feeney was president of the National League while the Giants were being sold. (Transcendental Graphics)

Moscone secured the restraining order against the sale of the Giants on January 12 and flew to the owners meeting in Phoenix the next day to serve it personally.

Did he have a local buyer for the Giants? the owners asked. Moscone identified two. One group was headed by Pizza Hut owner Raymond Rossi and Bob Short, the man who had moved the Senators from Washington to Texas. The other was spearheaded by Bob Lurie, son of real estate magnate Louis Lurie and a member of the Giants' board of directors. The owners assured Moscone that if the city produced a viable offer before Stoneham's lawyers overcame the restraining order, they'd vote to keep the team in San Francisco. "I'd love to get Walter O'Malley and Horace Stoneham alone in one room. I think we could thrash the whole thing out in short order," a glowing Moscone said after the meeting.

But neither ownership group held together long enough to make Stoneham a proposal. Superior Court Judge John Benson gave the city until noon on February 11 to find a new local buyer. Otherwise he would lift the restraining order and let the Giants go to Toronto.

Moscone worked the phones relentlessly. Four hours after the deadline he walked into Benson's courtroom between Short and Lurie, whom he'd brought together. After a round of questioning, Benson announced to a courtroom packed with 200 Giant fans that "the court considers the equities to be overwhelming on the side of the city and the court will issue a preliminary injunction." The spectators erupted in applause. Judge Benson had to remind them they weren't in Candlestick Park.

Emerging from the courthouse, Moscone shouted, "Bobby Thomson still lives!" For the rivalry, it was indeed a bottom-of-the-ninth miracle. But unlike 1951, this one satisfied the Dodgers, too.

The celebration was premature, however. Stoneham and the National League bosses still had to approve the sale, and though Stoneham said aye, the owners couldn't stomach Short, who had infuriated their American League brethren by moving, then abandoning, the Senators-Rangers. He could have a stake in the team, they decreed, but he couldn't be the managing partner. Short wouldn't invest unless he was the boss, so the deal fell apart. "I got on a conference call with the 11 other owners," recollected Lurie. "I requested that I have 48 hours to find a new partner. So they talked among themselves and came back and said, 'We'll give you five hours.'"

The rivalry looked dead after all.

Then, out of nowhere, 55-year-old Arizona cattleman Bud Herseth called Moscone's office and volunteered $4 million to keep the Giants in San Francisco. Moscone hooked up Herseth and Lurie, and the moneymen hastily worked out a partnership. "At five o'clock I got on the phone and I told the league about Herseth. Buzzie Bavasi knew somebody who knew Herseth. I said that I represented the two of us and that we will buy the club. So they voted and said yes," Lurie recalled. He and Herseth met for the first time a day later in San Francisco, where the millionaire meat packer's country boy persona created a sensation. "I know this is a business, and I will view it as such. But I want some recreation, too, and I think this will be more fun than loading cattle at the plant."

On March 4, 1976, in Lurie's office on the top floor of the Bank of America building, the city's tallest skyscraper, the sale of the Giants was closed. Lurie hired Bill Rigney, the Giants' first San Francisco manager, to manage the team again. The Giants played their first home game under the new ownership on April 9 against the Dodgers. They drew their largest crowd in 10 years.

19. 1978: "Let Them All In, Lock the Gates, and Go Play Somewhere Else"

On September 27, 1976, 64-year-old Walter Alston announced his retirement. His 23 consecutive years managing one team ranked second in National League history to the Giants' John McGraw. Only McGraw won more N.L. games than Alston's 2,040, and only McGraw won more pennants. Alston was the first Dodger manager to win a World Series, an achievement that eluded, among others, Hall of Famers Wilbert Robinson, Casey Stengel, and Leo Durocher, and then he did it three more times with ballclubs of radically different character. But because he was The Quiet Man he has seldom been equated with McGraw, and for most people he doesn't even come up to Stengel and Durocher. It's not the first time image has counted for more than results.

Alston's greatest gift to the Dodgers was stability, something they desperately needed as they changed cities, stadia, and styles. It was only fitting, then, that his legacy to Tommy Lasorda was the most enduring infield in baseball history.

Bill Russell arrived first. A raw but promising prospect in 1968, he nearly became a San Diego Padre in the expansion draft that winter, but Padre president Buzzie Bavasi, in a whopping conflict of interest, honored Dodger vice president Fresco Thompson's dying wish and drafted three non-prospects off the Los Angeles roster instead. Al Ferrara, Jim Williams, and Zoilo Versalles combined played 317 games for the Padres. Russell played 2,181 games for the Dodgers, more than anyone except Zack Wheat. He came up an outfielder, but in a decision that was to reverberate through

226

the Dodger organization for 30 years, Alston made him Maury Wills's successor at shortstop instead of hot-shot minor leaguer Bobby Valentine, a protégé of Tommy Lasorda.

Davey Lopes was much like Wills, a speedy middle infielder who started at another position (outfield) and took a long time to climb the minor league ladder. With second baseman Jim Lefebvre at the end of his career and top prospect Lee Lacy injured, Alston took a chance on Lopes in '73 and never regretted it.

The power-hitting Ron Cey, nicknamed "The Penguin" for his short legs and waddling run, forced his way into the third base job that same year. Workmanlike to the point of being taken for granted, by the time he left he'd hit more home runs in a Dodger uniform than anyone except Duke Snider, Gil Hodges, and Roy Campanella.

Cey's arrival left incumbent third baseman Steve Garvey with no place to play. Garvey possessed hitting skills the Dodgers craved after all those lean offensive years, but due to a shoulder separation from his college football days he threw poorly. First base was the logical spot for him, but the Dodgers already had a hitting first baseman in Bill Buckner. Alston decided to try Garvey at first anyway, moving Buckner to the outfield. On June 13, 1973, Garvey, Lopes, Cey, and Russell played the infield together for the first time. The Dodgers lost to the Phillies, 16–3. Undiscouraged, Alston 10 days later installed Garvey at first base permanently, and over the next eight and a half years the infield quartet propelled the Dodgers to four pennants, including Alston's last in 1974.

The Quiet Man also bequeathed Lasorda an imposing pitching staff led by Don Sutton (well on his way to becoming the all-time Dodger leader in wins, strikeouts, shutouts, and games pitched) and a pair of hard-hitting outfielders in Reggie Smith and Dusty Baker. Lasorda's mission was to take Alston's team, beefed up by the acquisition of center fielder Rick Monday, and overcome one of the most magnificent ballclubs ever assembled, Cincinnati's Big Red Machine. He did it by creating a new rivalry, threatening to fine his players if they wore anything red and engaging in a war of words with Red skipper Sparky Anderson. The Dodgers won the division by 10 games in 1977 and went to the World Series. "The rivalry in the '70s between the Dodgers and Reds was probably the best in the major leagues," recalled Los Angeles Times columnist Ross Newhan.

So when the 1978 season rolled around the Dodgers weren't thinking about that *other* rivalry, which had been moribund since Mays, McCovey, Marichal, and Perry moved on. (Marichal was finished in 1975, but the Dodgers invited him to try out. "You can't tell me he *liked* doing that," pitied one Giant booster. The Dominican Dandy made two starts for Los

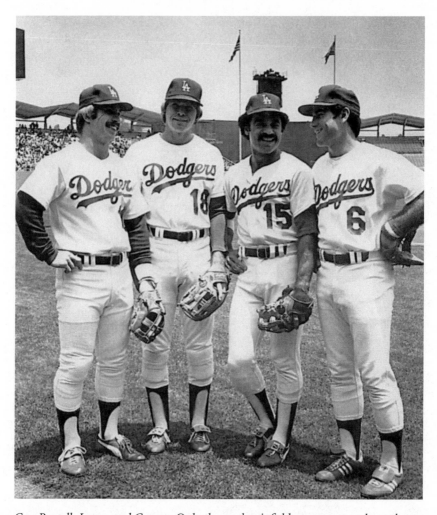

Cey, Russell, Lopes, and Garvey. Only three other infield quartets stayed together as long as five years: the 1906–10 Cubs (Tinker, Steinfeldt, Evers, and Chance); the 1948–52 Dodgers (Cox, Reese, Robinson, and Hodges); and the 1965–69 Cubs (Santo, Kessinger, Beckert, and Banks). (Courtesy Los Angeles Dodgers, Inc.)

Angeles, losing one, before retiring.) But the 1978 Giants had a tremendous young hitter in Jack Clark; a tremendous old hitter in Willie McCovey, returned from exiles in San Diego and Oakland; an underrated star in Darrell Evans; an overrated star in Bill Madlock; a staff ace in Vida Blue; a lefty-righty closer combo in Gary Lavelle and Randy Moffitt; and an instigator in John "The Count" Montefusco.

A Yankee fan from northern New Jersey, Montefusco never forgave the Dodgers for winning the 1963 World Series. He exacted revenge in his major league debut, September 3, 1974. Relieving starter Ron Bryant, who didn't retire a single batter, he gave up a run-scoring grounder but struck out the next two to get out of a jam. He then yielded just one run the rest of the game and hit a two-run homer in his first big league at-bat to catapult the Giants to a 9–5 victory.

From that day on Montefusco seldom missed an opportunity to antagonize the Dodgers. Before pitching the inaugural 1978 battle between the teams in Los Angeles, he told reporters, "I hate those guys. Every time Lasorda talks it gets a little deeper. I can't stand it." A near-capacity crowd turned out to see him get his comeuppance. Rick Monday slammed a pair of three-run homers off him, but the Giants went on a hitting spree of their own and won 10–7, stretching their surprising lead over the Dodgers to two and a half games. Montefusco responded to Dusty Baker's complaints about a knockdown pitch and a near-fight between Reggie Smith and Giant third base coach Jim Davenport with "the Dodgers don't know how to lose gracefully."

It was the Giants who lost ungracefully the next night, as the game was decided on a hotly disputed hit-batsman call with the bases loaded in the bottom of the ninth. When the Dodgers won the rubber game 4–1 behind Burt Hooton to pull within half a game of first place, the tone was set for the season, the best for the rivalry since 1962. Mused *Los Angeles Times* sports columnist John Hall, "The old rivalry was supposed to have joined the dinosaur ... now, the party reconvenes."

With, perhaps, too much booze and wacky weed. On Friday night, May 26, the Dodgers' first appearance of the year in San Francisco, the largest crowd ever to watch a night game at Candlestick pelted and taunted the Dodgers. During batting practice someone hit Lasorda with a paper cup. Later on, a fan earned an ovation for burning a Dodger flag. After McCovey hit a three-run homer, another fan paraded across the top of the Giant dugout with a sign reading "L.A. has the actors, S.F. the stars." Late in the game so many beer cans, rocks, and tomatoes rained on the Dodgers that the umpires threatened to call a forfeit. After the final out Reggie Smith climbed into the stands after a fan who'd been hurling racial epithets and beer at him; fortunately for the fan, teammates and security guards held Smith back. That the Giants won 6–1 seemed incidental.

Lasorda refocused his players in a team meeting before the next game, and behind Hooton the Dodgers went out and beat the Giants 3–1. The crowd was nowhere near as rowdy as the previous night. "Obviously, they can't handle a winner, but I don't think they're going to have to worry about having one for much longer," a still seething Smith said afterward.

John Montesfusco. He threw the last Giant no-hitter of the 20th century, on September 29, 1976, in Atlanta before a crowd of just 1,369. (Transcendental Graphics)

The next day Smith hit a homer off Montefusco and baited another record crowd (56,103) by taking a s-l-o-w trot around the bases. The fans responded by hanging him in effigy from the upper deck, then rocking the house as the Giants got a pinch-hit grand slam from Mike Ivie to win 6–5. Walking to the clubhouse door in right field after the game, Smith saluted jeering Giant fans with his middle finger.

"I wish I had taken even more time," he said of his home run trot. "My only satisfaction is that the win didn't go to Montefusco. He's a loud-mouthed braggart. People are going to stop believing him when he keeps telling them he's going to do this and that to the Dodgers. He hasn't done it yet and he won't as long as I'm here." Montefusco, asked whether he wanted to debate Smith, retorted, "I don't think Reggie is smart enough." Interjected Lasorda, "I could make a fortune buying him [Montefusco] for what I think he's worth and selling him for what he thinks he's worth."

And this was only May.

When the teams hooked up again in August, the Giants still had a lead of two and a half games over the Dodgers, who weren't even in second place; Cincinnati, despite injuries to Johnny Bench and Joe Morgan, had crept back into contention. More than 48,000 (42,084 paid) turned out for the chilly Thursday night opener at Candlestick. They were even uglier than the crowds in May. They showered apples, bananas, oranges, beer, ice, bottles, cups, cans, coins, golf balls, and firecrackers on Dodger

Reggie Smith. His teams had a .544 winning percentage in the 1,987 games he played, seventh best in major league history, just behind Willie Mays's .546. (Transcendental Graphics)

outfielders, at one point so menacing the Dodgers that the players armed themselves with bats and readied to defend their dugout. "There are three bad places in the league. In Philadelphia, the fans are loud. In New York, they're rowdy. But here, they're vicious," said Reggie Smith on a night when 48 fights left 13 security guards injured and several fans nursing stab wounds.

The Giants held a 4–3 edge with two out and the bases empty in the top of the ninth when the Dodgers' Lee Lacy lined one into the gap in right-center. Center fielder Larry Herndon caught the ball — but then right fielder Jack Clark collided with him, even harder than Jimmy Jordan had with Freddie Lindstrom back in 1936. The ball rolled out of Herndon's glove, and while the two Giants lay on the ground semiconscious, Lacy circled the bases. Umpire Jim Quick ruled there was no catch and that the game was tied. Those Giants who didn't run to their fallen teammates surrounded Quick and inflamed the crowd with their extended arguing. The fans quieted only after Darrell Evans singled home the game-winner in the bottom of the ninth.

The Dodgers could muster only two hits against Vida Blue the next night and fell four and a half behind. Not to take anything away from Blue's stellar performance, his 10th straight win, but the Dodgers seemed preoccupied by the fans' behavior. "I don't like to be threatened when I come to play. I don't think that's part of the game," said outfielder Billy North. Seconded catcher Joe Ferguson, "They're not good fans. They didn't support the team when it was bad."

Vin Scully, normally the paragon of diplomacy, said, "You know what they ought to do with the Friday night crowds here? They ought to let them all in, lock the gates, and go play somewhere else." He then added, "The fans at Ebbets Field and the Polo Grounds would never think of throwing things at the players."

Oh, Vin, what 20 years in Lotusland had done to your memory! Hank Sauer, the Giants' hitting coach, didn't deny that what happened in San Francisco was ugly, but he didn't let nostalgia muddy up the facts, either. "Many times in left field at Ebbets Field, I had to get out of the way of things thrown from the stands. The Polo Grounds wasn't much better."

Not just Scully, but the whole nation was aghast the next day when, with cameras from the Game of the Week rolling, a Giant fan tried to dump beer on Reggie Smith as he chased a foul fly down the right field line. The beer missed Smith, but Smith missed the ball, which could have affected the game. The endless replays embarrassed the city, leading the San Francisco Chronicle to editorialize defensively, "The disgraceful behavior of a very small group in the stands should not indict the vast majority of fans who attend to enjoy the game."

In the eighth the Dodgers put together a pair of runs to break a scoreless tie. But Bob Welch, making only his fourth career start, put two runners on for the Giants' young stud, 22-year-old Jack Clark, in the bottom of the ninth. Although he grew up in Azusa and Covina, Clark "was never a Dodger fan. I grew up a fan of the Giants—Mays, Tito [Fuentes], Juan Marichal, Gaylord Perry, all those guys." Now he had a chance to join his name with theirs, for it looked as though the entire season hinged on this confrontation. Lasorda walked to the mound. "Do you want this guy?" he asked his young pitcher. "I want him," answered Welch. "Then you got him," Lasorda said, and told him that if he was going to lose, to lose with his best fastball.

So Welch threw his best fastball. Three times. And Clark struck out swinging. The Dodgers won, 2–0. Then Burt Hooton twirled a four-hitter on Sunday to knock the Giants out of the lead for the first time in two months (Cincinnati took over) and restore the Dodgers' confidence.

When Alvin Dark made a lake of the Candlestick infield in 1962, Dodger fans responded with humor, blowing duck calls the next time San Francisco came to town. When Juan Marichal clobbered Johnny Roseboro in 1965, Dodger fans responded with class, hailing Willie Mays for stopping the ensuing donnybrook. How would they react to the Candlestick crowd's treatment of the Dodgers in 1978? With enthusiasm and civility. The August 10–13 four-game series drew more than 207,000 paying customers, and not a soul was hung in effigy.

In the first inning Jack Clark, facing Welch for the first time since that memorable strikeout five days before, homered to put the Giants up 1–0. But in the bottom of the inning Smith crushed a 435-foot shot to the back of the Dodger bullpen, igniting an onslaught that left Vida Blue — who had that 10-game win streak — a 12–2 loser. That tied the Giants and Dodgers for the division lead. When the Dodgers won the next night on a bases-loaded walk in the bottom of the ninth (delighting the largest Dodger Stadium crowd thus far that season) they had first place to themselves.

Welch's August 5 strikeout of Clark should have been the season's turning point, and the tag line to the game-winning walk on August 11 should have been "and the Dodgers never looked back." But once again the rivalry confounded narrative formulas. Over the next two games the Giants regrouped. They won a 3–2 nailbiter on Saturday, then won an 11-inning thriller on Sunday, overcoming two Smith homers against Montefusco ("Next time I'll throw him the resin bag," the chagrined Giant pitcher said) to regain the lead. "If the Dodgers had any doubts about us folding, this might have changed their minds," said Montefusco.

Doubt indeed plagued the Dodgers. The team that had cruised to a division title over the mighty Reds the year before suddenly couldn't shake off the Giants. In New York a week later, Steve Garvey asked Don Sutton whether the following quote, attributed to Sutton, was accurate: "All you hear about on our team is Steve Garvey, the all-American boy. Well, the best player on this team for the last two years ... is Reggie Smith. Reggie's not a façade or a Madison Avenue image. He's a real person." Sutton acknowledged its accuracy, and added a gratuitous remark about Garvey's celebrity wife Cyndy. According to Garvey, "I think he started poking me in the chest, and then I picked him up and threw him into the locker next to Tommy John's."

Said John, "I was in the clubhouse signing baseballs. They were wrestling, scratching, hitting — all real close. Someone yelled 'Stop the fight!' And Joe Ferguson said, 'Let 'em go. Maybe they'll kill each other.'"

The clubhouse wrangle belied Tommy Lasorda's boast that the Dodgers were one big, happy family. As Ferguson's comment showed, the Dodgers were a mutually jealous collection of stars, with a professedly mystified Garvey in the middle. But the fight got their juices pumping. By the time the Giants returned to Los Angeles for a two-game set on September 4, the Dodgers had surged a game ahead of them.

Giant manager Joe Altobelli arranged his rotation so Ed Halicki, who had won his last six starts at Dodger Stadium, pitched the first game. Halicki was tiring down the stretch, but he held firm early in this one, carrying a 4–0 lead into the bottom of the fifth. Then the Dodgers smashed seven hits and exploited two Giant errors to take a 5–4 lead that stood for the rest of the game. It was the eighth one-run decision in the 15 games the teams had played against each other.

Rain pushed the second contest back a day, giving Altobelli another rotation choice: did he want to send out scheduled starter Jim Barr, who hadn't beaten the Dodgers in four years, or Vida Blue on three days' rest? Despite the 12–2 beating he'd taken his last time out against L.A., Blue begged for the ball; he'd been wanting to pitch on a stepped-up schedule for weeks. But Altobelli, who had done a nearly perfect job to keep the Giants in contention, opted for Barr. "I don't lack confidence in any of our other pitchers. I don't want it to seem like [Blue] is the only guy here," he explained. So Barr got the start.

He didn't last four innings, and the Giants lost, 9–2, to fall three behind.

Although there were still three weeks to play, and the Giants had made up bigger deficits against the Dodgers, that was the game that decided the season. When the Dodgers arrived at Candlestick five days later, they had increased their lead to four. Even Giant fans sensed the season was over; the crowds of 35,965 and 38,073 were the smallest of the year for Dodger games.

What they saw galled them. The Dodgers cruised to a 7–2 victory against Blue in the first game, and in the second Davey Lopes doubled in the eighth and homered in the ninth to make the final score a decisive 8–0. Giant second baseman Bill Madlock admitted, "The Dodgers are sure of themselves, they don't have to think out there on the field. Everything they do is automatic. Just like clockwork. We're not like that."

The Big Red Machine closed strongly, but not strongly enough to overtake the Dodgers, who won the division by two and a half games and went on to the World Series, making Lasorda the first new manager since Gabby Street in 1930–31 to win pennants his first two seasons in the National League. The Giants, meanwhile, faded to third place, far enough back to lull some into believing the Reds and Dodgers really did have the more vital rivalry.

20. 1982: "Double Murder"

Under Tommy Lasorda, the Dodgers' relationship with Hollywood, always warm, turned tabloid hot. The new manager lined his office with photos of celebrities. He got Frank Sinatra to sing the national anthem before his first game, a win over the Giants. He invited Milton Berle, Walter Matthau, and other aging stars into the clubhouse, and even had sweaty insult comic Don Rickles perform in the dugout before a World Series contest (to hoots of "Ah, shove it," from Don Sutton).

The players also got into the act — literally. Steve Garvey hired the prestigious William Morris Agency to handle his endorsement requests. Other Dodgers appeared on TV shows ranging from *Family Feud* to *Fantasy Island*. New York sportswriters cracked that the Dodgers lost to the Yankees in the 1977 and 1978 World Series because "they spend more time in studio makeup than at batting practice."

Lasorda's obsession with the spotlight occasionally got him in trouble. After a disappointing 1979 he had angrily fired coach (and former player) Jim Lefebvre. In an echo of the falling out between John McGraw and Wilbert Robinson, Lefebvre signed on as a coach for the Giants. On Sunday morning, February 17, 1980, Lasorda and Lefebvre ran into each other at KNBC-TV, where they were taping separate interviews. Words were exchanged, and Lefebvre punched Lasorda in the mouth. So far as is known, Lefebvre is the only Giant ever to have had that satisfaction.

Lasorda answered criticism of his fame-seeking antics by winning. He led the Dodgers to a first-place tie in 1980 (the Astros won a one-game playoff for the division title) and finally beat the Yankees in the World

Series after the strike-divided 1981 season. So when the Dodgers sank 10½ games behind Atlanta on July 30, 1982, it wasn't Lasorda, winner of three pennants in five years, who felt the heat, but his veteran players. The Dodgers had refused to re-sign Don Sutton after 1980 and had shipped Davey Lopes to Oakland after 1981. Now came hints of wholesale changes after the 1982 season ended.

Reggie Smith thought the Dodgers were turning over their roster too fast. "Right away, there was a negative attitude in training camp. Several players have told me that," he revealed to reporters after the Dodgers lost a late-July game in San Francisco. He had good reason to speak out. The injury-plagued Smith had himself been a victim of the Dodger youth movement — and was now playing for the Giants. Out of respect for Smith's past contributions, Lasorda responded politely. "I don't agree with Reggie, but he's entitled to his opinion."

But then, Lasorda may also have decided it was time for someone else's words to motivate his players. If so, it was a brilliant decision. Two days after Smith's remarks the Dodgers went to Atlanta and whipped the Braves four straight. Then they met the Braves in Los Angeles and whipped them four straight again. Gloated one fan, "It is now clear that Sherman was a Dodger. How else could he have so easily marched through Georgia?" Over an amazing 11-day span, the Dodgers went from 10½ down to half a game in front.

The Giants came along with them, for they too found Reggie Smith inspiring. During the Atlanta collapse, he and fellow veteran Joe Morgan led the Giants on a 10-game win streak that brought them within four games of first place.

The Giants were not expected to contend in 1982. They'd finished just one game above .500 the year before, then traded away their *entire* starting rotation. Nor were they happy; manager Frank Robinson had a superb eye for talent, but an irascible manner. It took Robinson two months to sort out his pitching staff and figure out that Smith and Morgan made ideal intermediaries with his players. Even so, the Giants didn't rise above .500 until August 8.

Suddenly their four-game set with the Dodgers from August 12 through 15 had pennant implications. A sweep could tie them for first place, depending on what Atlanta did. But the Giants had lost 24 of their last 30 games at Dodger Stadium, including four at the beginning of the season. "It was always the attitude that we had to get out of L.A. without embarrassing ourselves," conceded Jim Lefebvre. But Morgan, who had put in all those years with the Big Red Machine, would have none of that. "The Dodgers used to intimidate the Giants. That was before I was here. The Dodgers don't intimidate me."

He scored the first run of the opener on a single by Smith. With the game tied 2–2 in the sixth, he tried to score again, this time on a fly to medium right. He arrived ahead of the throw, but catcher Mike Scioscia blocked the plate, causing the diminutive Morgan to bounce off him. Morgan repeatedly tried to touch home, and according to him, he finally got it with his left foot. But according to Scioscia, Morgan's foot was 18 inches from the plate when he tagged him. Umpire Eric Gregg sided with Scioscia.

As far as Reggie Smith was concerned, Gregg had declared it legal to block bases without the ball. So when speedy Steve Sax, the rookie second baseman from Sacramento ("I loved the Giants, but now I want to put them out of the race, get rid of them") singled in the bottom of the eighth, Smith hindered his access to the bag on pickoff attempts. Sax and first base coach Manny Mota complained. Manager Robinson came out to defend Smith. Fortunately the confrontation didn't escalate, but it did rouse Sax, who stole second to touch off a four-run rally. The 6–2 Dodger victory snapped the Giants' 10-game winning streak — and ended their fantasies about finishing the week in first place.

The next night the Dodgers jumped out to an early lead against Rich Gale, a 6'7" thrower. In the bottom of the fourth Gale hit Dodger right fielder Pedro Guerrero with a pitch. Guerrero cursed and pointed his finger at Gale as he reached first base, where Reggie Smith could have defused the situation by explaining that Gale was chronically wild. Instead Smith accused Ken Landreaux, the Dodger runner on second base, of stealing signs, called the errant pitch payback, and pointed his own finger at Guerrero. "The two edged closer, like a couple of playground rivals waiting for the other to take up the dare," the *Los Angeles Times* reported. Again, no escalation. And again the Dodger involved answered on the field, as Guerrero hit a three-run homer his next time up. Sax stole a base (setting the record for Dodger rookies) and homered, and Bob Welch knocked down nemesis Jack Clark as the Dodgers cruised to a 6–1 win. The only counter for the Giants? A solo shot by Smith.

Morgan and Smith toned down the bravado for the remainder of the series, and the Giants won 4–2 and 8–6 to close back within four. As valuable as the two veterans were, the real secret of San Francisco's success lay in its bullpen, which repulsed Dodger onslaughts in both games. The Giants would finish the season giving up more runs than they scored, but they won an amazing 17 games in which they trailed after seven innings (the Dodgers won just five), went 12–8 in games that were tied after seven, and blew only seven leads after the seventh.

When the Giants and Dodgers next met on September 24, the standings were virtually unchanged from five weeks before: L.A. up by one over Atlanta, by four over San Francisco. Tommy Lasorda missed the series opener with an intestinal flu. If the virus hadn't already given him *agita,* the game would have: the Dodgers took an early 2–0 lead but lost 3–2 as Giant relievers Al Holland and Greg Minton pitched no-hit ball over the last six innings. Declared Morgan, "There are no great teams in this division. The Dodgers are very good, the best team overall. But that doesn't mean they're going to win it."

Jack Clark. His 26-game hitting streak in 1978 is the Giants' longest in San Francisco. (Transcendental Graphics)

The next day the Dodgers were ahead 4–3 in the eighth with pitcher Fernando Valenzuela going for his 20th win. Shortstop Bill Russell reached down to catch a sinking line drive by Giant catcher Bob Brenly. Umpire Harry Wendelstedt — the same Wendelstedt who 14 years earlier had denied Dick Dietz first base after Don Drysdale hit him with a pitch, preserving Drysdale's record scoreless inning streak — ruled that Russell trapped the ball. A startled Russell, certain he'd made the catch, threw belatedly to first and pulled Garvey off the bag for an error. Against the next batter, Ron Cey made an error. Then the Giants' rookie center fielder, Chili Davis, hit a grounder to short that took a bad hop past Russell and tied the game. Lasorda brought in lefty Terry Forster to pitch to left-handed Joe Morgan, and Morgan ripped a game-winning single. The Giants' sinkerballing closer Greg Minton held on in the ninth for his 30th save.

"For us," said Reggie Smith, "this is the playoffs."

Because he'd won 17 of the last 18 games he'd started against the Giants, Burt Hooton pitched the final game of the set. He did well through four innings, but Morgan ignited a three-run rally in the fifth by walking and stealing his 23rd base (he was 39) and stalwart Darrell Evans capped it with a homer. "Rocking and reeling, this is the Dodger network," Vin Scully smarted after the third out.

But the Dodgers clawed back. With runners on first and second in the bottom of the sixth, Garvey, responding to cheers from a capacity crowd afraid he was playing his last home game in Los Angeles, singled to knock in a run. A walk to Cey and the bases were loaded.

Frank Robinson summoned reliever Al Holland, who hadn't given up a hit in his last 16⅔ innings. As Holland finished his warmups, Morgan strolled to the mound. "Let's have fun," he said, oblivious to the cries of 50,000 Dodger fans smelling pennant. The beefy Holland, a lefty facing a predominantly right-handed lineup, stopped the rally on a pop-up and long fly, and though the Dodgers ended his no-hit streak at 58 batters, he nailed down the Giants' first three-game sweep in Los Angeles since 1967.

Going into the final week of the season, then, the Dodgers clung to a one-game lead over both the Braves and Giants. But they and the Braves were faltering, whereas the Giants had momentum. The Giants also had the schedule on their side: they played their last seven games at home, including two against Atlanta and three against Los Angeles, the teams they had to beat. "We've got it coming together and the Dodgers are going the other way," said Morgan.

So what happened? Both teams choked. The Giants lost a pair to Atlanta. The Dodger losing streak grew to eight. With just three games left, the Giants and Dodgers were tied for second, one game behind Atlanta. The Braves would play mediocre San Diego. The Giants and Dodgers would play each other at Candlestick. One of them would win at least two and have a shot at tying or passing the Braves. The other would finish with nothing.

One night after a mere 13,082 paid to see the Giants against the Astros, 53,281 stuffed themselves into Candlestick for game one against the Dodgers. Through seven innings Jerry Reuss of the Dodgers and home-town boy Fred Breining of the Giants pitched shutouts, but in the eighth Breining faltered. He walked Steve Sax, gave up a single to Dusty Baker, and walked Garvey to load the bases. Left-handed Rick Monday came up. With lefty Al Holland ready in the bullpen, Frank Robinson ambled to the mound, looked at Breining, and made a fatal mistake.

"You dug this hole yourself, get out of it yourself," he said.

Monday hit Breining's third pitch over the right field wall for a grand slam, and the Dodgers won, 4–0. The Braves won also, meaning the Dodgers could still win the division, but all the Giants could hope for was a tie.

On Saturday, October 2, the 46,562 fans had barely settled into their seats when the Dodgers bombed the Giants right out of contention, plating six runs in the second inning. By the fifth it was 10–0, and Robinson, in a move that surprised even his players, conceded the game by yanking his regulars. The sole Giant highlight in the 15–2 rout: Morgan's 1,709th career walk, passing Mel Ott for the National League record.

Although Robinson conceded the game, and by extension the season, he wasn't conceding the Dodgers the pennant. He'd pulled his regulars, he explained, because he wanted them rested for the finale, which the Dodgers had to win to gain a share of first place (for the Braves had won again, clinching at least a tie). Said Morgan, "I don't want to sit around all winter with a 15–2 loss to the Dodgers on my mind."

It was October 3. On the same date in 1951, Bobby Thomson hit the Shot Heard 'Round the World. On the same date in 1962, the Giants snatched another pennant from the Dodgers. The 47,457 fans at Candlestick on October 3, 1982, knew they would see history. But which would it be, a Dodger killing or a Dodger redemption?

Lasorda started ace Fernando Valenzuela. "Here was a hero who did not speak English, did not have a good body, who came from a humble background, but who walked like a general," was how Jaime Jarrin, the Dodgers' Spanish language broadcaster (and Valenzuela's interpreter), explained Fernandomania, a craze that drew over 40,000 per start both home *and* away. Valenzuela was the bridge by which the Dodgers finally connected with L.A.'s large Mexican American community, which still remembered the desterrados of Chavez Ravine. As heir to the franchise's long tradition of storybook characters, he was the natural choice to break the curse of October 3.

He got a lead in the second when Ron Cey, like Garvey probably playing his last game as a Dodger, clanged a two-run homer off Giant starter Bill Laskey. But Valenzuela couldn't hold it, giving up a pair in the bottom of the inning. After that, however, he was untouchable, tuning out the crowd's urgent cries of *Beat L.A.!* to pitch hitless ball over the next four frames.

In the seventh the Dodgers got a chance to break the game open: bases loaded, one out, and Bill Russell up. Lasorda called for a squeeze. Russell squared, made contact — and fouled the ball off. On the next pitch he struck out. Valenzuela was due next. Should Lasorda keep his best pitcher in the game, or should he go for the runs? It was his biggest decision of the season, especially since the Braves had already lost, and the Dodgers still had a chance to tie for first. Valenzuela had thrown a lot of pitches, striking out nine and walking five in six innings. Believing him tired, Lasorda sent Jorge Orta to pinch hit.

Lasorda's move was even more puzzling than Frank Robinson's deci-

Fernando Valenzuela. Better known for glancing heavenward in mid-delivery than for throwing the best screwball since Hubbell. (Transcendental Graphics)

sion to leave Fred Breining in against Rick Monday two games earlier, for Valenzuela wasn't tired at all. After the game he said through Jaime Jarrin, "My arm was okay. It was very well. It felt very nice." And as a pinch hitter Jorge Orta was batting .154, 18 points *lower* than Valenzuela. Evidently, pitching coach Ron Perranoski interpreted Valenzuela's shoulder stretches in the on-deck circle as indications of tightness, and no one thought to ask a nearby Spanish speaker—fellow Mexican Orta, for instance, or Lasorda himself, who had learned the language playing in Cuba—to confirm Perranoski's perception. "I thought I was going to hit," Valenzuela said of his stretching. "I was getting ready."

Orta grounded weakly to second. The threat was over, and the Dodger ace was out of the game.

The Giants wasted no time taking advantage of reliever Tom Niedenfuer. Bob Brenly led off the bottom of the seventh with a single and pinch hitter Champ Summers doubled, sending Brenly to third. Niedenfuer hung around long enough to strike out Giant pitcher Greg Minton, then was replaced by lefty Terry Forster, who whiffed pinch hitter Jim Wohlford. With two outs, two on, and the game tied, Joe Morgan came to bat.

Just eight days earlier Morgan had lashed a game-winning single off Forster. With first base open Lasorda could have walked Morgan intentionally, but Jack Clark followed, so the Dodger manager elected to stick with the lefty-lefty matchup. Forster quickly got ahead in the count, one ball, two strikes. Then he attempted to throw one of his wicked sliders, which broke late and fast from left-handed batters.

But he got it a little high, and it didn't break that much.

Morgan hammered it with such force that it landed in the seats and bounced back on the field before he reached first base. The crowd hollered itself hoarse as he threw a fist in the air and exulted in what has since come to be known as the Little Shot Heard 'Round the World.

To their credit, the Dodgers refused to die, rallying in the eighth on doubles by Ken Landreaux and Dusty Baker to make the score 5–3. Steve Garvey came up as the tying run. Talk about storybook possibilities! But Brenly noticed Baker, on second base, tipping locations to Garvey. With the count 2 and 2, he and Minton decided to use Baker's chicanery against him. Brenly set up inside. Minton threw *outside*, and the stunned Garvey took a called third strike in what indeed turned out to be his last at-bat as a Dodger.

While Forster cried in the Dodger dugout, Minton pitched a routine ninth to end what *San Francisco Chronicle* columnist Lowell Cohn labeled a "morbid baseball weekend in San Francisco, a double murder." That it had been, for 1982 was the only year the rivals eliminated each other from contention at the season's very end.

21. 1992: "Tampa'd With"

Of all the twists in the rivalry's history, none would have been bigger than this: *Giant manager Tommy Lasorda.* Yet for a moment it was a possibility.

The catch being that it wouldn't have been in San Francisco.

The Giants had enjoyed their best five-year stretch of attendance from 1987 to 1991, averaging nearly 1.9 million customers per season. They'd come a long way from the time when Herb Caen could quip, "I envision the day when the announcer at Candlestick Park will say, 'And now, folks, here's the lineup. In left field, Joe Orengo. In center, Dave Falk. In right, Stu Adams. At first base, Blair Fuller. At third, Ida Brown, and behind the plate, Nick Geracimos.' The team? No, the attendance." But from owner Bob Lurie's perspective, the numbers were deceptive. The Giants still drew less than the National League average, and less than two thirds what the Dodgers drew. Back in New York, the Giants had topped the National League in attendance 24 times. In San Francisco, they'd never come close to leading the league. Something was holding the franchise back.

Many pointed to the Oakland Athletics, who cut into Giant attendance as soon as they arrived and averaged nearly half a million more fans per year during that '87 to '91 span. The Bay Area wasn't big enough to support two major league franchises, the wisdom went, and the Giants couldn't compete against an A's team that had won three league championships and featured Bash Brothers Mark McGwire and Jose Canseco. Others argued that New York, Los Angeles, and Chicago successfully nourished two franchises, so the problem wasn't the A's but the Northern California lifestyle: a preference for active rather than passive participation in sports and a surfeit of other entertainment options.

For Lurie, who bought out partner Bud Herseth in 1978, both these arguments had merit, but were secondary. The real impediment, he was convinced, was frigid, remote Candlestick Park. The first time Lurie announced his intention to sell the Giants, after a hapless 1984 season in which the team lost 96 games and suffered a 20 percent drop in attendance, *San Francisco Chronicle* columnist Glenn Dickey pegged it as "an obvious ploy to put pressure on the city to build a downtown stadium. Nothing gets done unless it seems to be an emergency; witness the public apathy toward talk of the Giants moving in 1976 until Horace Stoneham actually sold the club to Toronto interests."

Then-mayor Dianne Feinstein suggested the city dome Candlestick. No way, said Lurie, who embarked on a campaign—four, actually—to win voter approval for a new stadium. The first initiative, to build a park at Seventh and Townsend Streets, lost narrowly in November 1987 even though the Giants had won the National League West and set an all-time attendance record. The second, in 1989, called for a baseball-only park by the bay at China Basin; although the Giants had won the pennant and surpassed 2 million in attendance for the first time ever, the measure lost by 2,000 votes.

With that Lurie gave up on San Francisco—but not on the Bay Area. He noted the growing proportion of Giant fans coming from the South Bay and in 1990 proposed that Santa Clara County finance a new park via a 1 percent utility tax. The proposition lost county-wide, but won narrowly in San Jose. That encouraged Lurie to work with San Jose mayor Susan Hammer on one last stab, a June 1992 ballot measure that would increase utility taxes by 2 percent and, in addition to building a stadium, raise money for education and public safety.

Even the most spendthrift politician knew better than to propose a tax increase during a recession, but here were Lurie and Hammer doing just that. Liberal voters viewed it as a corporate subsidy hiding behind a social welfare initiative. Moderates worried about the additional traffic on Highway 237. Conservatives just didn't like the tax. Stadium advocates outspent opponents 85–1, but on election day got less than 46 percent of the vote.

So now Lurie gave up on the Bay Area, asking for and receiving permission from baseball commissioner Fay Vincent to shop the team elsewhere.

Establishment San Francisco still wanted the Giants. Mayor Frank Jordan, a former police chief with little political experience but strong ties to the city's wealthy elite, enlisted real estate mogul Walter Shorenstein to find local buyers. Shorenstein thought he had a possibility in cable TV tycoon H. Irving Grousbeck, but when Grousbeck demanded the city definitively commit to building a new ballpark, the deal fell through.

Which hardly surprised Lurie. On August 7, 1992, he went ahead and sold the Giants for $115 million to a group from Tampa, Florida.

The Gulf Coast excitedly planned for the Giants' arrival. The Sun-coast Dome would have to be fitted for baseball: turf, clubhouses, dugouts, foul poles, and, of course, luxury boxes. There would have to be new management, too, and who better for that than ... Thomas Charles Lasorda, best friend of Tampa Giants partner Vincent Piazza! (He was godfather to Piazza's son Mike, a promising Dodger prospect.) Lasorda would manage the team for a year, then become general manager, handing the field duties to longtime protégé Bobby Valentine. It was the perfect excuse for Tommy to exit Los Angeles, where he was enduring his worst season and was just one year shy of the age Walter Alston was put out to pasture.

Unnamed sources confirmed that Lasorda spoke hopefully of working with Piazza and Valentine in Tampa, but publicly Tommy disavowed interest. His contract with the Dodgers ran through 1993. And he still bled Dodger Blue.

Besides, it was premature to bank on the Tampa Giants. In San Francisco, the sense of emergency Glenn Dickey spoke of had finally set in.

First came the shock and fury. Sportswriter Bruce Jenkins, in a column so inflammatory his editors spiked it, told Lurie, the man who had saved the team 16 years earlier, "You've taken one of the most storied franchises in American sports, playing in the best city in the country, and moved it to a humidity-tortured sweatbox populated mostly by 88-year-olds and losers in cut-off jeans." And Scott Ostler, a defector from the *Los Angeles Times* to the *San Francisco Chronicle*, sneered even before the sale's official announcement that Lurie, "if he owned the cable cars, would sell them to Los Angeles to be converted into frozen yogurt stands."

Next came grief. *San Francisco Examiner* columnist Ray Ratto wailed that, among other consequences of the Giants' departure, "we lose our hatred for the Dodgers ... we lose Tommy Lasorda's long walk to and from the right field corner nine times a season." Pleaded the *Examiner* in an editorial, "Tradition should stand for something.... The Giants' historic rivalry with the Dodgers, which moved west with the teams, shouldn't be Tampa'd with."

But then San Francisco cast off its sackcloth and formulated a two-pronged plan to save the Giants. Mayor Jordan would mobilize public opinion to pressure major league baseball to reject the sale. Shorenstein would redouble his efforts to field a competitive bid.

Jordan took out full-page ads urging fans to write the commissioner's office. He launched a campaign to sell 15,000 season tickets. He sponsored Save the Giants rallies. The response was underwhelming. The ads produced about a thousand letters plus some calls and faxes, according to the commissioner's office. The ticket campaign brought in all of 237 deposits the first week, when enthusiasm was highest. (Tampa already had 27,000 season ticket deposits.) And an August 18 noontime rally at Union Square drew a mere 1,500 onlookers; perhaps the no-hitter Kevin Gross of the Dodgers threw at the Giants the night before caused even the most diehard San Francisco fans to lose heart.

Shorenstein fared better. He couldn't find another deep pocket in the Bay Area, but he did find George Shinn, owner of the National Basketball Association's Charlotte Hornets. Shinn proposed to put up $20 million of his own and secure a loan for $30 million more to get San Francisco halfway to its goal of a $100 million counteroffer. Shorenstein rounded up local partners to provide the rest of the money, but the deal was slapdash; it probably wouldn't weather examination at the September 9 owners meeting. If San Francisco was to keep the Giants, it would need what it got in 1976: more time, and a powerful ally within the baseball establishment.

It got both.

In the three years since he had taken office, commissioner Fay Vincent had done something to rile almost every owner. He increasingly showed signs of aspiring to the job's *stated* purpose, which was to act in the game's best interests, to the detriment of its *actual* purpose, which was to cover the owners' grubby intentions with a magisterial patina. The owners planned on going to extremes to defeat the players' union in upcoming negotiations. Would Vincent back them? They couldn't be sure, and if they couldn't be sure, they had to get rid of him, because otherwise he might undermine them. Led by Milwaukee Brewer owner Bud Selig, they mounted a drive to force him out.

Vincent fought hard to retain his job, but on September 7, just two days before the owners were to discuss the Giants, he resigned. The owners realized that without a commissioner the game's integrity would become suspect. That was a bigger problem than the future of the Giants, so San Francisco won a reprieve until October.

Then Jordan and Shorenstein found their powerful ally: Peter O'Malley, owner of the Dodgers since his father's death in 1979. If four N.L. owners voted against the Giants' move to Tampa, the sale would be killed. Shortly after the September meeting, O'Malley revealed that he would vote no. His stated reason was that the rivalry still mattered, and if — as was expected now that the owners had taken direct control of the game — the leagues were realigned into three divisions each, he wanted someone familiar besides the Padres in the National League West.

But now that the Dodgers drew 40,000 fans for *every* game, the rivalry wasn't as vital to the team's financial well-being as it used to be. There had to be deeper reasons for O'Malley's opposition. One was that baseball's television ratings were sagging, and with national contracts set to expire after 1993, it made no sense for the National League to trade down from the fifth-biggest market to the 20th. Another was that the National League had granted Miami an expansion team for 1993, and though the Marlins' prickly owner, Wayne Huizenga, publicly welcomed the Giants to Tampa with talk of a new rivalry, behind closed doors he made it clear he wanted exclusive rights to Florida, at least for the first few years while the Marlins struggled.

Peter O'Malley lacked his father's eloquence, but his word carried weight nonetheless. A day after he told the *Los Angeles Times* he preferred the Giants to remain in San Francisco, the owners' committee looking into the sale decreed that two key Tampa investors, Vincent Piazza and Vincent Tirendi, represented too much out-of-town money and needed to reduce their stakes in the partnership.

It was the break San Francisco had been waiting for, although if the owners were concerned about out-of-town money in the Tampa bid, what about George Shinn's role in the San Francisco package? Shorenstein assembled his group on October 5. When the roomful of minority partners heard Shinn say he intended to run the franchise on a shoestring, they sprang some grim news of their own: with help from Shorenstein, Jordan, sports agent Leigh Steinberg, and CBS executive Larry Baer, Safeway Stores chief executive Peter Magowan, a Giant rooter since his youth, had rounded up enough money to replace Shinn's, and Shinn was out.

San Francisco presented its $95 million, all-local bid to the National League on October 12. The owners said it wasn't enough, so the bid was raised to $100 million on October 28.

Lurie didn't like it. Not only was it $15 million below the Tampa bid, but it stipulated that he loan the partnership $10 million. True, that was also part of the deal with Tampa, but the Tampa group reportedly had new investors willing to pay off Lurie immediately. When the owners announced they would decide the Giant question once and for all on November 10, Lurie lobbied mightily for Tampa.

His fellow owners wholeheartedly sympathized with Lurie's desire to realize the maximum value of his franchise. But pitted against Peter O'Malley, what chance did he have? The N.L. lords voted 9–4 against the move to Tampa, leaving Lurie little choice but to accept the San Francisco group's lower offer. Before you cry for Bob, though, consider that he bought the team for under $10 million.

And that's how Giant and Dodger fans alike were spared the sight of Tommy Lasorda in black and orange.

PART VII

1993–2002: Do You Believe in Dustiny?

	Giants	Dodgers
Where They Played	Candlestick Park, 1993–99 Pacific Bell Park, 2000–02	Dodger Stadium
Owners	Peter Magowan Group	Peter O'Malley, 1993–98 The News Corporation, 1998–2002
Managers	Dusty Baker	Tommy Lasorda, 1993–96 Bill Russell, 1996–98 Glenn Hoffman, 1998 Dave Johnson, 1999–2000 Jim Tracy, 2001–02
Best Players	Matt Williams, Barry Bonds, Jeff Kent, Robb Nen	Eric Karros, Mike Piazza, Shawn Green
Wore Both Uniforms but Shouldn't Have	Brian Johnson	Orel Hershiser
Division Championships, League Championships, **World Championships**	*1997, 2000,* 2002	*1994, 1995*
Won-Lost vs. Each Other	63–73 (.463)	73–63 (.537)
Won-Lost vs. Rest of League	777–642 (.548)	746–672 (.526)

"I truly believe they [African Americans] *may not have some of the necessities to be, let's say, a field manager, or perhaps a general manager."*
So Dodger general manager Al Campanis told Ted Koppel of ABC's *Nightline* television program on April 6, 1987, during a show intended to honor the 40th anniversary of Jackie Robinson's major league debut. Given a chance to retract, Campanis only compounded his error: *"Why are black men, or black people, not good swimmers? Because they don't have the buoyancy."* The ugly remarks triggered a national debate over just how thoroughly major league baseball in general — and the Dodgers in particular — had integrated. The Dodgers had never appointed an African American manager or general manager at any level, and in their history had named only two black coaches to the big club (Jim Gilliam and Manny Mota). They had been using Robinson's legacy as a figleaf for decades.

Campanis's statement was all the more outrageous considering that the man destined to become baseball's most acclaimed African American manager played right under his nose for eight years.

In fairness to Campanis, few in baseball's hidebound oligarchy would have recognized the managerial potential of blues-blasting, motorcycle-riding outfielder Johnnie B. "Dusty" Baker. The line drives rocketing off Baker's bat from 1976 to 1983 put him in the Los Angeles top 10 in hits, home runs, extra base hits, total bases, and RBIs. Appreciative teammates nicknamed him Doctor Scald. But he was getting past his prime, and when unfounded rumors surfaced in 1984 that he sold cocaine to the hopelessly addicted Steve Howe, the Dodgers tried to unload him. As a 10-year veteran with five years on his current team, he had a right to veto trades involving him, and did — hardly the behavior of an organization man. So the Dodgers waived him.

The Giants picked him up. He stepped out of the dugout late on opening day at Candlestick and received a surprisingly warm hand. That was nothing compared to his homecoming, when 49,256 fans filled Chavez Ravine for Dusty Baker Night. They gave him a standing ovation as he strode to the on-deck circle to pinch hit in the top of the ninth, and cheered after he singled to give the Giants a 5–4 lead.

Though he played just one year in San Francisco, Baker made enough of an impression that the Giants hired him as batting coach in 1988. When new owners took over in late 1992 and needed to make a clean break with the past, they gambled on him as manager. "People ask me how I'm going to deal with the egos of today's players. They forget that in L.A., we had some major egos, and I was one of them," he said. And that wasn't the only lesson he'd learned with the Dodgers. "Tommy Lasorda taught me the power of belief and not being afraid to stick your neck out." At the same time, however, "I don't want to be a star manager. I played for a star manager, okay?"

What he became was the central figure in a role reversal that saw the Giants embrace tried-and-true Dodger values while the Dodgers lapsed into the disarray that had long typified the Giants.

As Walter Alston and Tommy Lasorda had done with him, Baker stood by slumping or injured players, eschewing the Herman Franks ethic that had led to the disastrous trade of Orlando Cepeda nearly 30 years before. Like Lasorda, he wore his emotions on his sleeve so the players knew exactly where he stood. And by staying calm through losing streaks and sticking around longer than any Giant manager since John McGraw, he brought much-needed stability.

But Baker also improved on the Dodger model, creating the most inclusive atmosphere in the major leagues. He always had at least one white, one black, and one Latino coach on his staff. He allowed girls and the players' sons to serve as batboys. He lent his support to Until There's a Cure Day, the first AIDS benefit staged by a professional sports team. The upshot? The Giants developed into a cohesive, overachieving unit, the most popular with fans since Mays, McCovey, and Marichal wore the uniform. Several players signed less-than-market-value contracts to stay in Baker's clubhouse. And the Giants became perennial winners for the first time in 30 years. Baker himself won three Manager of the Year awards.

Closer Rod Beck reputedly was the first to describe as "Dustiny" the gritty, spirited play that carried the Giants past the Dodgers for the division title in 1997 and continued to characterize them in subsequent seasons. Even Dodger fans believed in it. When Los Angeles looked for a new manager after 2000, hopes abounded that the momentarily unsigned Baker would abandon San Francisco and skip south.

Other than to fire Campanis and denounce his remarks, the Dodgers at first did little to make themselves more inclusive. But the tremendous contributions of free agent Kirk Gibson, hero of the 1988 World Series, encouraged them to sign more, and it was probably no coincidence that the next three stars they landed, Eddie Murray, Darryl Strawberry, and Eric Davis, were African American natives of Los Angeles. They proved disappointing, however, and that, combined with a belated understanding of L.A.'s increasingly multicultural character, led the Dodgers to pursue the idea of inclusion from another angle.

Every Dodger chief executive since Larry MacPhail had taken bold steps to popularize the game. From the earliest years of his reign, Peter O'Malley's ambition was to internationalize baseball's appeal. In 1995 he

Dusty Baker. "It hurt me, but it didn't surprise me," *he said of Al Campanis's* Nightline *remarks. (National Baseball Hall of Fame Library, Cooperstown, N.Y.)*

made Hideo Nomo the first Japanese big leaguer since the Giants' Masanori Murakami 30 years earlier. Even before Nomo arrived, the Dodgers brought up Chan Ho Park, the first Korean to play in the majors. By 1999 the Dodgers had players from 17 countries and U.S. territories in their organization.

Despite that laudable advance, plus division titles in 1994 and 1995 and every Rookie of the Year award from 1992 to 1996, the Dodgers came apart in the '90s, undone by big-money languor and a string of calamities. Darryl Strawberry left on the eve of the 1994 season to enter a drug rehabilitation program and was released with two years still on his contract. A traumatic labor dispute ended play that August and deprived the Dodgers of a shot at the World Series. In 1995 general manager Fred Claire called up Mike Busch, a replacement (strike-breaking) player, and touched off a clubhouse uproar; the Dodgers won the division, but fans, seeing Busch as a lunch-pail guy against 24 union bullies, hooted the team. Then in 1996 the chief villain in the Busch affair, union representative Brett Butler, himself became an object of sympathy when he developed throat cancer.

But the biggest blows were yet to come.

On June 24, 1996, 68-year-old Tommy Lasorda, rotund as ever despite well-publicized campaigns to lose weight, went to the hospital complaining of abdominal pain. Doctors discovered he'd had a heart attack. At first Lasorda insisted he'd return to the dugout, but the concern of his closest confidants and memories of friends who had died of heart attacks (including Don Drysdale, in 1993, at age 56) combined to dissuade him. He retired fourth all-time in continuous service to one team, behind Connie Mack, John McGraw, and Walter Alston. His four pennants trailed only Casey Stengel, McGraw, Mack, Joe McCarthy, and Alston. But more to the point was *Los Angeles Times* columnist Ross Newhan's assertion that "no manager has ever been — nor probably ever will be — more synonymously linked to his organization, nor more of an ambassador for it and his sport."

In San Francisco, *Examiner* columnist Ray Ratto asked, "So now who are we supposed to boo?"

Then on January 6, 1997, Peter O'Malley shocked the baseball universe by announcing he would sell the team. "Professional sports today is as high risk as the oil business. You need a broader base than an individual family to carry you through the storm," he explained. Moreover, if he were to die, his estate, i.e. the Dodgers, would be taxed at 55 percent, whereas by selling the team he would pay only 28 percent.

But like protestations that Al Campanis wasn't a racist, O'Malley's arguments didn't hold up. O'Malley *père* had invested roughly $20 million in the Dodgers for stock purchases and park construction. Forty-eight years later, O'Malley *fils* sold the team for $311 million, a more than 15-fold appreciation. And this didn't include the untold millions in *revenue* the family had pulled from the franchise. High risk? The Dodgers were a safer investment than an index mutual fund in the booming '90s. As for the inheritance tax rationale, O'Malley knew sportswriters were unlikely to call an attorney to learn about loopholes like trusts, through which his father first bought into the Dodgers.

So why did O'Malley want out, particularly when the 1994 strike was still suppressing franchise values? It could be that he really did doubt his family could keep Mike Piazza, Eric Karros, Raul Mondesi, Chan Ho Park, and Hideo Nomo together, especially after the White Sox signed Albert Belle to a five-year, $55 million contract. Reportedly he was also disappointed that the city of Los Angeles rejected his bid to build another stadium in Chavez Ravine for a National Football League franchise to replace the departed Rams.

But most likely O'Malley had grown weary of his colleagues. The game had been taken over by so-called "small-market" owners, whose twin ambitions were to humiliate the players and squeeze every nickel from the sport. They did not welcome O'Malley's participation on committees. They rejected his ideas for ending the 1994 strike. It seemed baseball no longer had a place for someone who raced sailboats as a boy, graduated from the Wharton School of Finance, and wore dark, custom-tailored suits to the office. So O'Malley sold the team to Rupert Murdoch's News Corporation, a media conglomerate that purveyed sleaze, sensation, and ballgames on its Fox Network and cable channels.

Just as the sale was approved, freshly retired Brett Butler ripped superstar Mike Piazza as "a moody, self-centered, '90s player." Though Butler later recanted, the new Dodger management heard him, especially after Piazza proclaimed himself "confused and disappointed" by a six-year, $80 million contract offer and demanded $100 million. On May 15, 1998, in the most spiteful Dodger trade since Maury Wills was packed off to Pittsburgh, News Corporation executives shipped Piazza to the Florida Marlins, who a week later dealt him to the Mets, run by Lasorda's surrogate son, Bobby Valentine.

A month later the new owners fired manager Bill Russell and general manager Fred Claire. Amid rumors that Valentine would become manager after the season, the normally reticent Russell alleged that Lasorda, promoted to the front office, had masterminded the ouster because Russell hadn't sufficiently appreciated Lasorda's help in getting him the job — or the advice Lasorda had been offering since. "Tommy's just vicious when he wants something. He did the same sort of thing when he was a coach under Walter Alston, and wanted Alston's job," Russell charged. To which Lasorda retorted, "In no way did I ever undermine him. All I've ever done is helped him and pulled for him."

Glenn Hoffman ran the team the rest of 1998, but then the Dodgers, who'd had just two managers in 43 years, searched for their third in six months. They hired Dave Johnson, a proven winner but a maverick bound to clash with a front office that signed 34-year-old pitcher Kevin Brown to a record seven-year, $105 million deal just six months after refusing to extend similar terms to the younger (and more popular) Piazza. Johnson lasted only two seasons.

These woes and others plunged the Dodgers into mediocrity. They still knew how to beat the Giants, winning the season series from them every year from 1993 to 2001, but that scarcely mollified their fans. Wrote the *Los Angeles Times*' Mike Penner: "The Dodgers Los Angeles once knew, the summer perennial that sent millions of kids to bed with their transistor radios, dreaming of Danny Goodman souvenir specials and fairy tales spun by Uncle Vinny, are no more. Everything those Dodgers stood for, everything Dodger blue once symbolized, has been buried behind home plate at Chavez Ravine, where Mike Piazza once squatted, where Dusty Baker once trotted."

Giant fans disagreed. What Dodger blue once symbolized hadn't been buried, it had moved north! Baker was theirs now, ensconced for the long term. The team contended annually. At the end of 2002, nine players—outfielders Barry Bonds and Marvin Benard, infielders Rich Aurilia, Jeff Kent, J. T. Snow, and Ramon Martinez, starting pitchers Kirk Rueter and Russ Ortiz, and reliever Robb Nen — had been on the roster the last five seasons or longer, creating a continuity reminiscent of the Boys of Summer. (The 2002 Dodgers had only three such players, Eric Karros, Adrian Beltre, and Mark Grudzielanek.) Most important of all, they copied Walter O'Malley's formula for success and built their own stadium. Pacific Bell Park opened in 2000, and for the first time on the West Coast the Giants outdrew the Dodgers.

In 1993 the National League expanded from 14 to 16 teams and switched to a balanced schedule, reducing Giant-Dodger games from 18 annually to 12 or 13. (In 1997, the only pennant race between the rivals during this period, they played just two games against each other after July 13.) Then in 1997 the lords of baseball introduced interleague play, hoping to nurture new rivalries like the Giants-Athletics and Dodgers-Angels. Though the crosstown rivalries generated some sparks, they failed to displace the Giants and Dodgers. "As long as the Dodgers are in existence, the people in San Francisco will hate them," rued Athletics general manager Billy Beane.

This remained true even as San Francisco and Los Angeles grew so alike that, topography and tourist attractions aside, casual eyes found them increasingly hard to distinguish. In the wake of the Rodney King riot, Los Angeles tried to integrate as matter-of-factly as San Francisco, with mixed results; in 1997 two thirds of the populace believed race relations remained poor. And with the advent of the Internet, which brought countless dot-com start-ups to the South of Market area, San Francisco approached Los Angeles as a force in the world economy (though the "dot-bomb" recession beginning in late 2000 blunted that advance). Both regions burst with vitality and wealth. Both struggled with skyrocketing housing costs, perpetually clogged freeways, and overcrowded schools.

Politically, Los Angeles joined San Francisco as a Democratic bastion. The six core Bay Area counties (Alameda, Contra Costa, Marin, San Francisco, San Mateo, and Santa Clara) gave Democrat Al Gore nearly 900,000 more votes than Republican George W. Bush in the 2000 presidential election, and the five core counties of Greater Los Angeles (Kern, Los Angeles, Orange, San Bernardino, and Ventura) gave Gore 600,000 more votes than Bush. If not for San Francisco and Los Angeles, in other words, Bush would have won the national vote by a million (instead of losing by half a million) and garnered California's 55 Electoral College votes, rendering Florida's tainted results moot.

All of which suggested that the Bay Area and Greater Los Angeles follow the example of France and Germany after World War II and forsake their longstanding rivalry in favor of cooperation.

Well, maybe. But maybe not.

When the Giants played their last night game at Candlestick Park, they asked their opponents— the Dodgers—for a favor. The Dodgers obliged, and so, shortly before the game began, Thomas Charles Lasorda emerged one last time from the visitors' clubhouse in right field. Wearing a Dodger blue jacket on which his name was spelled *Lasodra,* "the most fun guy in the world to hate," as Giant broadcaster Mike Krukow called him, strolled toward the infield while the public address system blared "That's Amore." After a stop by first base to shake hands with Giant owner Peter Magowan, the former Dodger manager stood alone in the infield, doffed his cap, raised his arms skyward, and soaked up the vitriol as if it gave life. Like Robinson watching Thomson touch each base or Roseboro reeling from Marichal, the image of the 72-year-old Lasorda provoking an Orwellian two minutes' hate from 50,000 people captured the essence of the longest running sports rivalry in American history — and a complicated piece of human nature.

Because hate is not the opposite of love. (Indifference is.) Like love, hate is a handhold in a universe too sheer for comprehension. From it we fix our place, distinguish good from bad, and contextualize ourselves — the basic building blocks of psychological survival. Which is why hatred endures. How often we think, *if only we could rid ourselves of what we hate, our lives would be much better,* when in fact we'd feel empty without that potent rival to define ourselves against, and would, in short time, find a new one to replace it. We *need* what we hate.

Sophisticates in New York, San Francisco, and Los Angeles disdain sports and sports fans, yet it's hard to imagine a more civilized sublimation of the primal urge to hate. As we've seen, an athletic rivalry *can* break out in violence. But on the whole it's downright Gandhian compared to the slaughter and oppression that are humankind's traditional responses to rivalry. At times it even has comedic overtones. For who could honestly believe Lasorda was spoiling for combat that evening, and the crowd literally braying for his blood? They were antagonists, yes, but also actors reprising signature roles with a wink and a nod. As Mike Krukow observed, it was *fun* for Giant fans to hate Lasorda. And if Lasorda truly felt threatened, he never would have agreed to that last walk — or to leading the crowd (off-key) in a seventh-inning rendition of "Take Me Out to the Ballgame" that climaxed with the line, "And it's root, root, root for the *Dodgers.*"

Question was, would this complex, entertaining relationship between the Giants and Dodgers survive another transplant, not between cities, as in 1958, but from Candlestick to Pacific Bell Park? Giant fans had carried the rivalry for a generation, but now the ballpark demographic would change radically. The new stadium had 20,000 fewer seats. Its ticket prices averaged a whopping 75 percent more than Candlestick's, and season ticket holders had to ante up thousands of dollars for so-called seat licenses. The bleacherites who stomped, clapped, cheered, and bowed from the waist crying "We are not worthy!" to Barry Bonds could not afford those prices, as the well-compensated Bonds himself acknowledged.

Although the first regular season game at Pac Bell would be played against the Dodgers, the Giants' debut there would be a March 31, 2000, exhibition against Milwaukee, a sop to commissioner Bud Selig, who had owned the Brewers for 28 years before turning them over to his daughter. A capacity crowd of 40,930 turned out, a mixture of middle-aged corporate functionaries and 20-something dot-commers. They knew baseball, but they weren't passionate about it, certainly not as passionate as they were about money. Between complaints about the lines for concessions and bathrooms, they talked business and yakked on their cell phones. Occasionally they asked a more attentive neighbor who was winning.

Add a beachball or two and they'd be just like those Dodger crowds that smiled and said "whatever" to the notion that they weren't true fans. If this was a preview of the regular Pac Bell audience, the rivalry was doomed. And yet ...

It was in the eighth inning, at 10:15 p.m. The Giants had taken a big lead over the Brew Crew, and the see-and-be-seen element had left to get a jump on traffic (or go back to the office). It started where it should have, in the bleachers. A few voices at first, then a small chorus. In the unseasonably warm, still air, it carried across the park, an affirmation that true passion transcends every obstacle:

Beat L.A.! Beat L.A.!

22. 1993: "A Ralph Branca Walk"

Dusty Baker's June 1993 Los Angeles debut as manager of the Giants was ruined by a two-out, bottom-of-the-ninth, pinch-hit grand slam by Dave Hansen that gave the Dodgers a 4–0 win. The rest of the series was ruined by the death of Roy Campanella.

Campy had surprised everyone by living 35 years after his paralyzing accident — and by maintaining the sunny spirit that made him so beloved in Brooklyn. Although he never played in Los Angeles, West Coast Dodger fans instantly adopted him, setting the major league attendance record by pouring into the Coliseum 93,103 strong for Roy Campanella Night, a May 7, 1959, exhibition against the Yankees. The O'Malleys flew Campy to spring training every year, where he tutored catchers and dispensed wisdom. "Roy coached me all the time when I was here, he and Jim Gilliam," Baker recalled. "They used to talk to me all the time, about baseball things, about life things, everything."

Baker attended Campy's funeral, where "I saw Steve Garvey and Ron Cey and Reggie Smith and a lot of the guys I played with. I got to visit with some of the Dodger greats, like Koufax, we had a long talk, and Erskine and Duke Snider. They all wished me luck, told me 'I'm proud of you,' and a lot of the guys said, 'I hope you guys win.'"

What, Dodger immortals hoping the *Giants* win? "Who knows? They may tell Tommy the same thing," Baker speculated.

Or maybe they recognized that the Dodgers, coming off their worst season in California, would be lucky to break .500, whereas Baker's Giants, despite losing two of three that trip to Los Angeles, ended June seven games in first place. So why not pull for their old colleague?

Even current Dodgers liked what they saw of the Giants. "The biggest difference in the Giants this year is the pitching," observed leadoff man (and former Giant) Brett Butler. Concurred Eric Davis, "The 1987 and 1989 [division-winning] clubs were built on offense. Now, they have the pitching, and that's what championships are built on."

Butler and Davis had a point. Bill Swift and John Burkett became the Giants' first 20-win combo since Marichal and Perry in 1966, and the bullpen, led by scraggly-maned Rod Beck, was the most effective since 1982. But the hitting had improved, too. Third baseman Matt Williams raised his average and cut down his strikeouts while increasing his power. Robby Thompson had a career year. Will Clark and Willie McGee performed below established levels, but still racked up numbers most players would be proud of. Even defense-minded catcher Kirt Manwaring hit .275.

And then there was Barry Bonds.

Even before hiring Baker, new Giant owner Peter Magowan signed Bonds, son of former Giant outfielder Bobby Bonds, godson of Willie Mays, and two-time Most Valuable Player, to what was then the most lucrative contract in baseball history, six years at $43.75 million. Bonds was surly with the press and aloof from his teammates. He'd had confrontations with his manager in Pittsburgh, the well-respected Jim Leyland. But Baker established an understanding with him, and Bonds flourished as never before. "Ted Williams was never the player that this guy is," raved sabermetric guru Bill James. In 1999 the *Sporting News* named Bonds Player of the Decade.

The haughty Atlanta Braves, figuring they'd stroll to a third consecutive division title after adding Greg Maddux to their formidable rotation, were caught off guard by the resurgent Giants. Trailing by nine games on July 20, they plundered the Padres for first baseman Fred McGriff, who hit .310 with 19 homers the rest of the way to invigorate the sagging offense. They climbed to within seven and a half by August 23, then won three straight at Candlestick to cut the Giants' lead to four and a half. In Atlanta a week later, they beat San Francisco two of three to close within three and a half. Then the bottom fell out for the Giants: starting on September 7, they lost eight in a row, their worst home losing streak since 1972. Over that same span the Braves went 8–1 to take a four-game lead.

It was crunch time for Dusty Baker. His pitchers were worn out, some of his best hitters nursed injuries, and the Braves looked unstoppable. He responded with a tranquility that would have mystified McGraw, Durocher, or Lasorda. "You wouldn't be human if you didn't feel the highs and lows," he explained a few years later. "[But] this isn't life or death. We're like

Barry Bonds. The first player in the long history of the Giants to hit more than 30 homers in his first year with the team. (National Baseball Hall of Fame Library, Cooperstown, N.Y.)

those surfer dudes out on the ocean. When you get up on a good wave, you ride it as long as you can." His calm reassured the players, who caught a fresh wave and won six of seven on the road, then five of six at home to reach 100 victories and close within a game of Atlanta with four to play.

Four to play, that is, in Los Angeles. Where the Giants wouldn't be greeted by well-wishing Dodger alumni, but by Tommy Lasorda and players who remembered the Giants' sweep at the end of 1991 to deny *them* a title over the Braves.

Anxious Giant fans trash-talked their rivals. "[Dodger crowds] don't care. You can walk around in Giants paraphernalia and they won't even throw things at you. It's a stadium filled with 45,000 people who don't care," accused one. His friend seconded, "It's a city filled with 13 million people who don't care." Angelenos responded by ... well, not caring. "After riots and recession and all the self-criticism, self-hatred even, that came with them, this nattering from the north seems silly, out of place, dated," yawned *Los Angeles Times* columnist Peter H. King. Tommy Lasorda was downright gracious. "Dusty Baker played for me for a long time and he helped make it possible for me to manage a world championship team. What am I going to do, say I want to knock Dusty out of it? No way."

Thousands of Giant fans invaded Chavez Ravine for the Thursday night opener of the climactic series. Soothed (or stunned) by the superior surroundings, they conducted themselves civilly; not a single punch was thrown while Dodger fans cheered news of a Brave rally against the Houston Astros.

When the rally fell short and the Braves lost, the Giants had a chance to tie for first. They carried a 3–1 lead into the bottom of the ninth, but closer Rod Beck was sore-hipped and running on fumes, having appeared in nearly half the team's games. After Mike Piazza singled, first baseman Eric Karros, a UCLA grad whose Brooklyn-born father worshipped Gil Hodges, powdered one down the third base line. But Matt Williams snatched it cleanly and erased Piazza on a double play. Once Beck secured the last out for the save, the large contingent of Giant fans stood and cheered.

"Now we control our own destiny," said Williams. What he meant was that if the Giants took the next three from the Dodgers, they guaranteed themselves at least a tie for first. What he didn't know was that the Giants hadn't swept a four-game series on the Dodgers' turf in 70 years.

The next night the Dodgers beat every Giant except Barry Bonds. Starting pitcher Ramon Martinez yielded a three-run homer to Bonds in the third. Lasorda elected to pitch to Bonds in the fifth with the score tied, runners on second and third, and .238 hitter Dave Martinez on deck. Even after rookie left-hander Omar Daal fell behind two balls, no strikes, Lasorda refused to signal an intentional walk. "You're asking [Daal] to throw strikes with nobody out and the bases loaded. That's not good baseball," he explained. But Daal seemed to prefer bad baseball, intending ball three with a breaking pitch low and away. Bonds nailed it anyway for his second three-run homer of the night. After Bonds knocked in his seventh run with a double off southpaw Steve Wilson, the *Los Angeles Times'* Ross Newhan theorized that Lasorda was trying to show general manager Fred Claire just how desperately the Dodgers needed to improve their left-handed pitching.

Bonds—er, the Giants—carried an 8-5 lead into the bottom of the ninth. Beck took the mound again. The Braves had won against the expansion Colorado Rockies, adding to the pressure on the exhausted closer. Dave Hansen stroked his fourth hit of the game to lead off. After Piazza lined out, Karros got even for the night before, smashing a homer. Shrugged Beck, "I was aiming for the middle of the plate and hoping I'd catch the corner. I found the middle of the plate." But he gutted his way through the last two outs for the 8-7 win and his 47th save. The Giants were still tied for first. Talk of a playoff—not with the Dodgers for once, but with the Braves—ran rampant.

But the Dodgers' spoiler role became easier now that San Francisco's top two starters, Swift and Burkett, had pitched their turns. All season long the bottom of the rotation had been the Giants' weakness. Baker tried nine hurlers in the other three spots, none of whom made more than 18 starts. He settled on lefty Bryan Hickerson for game three.

Spotted a 2-0 lead, Hickerson injured his ribs and was gone by the end of the third, having allowed the Dodgers to tie. Baker brought in Jeff Brantley, who kept the Dodgers quiet for four innings. Meanwhile, the Giants rallied against Orel Hershiser. San Francisco was up 5-3 in the eighth when the Dodgers loaded the bases with two out. Baker brought in Rod Beck for the sixth straight game.

Lasorda countered with Dave Hansen, the pinch-hitting specialist whose grand slam had ruined Baker's managerial debut in Los Angeles, and whose four-hit, three-run, three-RBI game the night before nearly overcame Bonds's barrage. Hansen belted a ball deep to right. "I had no idea where it would land," Beck recounted. "I'd given up so many lately, it could have gone out." Right fielder Dave Martinez raced to the corner. He caught the ball just a few feet short of its becoming another grand slam. The Dodgers went quietly in the ninth, and the Giants remained tied with the Braves, who had clobbered the Rockies. Dodger Stadium reverberated with cries of *Beat L.A.!* It was all those Giant fans, now just one win from postseason play.

Hearing that chant in their own park gave the Dodgers yet another incentive to win the Sunday finale. They were also trying to stay at .500, a significant achievement for a team that had lost 99 the year before.

Oh, and one more thing: it was October 3, the darkest date in Dodger history. Giant owner Peter Magowan flew in Bobby Thomson and Willie Mays to watch the game from his box. Joe Morgan was there too, calling the game from the broadcast booth.

The Dodgers didn't fly in any old heroes. They just let Tommy be Tommy.

Lasorda had been a Dodger through all those nightmarish October 3rds. In 1951 he was a pitcher for the team's top farm club. In 1962 he was a scout. In 1982 he was the manager. At a team meeting he talked to his players about the rivalry, recounting each humiliation. He then recalled how the Giants eliminated them in 1991, and Will Clark's boast that, though injured, he would play against the Dodgers for the sheer pleasure of beating them. "He didn't want to beat us any more than we wanted to beat him," Lasorda bellowed, and sent his players onto the field with "This could make my year!"

Kevin Gross—the same Kevin Gross who had no-hit the Giants a year earlier, just as San Francisco was mounting an effort to stop the Giants from moving to Tampa — started for Lasorda. Baker had spent days mulling his choice of starters. His options: washed-up veterans Scott Sanderson and Jim Deshaies, or 21-year-old rookie Salomon Torres. Though possessed of good stuff, Torres had been in the big leagues just five weeks and had failed to survive the second inning in two of his prior three starts; he was also the only Giant starter to lose a game since September 15. But Baker settled on him, with the proviso that "we'll have everyone ready, just in case."

In Atlanta, the Braves beat the Colorado Rockies, 5–3. The Giants had to win, or else.

The game was scoreless through the first two, but in the bottom of the third Gross led off with a single, went to second on a sacrifice, to third on a groundout, and scored on a single by Hansen. Then Hansen scored on a Karros double. In the fourth the Dodgers turned two walks and a single into another run, knocking out Torres. San Francisco's Trevor Wilson squirmed out of the jam and the Giants plated a run in the top of the fifth to trail 3–1. They'd get the rest later; wasn't that how October 3 always worked?

Mike Piazza led off the bottom of the fifth. His father, Vince, thwarted a year earlier in his bid to purchase the Giants for Tampa, watched in glee as Piazza hit the very first pitch from reliever Dave Burba over the fence in right center field. A flustered Burba walked Karros. He got an out on a pop fly, but then former Giant Cory Snyder, an all-or-nothing hitter, got all of Burba's next pitch for yet another homer to right center. "Snyder's home run killed our morale. We could have dealt with a three-run deficit, but all of a sudden it's five," conceded Beck.

While Gross cruised, the Dodgers poured it on. Karros singled in the sixth to make it 7–1. In the eighth Piazza struck again, blasting a three-run homer. Karros tripled, and then Raul Mondesi homered to make it 12–1. A frustrated Jim Deshaies threw two knockdown pitches at Snyder. The Dodgers rushed to the top of their dugout, but nothing came of it. Why bother? They already had what they wanted: a victory to seal a .500 season, the biggest Dodger takedown of the Giants since 1934, and a decisive end to the Curse of October 3.

Dodger partisans taunted the Giant rooters in their midst by performing the Tomahawk Chop, trademark ritual of Brave fans. Vince Piazza hugged his son and said, "I just wish all the dads in the world could feel what I'm feeling." He wasn't the only one to wish feelings on others. Proclaimed Tommy Lasorda, "I want all those fans in San Francisco to feel like we felt in 1991, and 1951, and 1962." (He then phoned Dusty Baker to offer his condolences.) Vin Scully, after mentioning that he'd seen Bobby Thomson and congratulated him on the anniversary of his homer, couldn't resist smirking, "I don't think Bobby's feeling as good right now as he was then."

The Giants won 103 games in 1993, their best total in San Francisco. It was also the record for victories by a National League rookie manager, which earned Baker his first Manager of the Year award. But thanks to the Dodgers, Giant fans would remember the season for how it ended: in what *San Francisco Chronicle* columnist Bruce Jenkins called "a Ralph Branca walk, back to the cruel barbs of civilization and plenty of soul-searching back home."

23. 1997: "They Blew Sincere Kisses to Their Sport"

In 1997 the Giants and Dodgers battled for the division title down to the last week of the season. It was their first such fight in 15 years, and all the more gratifying for its unforeseeability.

The 1996 Giants had finished a dismal 23 games out of first. New general manager Brian Sabean, perceiving the team as two superstars and bodies filling uniforms, decided to trade one of the superstars for several good players. Most fans preferred that standoffish Barry Bonds go, but on November 13, 1996, Sabean dealt blue-collar favorite Matt Williams and reserve outfielder Trenidad Hubbard to Cleveland for second baseman Jeff Kent, shortstop Jose Vizcaino, and relievers Julian Tavarez and Joe Roa. It was immediately deemed the worst trade in San Francisco history. A besieged Sabean called a press conference to insist that "I am not an idiot."

The Dodgers had finished first in 1994, first in 1995, and second by just one game in 1996. But new manager Bill Russell wasn't as entrenched as Tommy Lasorda, and Peter O'Malley's announcement that the team was for sale hurt clubhouse morale. Then the diversity problem returned. On the 50th anniversary of Jackie Robinson's breaking the color barrier, the Dodgers were embarrassed by the revelation that they were the only major league team without a front-line African American player (the only one on the roster was reserve outfielder Wayne Kirby). Closer Todd Worrell expressed fear that a damaging cliquishness had taken root in the multilingual clubhouse. As if to prove his point, pitcher Ismael Valdes got into a fight with Eric Karros early in the season, and in the second game of the year between the Giants and Dodgers, a 5–4 Giant win at Dodger Stadium, Valdes and Russell exchanged shoves in the dugout. Later that week Pedro Astacio, another starter miffed by Russell's quick hooks, lunged at the manager.

Despite the discord, the Dodgers reached the All-Star break at 45–42, second (by six games) to the surprising Giants. Sabean indeed was no idiot; prickly perfectionist Jeff Kent hit better than the departed Williams and instilled a yes-we-can attitude in his teammates. The Dodgers were showing they had the talent to overcome their lack of spirit. The Giants were showing they had the spirit to overcome their lack of talent. Which would prevail? Right after the All-Star break, they squared off for four games in Los Angeles.

The Dodgers slaughtered the Giants 11–0 in the opener behind Chan Ho Park. The next night Hideo Nomo went eight en route to a 6–2 win. Before game three, Dusty Baker invited Sandy Koufax to the Giant clubhouse, where the Dodger legend shared his wisdom with lefties Kirk Rueter (victim of the 11–0 shelling) and Shawn Estes (loser of the All-Star game four days before). But it was the Giant hitters who took inspiration, pummeling relievers Worrell and Antonio Osuna for seven runs in the ninth to claim an 8–5 victory.

That left game four. If the Giants won, they'd escape L.A. with a split and remain six ahead. If the Dodgers won, they'd rise to within four and seize the momentum. With Koufax's words ringing in his ears, Estes took the ball for the Giants against 20-year-old Dennis Reyes, the first lefty to start a game for the Dodgers in more than four years. (Maybe they should have offered Koufax a contract.) After 115 laborious pitches, Estes departed in the top of the sixth trailing 6–3. Reyes, meanwhile, pitched as if *he'd* gotten the Hall of Fame pep talk, baffling every Giant hitter except Bonds, who clanged him for a two-run homer in the first and walked, stole second, and scored in the fourth to account for all the Giants' runs. The 9–3 Dodger win hit the Giants in their collective solar plexus, and by the end of July, the Dodgers were in first place.

Over the next month and a half the Giants never fell more than two and a half back. The long, tight battle wore on both teams. The Dodgers lost five in a row to fall out of the lead, only to have the Giants lose four in a row to hand it back. Going into the last series of the year against each other, a two-game set in San Francisco on September 17 and 18, the Dodgers clung to a two-game edge.

Though losing both would put the Giants four down with nine to play, Dusty Baker denied the games were must-wins. "You say 'must' on anything, you put pressure on yourself. What happens if you don't win the first one, is it over then?" The Dodgers, coming off three straight victories in St. Louis, felt relaxed and confident, but in Los Angeles anxiety ran high. The *Times* ran an article on the rivalry in which six Dodger legends were asked to name their most memorable Giant-Dodger game. Four of them — Don Newcombe and Vin Scully (October 3, 1951), John Roseboro (August 22, 1965), and Bill Russell (October 3, 1982) — picked games the Dodgers *lost*. (Tommy Lasorda and general manager Fred Claire picked October 3, 1993.)

On a cool Wednesday night, Candlestick Park — rechristened 3Com Park at Candlestick Point as part of a municipal revenue scheme — filled with over 56,000 fans (50,921 paid). They were screaming *Beat L.A.!* even before the first pitch. Grinned Dusty Baker, "Maybe they're just getting us ready for the playoffs." Fearing for his safety, Tommy Lasorda refused to sit in the stands.

Finesse pitcher Kirk Rueter started for the Giants, power pitcher Chan Ho Park for the Dodgers. With one out and one on in the bottom of the first, Bonds strode to the plate. On a two-two count Park threw a fastball down, a waste pitch, but Bonds belted it off the facing of the upper deck to give the Giants a 2–0 lead. The self-conscious slugger did a 360-degree spin and pumped his fists as he left the batter's box.

But those were the only runs the Giants got, and for the rest of the game they had to make them stand. Pitching with a bloody blister on his index finger, Rueter kept the Dodgers off balance until the fifth, when Raul Mondesi blasted one over the left field bleachers to make the score 2–1. With one out in the sixth, Rueter yielded successive singles to Eric Young and Otis Nixon. Piazza flied to center for the second out, but Eric Karros hung tough. After Rueter got a second strike the crowd stood and cheered. Rearing back with what little extra he had, he snapped a curve that Karros missed to end the rally. Rueter then preempted a threat in the seventh by turning a Todd Zeile comebacker into a double play.

Having squeezed every last out from Rueter, Baker went to his bullpen for Roberto Hernandez. Acquired from the White Sox just before the July 31 trade deadline, Hernandez, a closer in Chicago, had an uneasy relationship with incumbent Rod Beck, whose velocity had markedly decreased. After Hernandez disposed of the Dodgers in the eighth on 15 pitches, Beck expected to close out the ninth. But with the Dodgers' number four, five, and six hitters coming up, Baker elected to stick with the flame-throwing Hernandez. He was more of a contrast to Rueter, and Karros, Mondesi, and Zeile had little experience against him, whereas they'd been facing Beck for years. Hernandez justified Baker's faith by fanning Karros and Mondesi, then inducing Zeile to ground out.

Eric Karros. His father caught a Don Newcombe home run off Sal Maglie at the Polo Grounds. (Courtesy Los Angeles Dodgers, Inc.)

The crowd went wild — too wild for the Dodgers. "We had some crowds like this a couple of times in '93, but I don't think even those were as loud as this one," said Darren Lewis, once the Giants' center fielder (and favorite of Dusty Baker, who named a son after him), now a Dodger reserve angry at the paper cups and *Beat L.A.!* signs thrown his way late in the game. "The crowd was vicious. They were yelling at me, screaming at me. You name it, I heard it." Mike Piazza got the same treatment and then some. "It was kind of flattering, I guess," he said. Summed up manager Russell, "This is about as close as you're going to get to a playoff game without really being there."

San Francisco partisans overlooked the nasty crowd behavior and focused on the quality of play. Wrote the *Examiner's* Gwen Knapp, "The Giants and Dodgers gave us baseball at its finest. They blew sincere kisses to their sport."

An even bigger audience — at 52,140, the largest paid attendance in three years — turned out for the second game on Thursday afternoon. Otis Nixon, who had hit just nine home runs in 4,500 career at-bats, pounded a solo shot off Giant starter Terry Mulholland in the top of the first to quiet the crowd. But the Giants got the run back in the bottom of the frame on a Bonds triple and Glenallen Hill single against knuckleballer (and Bay Area native) Tom Candiotti.

The Giants seemingly put the game away in the middle innings. First baseman J. T. Snow slammed a solo shot in the fourth, and in the fifth Bonds struck again, yanking a Candiotti floater into the right field stands for a three-run homer and a 5–1 lead. But the Dodgers battled back. In the sixth Nixon reached on an error by Gold Glover Snow, advanced to second on a wild pitch, scooted to third on a Piazza groundout, and scored when Eric Karros rapped an opposite-field single. Then Todd Zeile belted a double and Karros rounded the bases to bring the Dodgers within two. An inning later, the Dodgers jumped on reliever Julian Tavarez to put men on first and third with one out. Baker gambled that Roberto Hernandez had another overpowering performance in him, but Piazza, capping the greatest offensive season ever for a catcher, slapped a Hernandez offering into left for a single to tie the score at five.

Neither team scored in the eighth. Neither team scored in the ninth. The battle of spirit versus talent would need extra innings to decide.

Beck started the 10th. The struggling closer was greeted with a murmur of boos. The murmur grew into a roar as Piazza lifted a low and away 1–2 pitch down the right field line for a single, Karros knocked an inside fastball to left for another single, and Mondesi lined a 2–0 offering to right to load the bases with no outs.

Faced with his biggest managerial decision since the last game of 1993, Dusty Baker "started out, then he stopped, then he hesitated again, then he went out. I remember he said, 'Shit, I'm gonna go out and say something,'" recalled pitching coach Dick Pole. To the crowd's dismay, Baker didn't pull Beck. "I just said, 'Dig as deep as you can with whatever you've learned as a pitcher. You're the guy,'" Baker revealed.

Beck got two quick strikes on Todd Zeile. "He has the forkball and the slider. I was just protecting," said Zeile, who took a surprise fastball on the inside corner for a called strike three.

Now it was Bill Russell's turn to make a huge decision: with the pitcher's spot due next, he needed a pinch hitter. He scanned his bench and chose Eddie Murray, the 41-year-old future Hall of Famer snatching a few last swings with his hometown club. It made good sense. Murray was a switch hitter with two hits and three RBIs in five prior pinch-hit opportunities.

As the Giant infield crept in to cut off the run at the plate, second baseman Jeff Kent had an inspiration. "I played with Eddie Murray [in New York], and he's always been a great RBI man, especially with the bases loaded. I asked him about it. And he said he always tried to hit the ball up the middle, so I was shading him there." Beck too had his thinking cap on. "Eddie Murray has driven in a lot of runs, and he's feasted on first-pitch fastballs. He wasn't going to get one from me."

So Beck threw a splitter. Murray pounced on it — and hit a one-hopper right to the repositioned Kent. Dodger fans world-over groaned as Kent threw home for an out at the plate, then catcher Brian Johnson relayed to first for a double play. With the season on the line, the Dodgers had loaded the bases with nobody out and failed to score.

Todd Worrell quelled the Giants in the 10th. Beck came back for the 11th and retired the Dodgers in order. Worrell whipsawed through the Giants in the bottom of the inning. Beck, going three frames for the first time in five years, retired the Dodgers with nary a peep in the 12th. The game, already four hours old, looked like it would go on forever.

Russell brought in his sixth reliever of the day, veteran lefty Mark Guthrie. First batter: the catcher, Johnson, not much of a hitter despite a couple of knocks that afternoon. Johnson hadn't become a Giant until mid July, but his Bay Area roots ran deep: he'd gone to high school in Oakland and had quarterbacked the Stanford football team.

The first pitch from Guthrie, a fastball, was a strike down and in. Johnson drove it deep to left. The wind pushed it back, but not enough. It landed in the stands for one of the most cathartic home runs in Giant history, as Los Angeles Times sportswriter Mike Downey recognized: "Third base coach Sonny Jackson of the Giants was waiting to escort Johnson around third and on his way to home, much the way Leo Durocher did 46 years ago for Bobby Thomson." The crowd went delirious, stamping its feet, shouting, and clapping while the team gathered at home plate and Barry Bonds hoisted Dusty Baker in the air.

All it did was tie the rivals with nine to play, but the 6–5 Giant victory proved decisive. The deflated Dodgers went home to face Colorado and lost three straight as boos echoed through the Taj O'Malley. "It's a bad time to lose five in a row," conceded Russell. Meanwhile the Giants, in San Diego, won three of four to go two and a half up with five to play. On September 24 Brian Johnson hit another game-winning homer to keep the Giants' margin at two and a half. The Dodgers won 9–5 in Colorado the next night, and the night after that they pounded six homers to beat the Rockies 10–4. But the Giants bashed the Padres 17–4 on September 26 to clinch a tie, and the next night they won 6–1 to claim the division.

By rights, the Dodgers should have won. Their pitching staff logged an ERA seven tenths of a run per game lower than the Giants, led the league in strikeouts, and trailed only the indomitable Braves in opposition on-base percentage. Offensively, for the first time in 20 years four Dodger hitters slammed 30 or more homers: Piazza (40), Karros (31), Zeile (31), and Mondesi (30). They outscored their opponents 742–645, whereas the Giants, incredibly, scored *fewer* runs than their opponents, 784–793, making them only the third team in the 20th century to win a pennant or division while being outscored, the others being the 1984 Royals and 1987 Twins.

But that last statistic is misleading. The Giants lost a lot of blowouts (the Dodgers beat them 11–0 twice), but had an unearthly facility for winning the close ones, compiling a 43–20 record in games decided by two runs or less. They were 11–3 in extra-inning contests. They never lost more than four in a row. In short, they fully absorbed their manager's even-keeled tenacity. It was a quality missing in their talented but fragmented rivals.

24. 2002: "The Sort of Stuff Around Which the Game Has Been Built"

When the National and American Leagues reconfigured into three divisions in 1994 they added an extra round of playoffs, with the best second-place team in each league — known as the wild card — advancing to the postseason along with the division winners. The idea was to increase the number of pennant races, raise attendance and TV ratings, and bring to baseball the excitement supposedly generated by the interminable playoff rounds of the other major professional sports.

But it often had the opposite effect. With fewer teams in each division, superior clubs more easily dominated; in 2002 Atlanta's jaded Braves won the National League East by 19 games, their 11th straight division crown. And the suspense of a close race could be ruined by the knowledge that the loser would go to the playoffs anyway; the 2002 Oakland Athletics and Anaheim Angels wrestled over the American League West into the last week of the season, but the only thing at stake was whom they would face in the opening playoff round.

Occasionally, though, the plan worked as intended. Such was the case with the 2002 Giants and Dodgers. A sensational August virtually clinched first place in the National League West for the Arizona Diamondbacks, but the wild card berth was still up for grabs, and barring a last-minute surge from the Houston Astros, either the Giants or Dodgers would get it. The Dodgers arrived at Pac Bell Park on September 9 just one game in front of the Giants with only 20 left.

"It's almost a playoff atmosphere," marveled Giant third baseman

David Bell after his two-run homer in the sixth put the Giants ahead and clutch relief work from Felix Rodriguez and Robb Nen preserved a 6–5 victory. (Nen's save tied him with Rod Beck for the franchise career record.) It was the Giants' fourth consecutive win and the Dodgers' fourth loss in five games, but nobody spoke of momentum. "You know they're not going to quit," Giant manager Dusty Baker said of the Dodgers. "They're not right there because they quit." Nonetheless, in front of another sellout crowd the next night, the Giants triumphed 5–2 to take over second place.

Time for Dodger manager Jim Tracy to play his hole card: Hideo Nomo. The Japanese pitcher with the balletically contorted delivery had been a Giant killer since his major league debut on May 2, 1995, when he yielded just one hit and struck out seven in five innings at Candlestick. After more than four years with other teams, he returned to the Dodgers in 2002 figuring to hold down the fourth or fifth spot in the rotation, but injuries to Kevin Brown, Andy Ashby, and others made him the ace by default. Starting the most important game of the season, he paced the Dodgers to a 7–3 win that knotted the rivals less than three weeks from season's end. "The Dodgers and the Giants with something at stake, late in the season, is the sort of stuff around which the game has been built," savored Mike Bauman, national columnist for major league baseball's Web site.

The race prompted other sportswriters to recount (not always accurately) the highlights of the rivalry's long history — with a few concluding it had been much better in the old days. Using Vin Scully as his chief source, Mike DiGiovanna of the *Los Angeles Times* asserted, "The violence and contempt that marked this rivalry from its origins in New York and for several decades on the West Coast has subsided." And an article in the *New York Times* titled "The Bitter Rivalry That Is No More" read like an obituary. Its author, Ira Berkow, built his case on the testimony of another nostalgic member of the Dodger family, 76-year-old Don Newcombe. "The rivalry as we once knew it doesn't exist anymore. Maybe to the media. Maybe to some fans. But to the players? Absolutely not. It's like any other series against any other opponent to them," the former Brooklyn great pronounced.

Probably true. But neither article probed too deeply as to why. The sensibilities and demographics of baseball players had evolved enormously since the 1950s. In 2002 the average player earned more than $2 million a year, making him think twice before engaging in brawls and beanball exchanges that could endanger his career. Several members of each team hailed from other countries and knew little of America's baseball history and regional animosities. And since Newcombe's time, more players came from California; how was Giant manager Dusty Baker, himself a former Dodger star, to convince a clubhouse full of Southern Californians—Marvin Benard, Jeff Kent, Robb Nen, Russ Ortiz, J. T. Snow, Tim Worrell—to hate the Dodgers?

Besides, as Newcombe himself noted, the rivalry existed on several levels. Though the players were important, they were also the rivalry's most transient participants. More enduring were the front offices, the media, and the fans. And on those levels, the rivalry flourished.

In 2001, having finished behind the Giants four straight seasons for the first time since 1935–38, the Dodger front office took up the burden of rivalry underdog. Brooklyn-born board chairman Bob Daly sought to re-instill tradition, which meant hating the Giants back. Players and front office alike fumed on April 17, 2001, when the Giants stopped play for 10 minutes to honor Barry Bonds's 500th homer, a blast off L.A.'s Terry Adams into the waters behind Pac Bell Park's right field stands. When the Giants proposed both teams wear period uniforms to commemorate the golden anniversary of the Shot Heard 'Round the World, Daly refused. "It's crazy. I have no problem with the Giants celebrating their championship, but do they have to do it when we are in town?" And as Bonds neared the single-season home run mark of 70, the Dodgers wouldn't hear of congratulatory gestures if he broke the record in L.A. "We don't believe our fans want to sit through a ceremony for the Giants in Dodger Stadium," huffed senior vice president Derrick Hall.

Giant-hating caught on in the media. "The ugliest scratches on this wonderful antique rivalry have always been caused by the Giants. They stole the signs. They drowned the basepaths. Marichal hit Roseboro," denounced the Los Angeles Times' Bill Plaschke. Dodger fans finally got into the act, too. After years of crowds that "probably would have greeted Attila the Hun with polite applause," as Times columnist Allan Malamud put it, Dodger Stadium shook with chants of "Giants suck!" at key moments. The popular enthusiasm did not escape the supposedly blasé players. "The stadium will be rocking, so we've got to put on a show," acknowledged Dodger center fielder Marquis Grissom before a September showdown with the Giants at Chavez Ravine.

In Northern California, passion for the rivalry ran as high as ever. The Giant front office, which had canceled the 2001 celebration of the Shot Heard 'Round the World out of respect for the tragic events of September 11, rescheduled it for July 28, 2002. Once more the Dodgers refused to wear old Brooklyn uniforms. "They didn't want to come out here and hear Russ Hodges again," chuckled Bobby Thomson, one of 12 survivors of the 1951 Giant team honored that afternoon. One fan's posting on the Giants' Web site said of the team's colors, "The orange represents the color of the Golden Gate Bridge; the black represents a dark and bitter hatred for the Los Angeles Dodgers." Another fan told the *Los Angeles Times* before the showdown at Chavez Ravine, "We're fighting the Civil War all over again, and like it did before, the north is going to win again." No wonder Sam Walker, in a *Wall Street Journal* think piece, asserted that the Giant-Dodger rivalry "hasn't been so hot since the days of Ebbets Field and the Polo Grounds."

The Dodgers won the opener when Marquis Grissom made a leaping catch at the wall in the ninth to rob Rich Aurilia of a homer, preserving L.A.'s 7–6 margin. But they lost the second game 6–4 after Omar Daal, another pitcher back from years in exile, proved he still couldn't get Barry Bonds out when it mattered; the Giant left fielder ripped him for a double that sparked a four-run second inning. In the third game, the Giants were leading 7–4 with two outs in the bottom of the ninth when Eric Karros stepped in as the tying run. Karros, a .450 lifetime hitter against Giant closer Robb Nen, struck out to end the game. The Dodgers salvaged the finale by a 6–3 margin behind a route-going performance by Odalis Perez. It was the only game that took less than three and a half hours to play.

The Dodgers emerged from the series trailing the Giants by one. They battled tenaciously over the season's final week and a half, moving Giant outfielder Tom Goodwin, a former Dodger still receiving checks from his old team, to acknowledge, "They showed a lot of heart." But the Giants didn't lose another game. Their 2–1 win over the Astros on September 27 clinched a tie for the wild card berth. "*Beat L.A.!*" shouted the capacity crowd at Pac Bell Park, unaware that at that very moment in Los Angeles, Brooklyn native Paul LoDuca was smashing a walk-off homer in the bottom of the 10th to keep the Dodgers alive. When the Giants clinched the next day, the crowd again briefly chanted "*Beat L.A.!*"

The 2002 race was for second place, hardly qualifying it as a rivalry classic like 1951 or 1962. But the Giants made the most of their success, winning two playoff rounds to reach the World Series, where they faced the Anaheim Angels. Managed by former Dodger Mike Scioscia, the American League's Southern California entry beat the Giants in seven games. Ten days later, Dusty Baker and the Giants parted ways, ending the rivalry's latest incarnation. No one can predict what will happen next, but this much is certain: as they have for generations, Giant and Dodger fans will continue to pass down the lore and passion that keeps baseball's best rivalry thriving.

Select Bibliography

BOOKS

Adelman, Melvin. *A Sporting Time*. Urbana: University of Illinois Press, 1986.

Alexander, Charles C. *John McGraw*. New York: Penguin, 1988.

Allen, Lee. *The Giants and the Dodgers: The Fabulous Story of Baseball's Fiercest Feud*. New York: Putnam's, 1964.

Angell, Roger. *Five Seasons*. New York: Warner, 1977.

Barber, Red, and Robert Creamer. *Rhubarb in the Catbird Seat*. Garden City, NY: Doubleday, 1968.

Bartell, Dick, with Norman L. Macht. *Rowdy Richard*. Berkeley, CA: North Atlantic Books, 1987.

Bavasi, Buzzie, with John Strege. *Off the Record*. Chicago: Contemporary Books, 1987.

Bouton, Jim, edited by Leonard Shecter. *Ball Four*. New York: Macmillan, 1990.

Burrows, Edwin G., and Mike Wallace. *Gotham: A History of New York City to 1898*. New York: Oxford University Press, 1999.

Caen, Herb. *One Man's San Francisco*. Garden City, NY: Doubleday, 1976.

_____. *Only in San Francisco*. Garden City, NY: Doubleday, 1960.

Cashmore, Ellis. *Making Sense of Sport*. London and New York: Routledge, 1990.

Cepeda, Orlando, with Herb Fagen. *Baby Bull: From Hardball to Hard Time and Back*. Dallas: Taylor Publishing, 1998.

Davis, Mike. *City of Quartz: Excavating the Future in Los Angeles*. New York: Vintage, 1992.

Delsohn, Steve. *True Blue: The Dramatic History of the Los Angeles Dodgers, Told by the Men Who Lived It*. New York: Morrow, 2001.

Dodgers Media Guide. Tempe, AZ: Ben Franklin Press, 1999.

Drysdale, Don, with Bob Verdi. *Once a Bum, Always a Dodger*. New York: St. Martin's, 1990.

Durocher, Leo, with Ed Linn. *Nice Guys Finish Last*. New York: Simon & Schuster, 1975.

Durso, Joseph. *Casey & Mr. McGraw*. St. Louis: Sporting News, 1989.
Einstein, Charles. *Willie's Time*. New York: Lippincott, 1979.
Eskenazi, Gerald. *The Lip: A Biography of Leo Durocher*. New York: Morrow, 1993.
Frommer, Harvey. *New York City Baseball: The Last Golden Age: 1947–1957*. New York: Macmillan, 1980.
Garvey, Steve, and Skip Rozin. *Garvey*. New York: Times Books, 1986.
Gewecke, Cliff. *Day by Day in Dodgers History*. New York: Leisure Press, 1984.
Giants Media Guide. Walnut Creek, CA: Diablo Publications, 2002.
Golenbock, Peter. *Bums: An Oral History of the Brooklyn Dodgers*. Chicago: Contemporary Books, 1984.
Goodwin, Doris Kearns. *Wait Till Next Year: A Memoir*. New York: Simon & Schuster, 1997.
Graham, Frank. *The Brooklyn Dodgers: An Informal History*. Carbondale, IL: Southern Illinois University Press, 2002.
_____. *The New York Giants: An Informal History of a Great Baseball Club*. Carbondale, IL: Southern Illinois University Press, 2002.
Greenwald, Hank. *This Copyrighted Broadcast*. San Francisco: Woodford Press, 1999.
Guschov, Stephen D. *The Red Stockings of Cincinnati: Baseball's First All-Professional Team*. Jefferson, NC: McFarland, 1998.
Helyar, John. *Lords of the Realm*. New York: Villard, 1994.
Hession, Joseph. *Giants: Collector's Edition*. San Francisco: Foghorn Press, 1993.
Higbe, Kirby, with Martin Quigley. *The High Hard One*. Lincoln: University of Nebraska Press, 1998.
Holmes, Tommy. *Dodger Daze and Knights*. New York: David McKay, 1953.
Honig, Donald. *The Los Angeles Dodgers: The First Quarter Century*. New York: St. Martin's, 1983.
Hynd, Noel. *The Giants of the Polo Grounds*. New York: Doubleday, 1988.
James, Bill. *The Bill James Baseball Abstract, 1983*. New York: Ballantine, 1983.
_____. *The Bill James Player Ratings Book, 1994*. New York: Macmillan, 1994.
_____. *The New Bill James Historical Baseball Abstract*. New York: Free Press, 2001.
Kahn, Roger. *The Head Game: Baseball Seen from the Pitcher's Mound*. New York: Harcourt, 2000.
Kavanagh, Jack, and Norman Macht. *Uncle Robbie*. Cleveland: Society for American Baseball Research, 1999.
Kirsch, George B. *The Creation of American Team Sports*. Urbana: University of Illinois Press, 1989.
Lansche, Jerry. *The Forgotten Championships: Postseason Baseball, 1882–1981*. Jefferson, NC: McFarland, 1989.
Lasorda, Tommy, with David Fisher. *The Artful Dodger*. New York: Avon, 1985.
Mandel, Mike. *SF Giants, An Oral History*. Self-published, 1979.
Marichal, Juan, with Charles Einstein. *A Pitcher's Story*. New York: Doubleday, 1967.
Mays, Willie, with Lou Sahadi. *Say Hey: The Autobiography of Willie Mays*. New York: Simon & Schuster, 1988.
McGraw, John J. *My Thirty Years in Baseball*. Lincoln: University of Nebraska Press, 1995.
McNeil, William F. *The Dodgers Encyclopedia*. Sports Publishing, 2001.

Meany, Tom, ed. *The Artful Dodgers*. New York: Grosset & Dunlap, 1966.

Miller, Marvin. *A Whole Different Ball Game*. New York: Birch Lane Press, 1991.

Monteleone, John J., ed. *Branch Rickey's Little Blue Book*. New York: Macmillan, 1995.

Neft, David, Richard Cohen, and Michael Neft. *The Sports Encyclopedia: Baseball*. New York: St. Martin's Griffin, 1998.

Northern California Baseball History. Cleveland: Society for American Baseball Research, 1998.

Parrott, Harold. *The Lords of Baseball*. Atlanta: Longstreet Press, 2001.

Peters, Nick. *Miracle At Candlestick!* Atlanta: Longstreet Press, 1993.

Plaut, David. *Chasing October: The Dodgers-Giants Pennant Race of 1962*. South Bend, IN: Diamond Communications, 1994.

Prince, Carl E. *Brooklyn's Dodgers: The Bums, the Borough, and the Best of Baseball*. New York: Oxford University Press, 1996.

Riess, Steven A. *Touching Base: Professional Baseball and American Culture in the Progressive Era*. Westport, CT: Greenwood Press, 1980.

Ritter, Lawrence S. *The Glory of Their Times*. New York: Vintage, 1985.

Roseboro, John, with Bill Libby. *Glory Days with the Dodgers (and Other Days with Others)*. New York: Atheneum, 1978.

Rosenbaum, Art, and Bob Stevens. *The Giants of San Francisco*. New York: Coward-McCann, 1963.

San Francisco Giants, 1958–1982: Silver Anniversary Yearbook. San Francisco: Woodford Associates, 1982.

Schoor, Gene. *The Complete Dodgers Record Book*. New York: Facts on File, 1984.

Schott, Tom, and Nick Peters. *The Giants Encyclopedia*. Champaign, IL: Sports Publishing, 1999.

Sherif, Muzafer, et al.: *The Robbers Cave Experiment*. Middletown, CT: Wesleyan University Press, 1988.

Smith, Curt. *Voices of the Game*. South Bend, IN: Diamond Communications, 1987.

Smith, Red. *Red Smith on Baseball: The Game's Greatest Writer on the Game's Greatest Years*. New York: Ivan R. Dee, 2000.

Snider, Duke, with Bill Gilbert. *The Duke of Flatbush*. New York: Zebra, 1988.

Stein, Fred, and Nick Peters. *Giants Diary: A Century of Giants Baseball in New York and San Francisco*. Berkeley, CA: North Atlantic Books, 1987.

Sullivan, Dean A., ed. *Early Innings: A Documentary History of Baseball, 1825–1908*. Lincoln: University of Nebraska Press, 1995.

Sullivan, Neil J. *The Dodgers Move West*. New York: Oxford University Press, 1987.

Thomson, Bobby, with Lee Heiman and Bill Gutman. *The Giants Win the Pennant! The Giants Win the Pennant!* New York: Kensington, 1991.

Thorn, John, and Pete Palmer, eds. *Total Baseball*. New York: Warner, 1989.

Thorn, John, et al., eds. *Total Baseball*. 6th ed. New York: Total Sports, 1999.

Thornley, Stew. *Land of the Giants: New York's Polo Grounds*. Philadelphia: Temple University Press, 2000.

Tygiel, Jules. *Baseball's Great Experiment: Jackie Robinson and His Legacy*. New York: Oxford University Press, 1997.

Weaver, John D. *Los Angeles: The Enormous Village, 1781–1981*. Santa Barbara, CA: Capra Press, 1980.

White, G. Edward. *Creating the National Pastime: Baseball Transforms Itself, 1903–1953*. Princeton, NJ: Princeton University Press, 1996.

Williams, Peter, ed. *The Joe Williams Baseball Reader.* Chapel Hill, NC: Algonquin Books, 1989.
Wills, Maury, and Mike Celizic. *On the Run.* New York: Carroll & Graf, 1991.
Wills, Maury, with Steve Gardner. *It Pays to Steal.* Englewood Cliffs, NJ: Prentice-Hall, 1963.
Zimbalist, Andrew. *Baseball and Billions.* New York: Basic Books, 1992.
Zimmerman, Paul. *The Los Angeles Dodgers.* New York: Coward-McCann, 1960.

PERIODICALS

American Mercury
Brooklyn Eagle
Dodgers Magazine
Giants Magazine
Los Angeles Times
New York Herald Tribune
New York Review of Books
New York Times
New York World-Telegram
New Yorker
San Francisco Call-Bulletin
San Francisco Chronicle
San Francisco Examiner
Saturday Evening Post
Sport Magazine
Sporting Life
Sporting News
Sports Illustrated
USA Today Baseball Weekly
Wall Street Journal

WEB SITES

Andelman, Bob, Stadium for Rent: Tampa Bay's Quest for Major League Baseball. <http://www.andelman.com>
BaseballLibrary.com. <http://www.pubdim.net/baseballlibrary>
Brooklyn Chamber of Commerce. <http://www.brooklynchamber.com>
Brooklyn Dodgers: The Boys of Summer. <http://www.bayou.com/~brooklyn/>
Brooklyn Historical Society. <http://www/brooklynhistory.org>
California Historical Society. <http://www.californiahistoricalsociety.org>
ESPN. <http://www.espn.com>
Encyclopedia Britannica Online. <http://www.eb.com>
Los Angeles Dodgers. <http://losangeles.dodgers.mlb.com>
Munsey & Suppes Ballparks. <http://www.ballparks.com>
Retrosheet. <http://www.retrosheet.org>
San Francisco Giants. <http://sanfrancisco.giants.mlb.com>

Sporting News. <http://www.sportingnews.com>
State of the Cities Data Systems. <http://socds.huduser.org>
Total Baseball. <http://www.totalbaseball.com>
United States Bureau of the Census. <http://www.census.gov>

BROADCASTS AND RECORDINGS

Krukow, Mike. Interview on The Gary Radnich Show, KNBR AM-680, San Francisco, September 28, 1999.
_____. Interview on The Gary Radnich Show, KNBR AM-680, San Francisco, September 30, 1999.
KSFO Presents "The Giants Win the Pennant": Hi-Lites of the 1962 Baseball Season. Narrated by Russ Hodges and Lon Simmons. LP. Fantasy GB-1962.

Index

Page numbers in *italics* indicate photographs

285